CHINA BLOODIES BULLETLESS BORDERS

CHINA BLOODIES BULLETLESS BORDERS

Col Anil Bhat, VSM (Retd.)

PENTAGON PRESS LLP

China Bloodies Bulletless Borders
By Col Anil Bhat, VSM (Retd)

ISBN 978-93-90095-47-6

First Published in 2022

Copyright © RESERVED

All rights reserved. No part of this publication may be reproduced, stored in a retrieval system, or transmitted in any form or by any means, electronic, mechanical, photocopying, recording or otherwise, without the prior written permission of the Publisher.

Disclaimer: The views and opinions expressed in the book are the individual assertion of the Author. The Publisher does not take any responsibility for the same in any manner whatsoever. The same shall solely be the responsibility of the Author.

Published by
PENTAGON PRESS LLP
206, Peacock Lane, Shahpur Jat
New Delhi-110049
Phones: 011-64706243, 26491568
Telefax: 011-26490600
email: rajan@pentagonpress.in
website: www.pentagonpress.in

Cover by Ajay Patel
Printed at Aegean Offset Printers, Greater Noida, U.P.

Dedicated to All Ranks of Indian Army, Navy and Air Force and security forces, who have defended India's borders with China since after Independence in the world's highest altitudes, toughest terrain and freezing temperatures against a most unreasonable and hegemonic enemy and all those who laid down their lives, including some whose unfound or inaccessible bodies still lie frozen in time in those snows.

Map of China's Hegemonic Greed

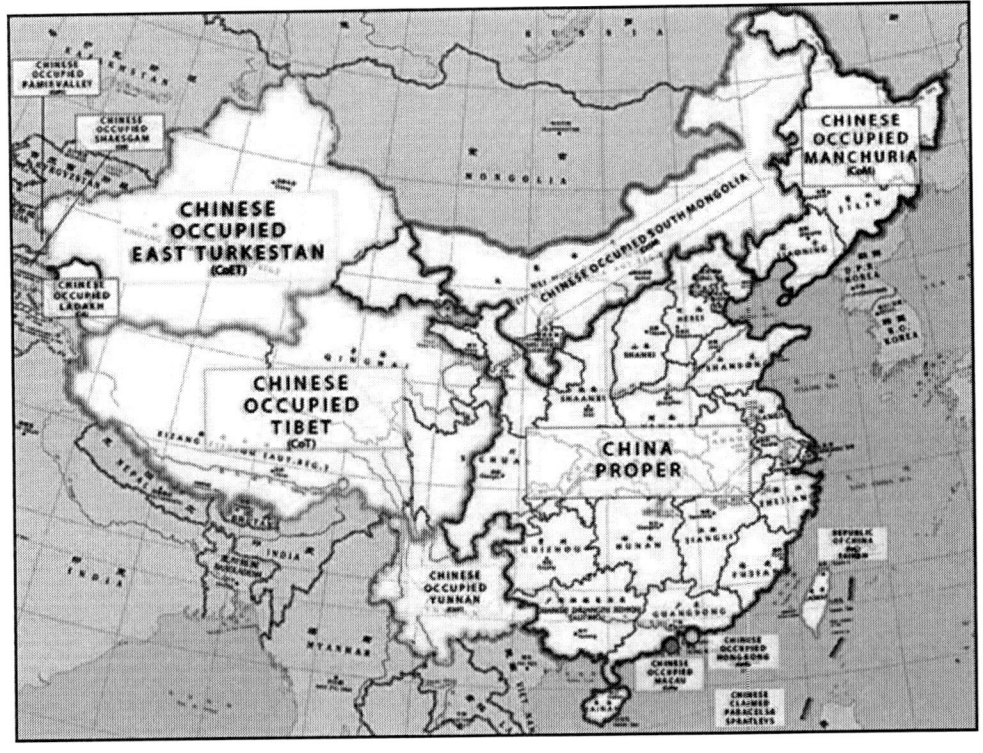

Contents

	Foreword	*ix*
	Preface	*xiii*
	Acknowledgements	*xvii*
1.	The Run-up to the 1962 Sino-Indian War	1
2.	The 1967 Nathula-Chola Skirmishes, which became a Game Changer	27
3.	1967-2007: Tulung La and Sumdorong Chu - Specializing in Bulletless Bouts and Dialogue	68
4.	2007-2017: Intrusions Galore and Dra'goon' Diplomacy	94
5.	Doklam	124
6.	Wuhan and Mamallapuram Summits followed by the Wuhan Virus	147
7.	Galwan and Kailash Range	176
	Afterword by Maroof Raza	207
	Photographs	221
	Index	237

FOREWORD

India-China boundary question has been a complicated and vexed issue. The contours of this question have gone through many stages of evolution. Immediately after India and China became republics in the late 1940s, this issue started affecting the bilateral relations between both the countries. During exchanges between leaders of both the countries in the initial stages, they tried to express each other's views on this issue. However, there were differences in the way India and China looked at the boundary question right from the beginning.

This book by Lt Col Anil Bhat, VSM (Retd) is an effort by him to give a context to the build up to the 1962 war and some of the major events that took place along the LAC from then till now. He explains the background to the incidents with the help of personal interviews, official statements and the agreements that have been signed between India and China. His own interpretation of these events is coming across strongly in this book.

The different approaches to protect the sovereignty and territorial integrity of the India-China boundary resulted in the India-China war of 1962. This war left an indelible mark on the bilateral relations and also affected the thinking and psyche towards each other in both the countries. The effects of this war are visible even today. Immediately after the war, India started standing up to any effort by China in changing the status quo on the Line of Actual Control (LAC). The LAC itself has not been mutually accepted by both sides since 1962.

Immediately after the war, the diplomatic relations between India and China went into a limbo. After a hiatus of 14 years, the ambassadorial relations were established again in 1976. In the early 1980s when the discussions on the boundary started, the pre-requisite was maintenance of peace and tranquility along the border.

The visit of Mr. Rajiv Gandhi to China in 1988 sought to give a boost to the bilateral relationship. Consequent to that visit, a number of agreements were signed between India and China. The 1993 Agreement on the Maintenance of Peace and Tranquility along the Line of Actual Control in the India-China Border Areas, the 1996 Agreement Between the Government of the Republic of India and the Government of the People's Republic of China on Confidence-Building Measures (CBMs) in the Military Field Along the Line of Actual Control in the India-China Border Areas, the 2005 Agreement between the Government of the Republic of India and the Government of the People's Republic of China on the Political Parameters and Guiding Principles for the Settlement of the India-China Boundary Question and the 2013 Agreement between the Government of the Republic of India and the Government of the People's Republic of China on Border Defence Cooperation were signed between both the countries. In between, a number of standard operating procedures were also established to avoid untoward incidents along the LAC.

During the period between 1976 and 2020, a few major incidents took place along the LAC. The 1986 incident of Sumdorong Chu was the first and a major one. This was followed by a face-off in the area of Depsang in 2013, Chumar in 2014, Dolam (also known as Doklam) in 2017 and the incidents of eastern Ladakh in 2020. During the Dolam incident of 2017 there was an incident on the Northern Banks of Pangong Tso. From the above, it can be seen that China has been trying to apply pressure on the LAC in eastern Ladakh from 2013 onwards. However, for almost 45 years after the Tulung La incident of 1975, there was no firing or fatalities along the LAC.

Starting from the 1990s till recent times there was also an improvement in the India-China bilateral relations. The reason for that was an understanding that the boundary question, being a complicated one, should be progressed in addition to the improvement in India

China relationship in other areas. This was again based on the prerequisite that peace and tranquility is maintained on the LAC. Another factor that brought in some stability in the India China relationship was the informal summits that took place in Wuhan and Mamallapuram in 2018 and 2019 respectively. However, actions of China in the summer of 2020 have jeopardised this relationship. China repeatedly taking the issue of Jammu and Kashmir to the UN, not supporting India's candidature for a permanent seat in UN Security Council and India's entry into the Nuclear Suppliers Group despite the latter's stellar non-proliferation credentials and vetoing the proscribing of known and wanted terrorists repeatedly have been the dampeners in this relationship.

India and China were expected to be the engines of growth to make this century an Asian Century. The Asian Century was also premised on the fact that India and China will grow in a complementary manner. Events of 2020 have jeopardized that belief. Even prior to the events in eastern Ladakh, an effort was visible to move the supply chains away from China because of the disruption that could be caused due to over dependence on a particular country for critical supplies. The world is going through a technological divide that will have its effects on the Asian continent also.

While India is looking at peace and tranquility along the border as the most important factor in this relationship, the Chinese side seems to be more interested in dealing with the LAC issue separately and progress the economic relationship simultaneously. This mismatch in the interests is something that needs to be resolved. In any case, India cannot and will not compromise on the sovereignty and territorial integrity.

The CBMs that have been in place for some time now, seem to have been rendered ineffective by the events of the summer of 2020. There is a need to revisit these measures and ensure that these are made effective.

Dr S Jaishankar, External Affairs Minister of India has clearly articulated the way ahead in his keynote speech in an Institute of China Studies event on 28 Jan 21. Three mutuals (respect, sensitivity and interests) and eight propositions (agreements should be adhered to in their entirety, LAC must be strictly adhered to and respected, peace and tranquility on the border areas is the basis on which the bilateral relations can be developed, multipolar Asia is one of the essential constituents of a multipolar world, mutual sensitivity to interests concerns and priorities of each other, not ignoring each other's aspirations, management of divergences and differences and civilisational states like India and China must take a long view) enunciated by him seem to be the way to go.

Having said that, this book brings out the fact, that there can be a number of approaches towards understanding these events. The author's approach is one of them. For those who want to understand the India China relations from that perspective, this book will be useful. The lessons learnt from these events may be the source for another study in the future. Disengagement from Pangong Tso and Gogra has taken place in February and August, 2021 respectively. However, there are other friction points that remain to be resolved. The background to the events provided in this book may help in understanding China and may assist in dealing with the present situation.

Lt Gen S L Narasimhan PVSM, AVSM*, VSM, PhD (Retd)
Member, National Security Advisory Board

New Delhi
14 September 2021

Preface

The period after the 1962 Chinese Aggression was marked by aggressive posturing by the PLA, based on its convenient/warped perceptions about the Line of Actual Control, which it very often claimed that the Indian Army had crossed and stepped into Chinese territory. That is a great irony because it is Tibet, all of which China took over by force by the late 1950s, after which PLA began with gobbling Aksai Chin and thereafter constantly nibbling at many parts of Indian territory.

In 1967, when Indian Army decided to mark the disputed border line in Sikkim with barbed wire to avoid frequent bickering, it greatly annoyed the Chinese. PLA began firing at Indian Army patrols and troops laying barbed wire. And after some time it stepped up from firing with small arms to heavy mortars-that is full-fledged artillery. Indian Army's response with artillery came only after then Prime Minister Indira Gandhi's approval. She also held charge of the Defence Ministry then.

The shock of confronting Indian Army in skirmishes at Nathu La and Cho La in 1967 ending with almost 400 PLA soldiers killed and a convoy of vehicles and many bunkers destroyed, resulted in PLA pressing for resolving all border disputes by discussion and not using firearms against each other. This continued for 53 years till September 2020, when Chinese soldiers fired a few rounds in the air. In 1975, PLA ambushed an Assam Rifles patrol, killing four riflemen, not with firearms but by torture. In fact, after the skirmishes mentioned, Chinese troops continued intrusions across the Line of Actual Control (LAC) into Indian territory on an almost daily basis while pressing for not using firearms and got this included as a clause in the 2nd and 3rd agreements on "peace and tranquility" along the disputed LAC out of the five agreements, which were in 1993, 1996, 2005, 2012 and 2014.

For the first time after decades, in May-June 2020, that too during the pandemic, caused by China itself, PLA, still did not use firearms, but resorted to using medieval barbaric weapons, initially only injuring many but eventually killing by the same weapons 20 Indian Army personnel on June 15, 2020. They did not expect an immediate backlash of fierce revenge by Indian Army troops which, it is believed, killed many more than the 43 PLA troops, as initially reported in media-and without using firearms. One young Indian soldier, Gurtej Singh, reportedly barehandedly killed twelve Chinese soldiers and sacrificed his life in the process.

Since after the 1967 skirmishes, PLA steadily continued intrusions/transgressions/incursions, but resorting mainly to "bullet-less border management". This off and on involved grappling/wrestling/pushing, but always ended in resolution by dialogue at the border itself or that and also by diplomatic discussion between new Delhi and Beijing.

Bullet-less border management may be a better option than that of firing at each other resulting in death or injury, but it is not easy to implement for prolonged periods, particularly, when an adversary like the PLA constantly crosses the disputed border or objects to Indian troops entering an area perceived by China as its own. Indian Army practiced this method which requires much restraint, for 53 years, till PLA's macabre and bloody attack on June 15, 20.

Taking advantage of the pandemic- caused by the release of a deadly virus reportedly from Wuhan Institute of Virology accidentally or deliberately, but as part of a programme of research/experimentation of biological weapons, PLA finally began the process of breaking this arrangement on May 05, 2020. While on May 05 and May 09, it tried grabbing land armed with crude medieval weapons, causing injuries, on June 15, 2020, when it killed 20 Indian soldiers, including their commanding officer, it completely broke all agreements/summits of peace and tranquility.

The resolution of the Doklam stand-off without the use of firearms and only grappling/wrestling and eventually dialogue in September 2017, only reinforced my theme and also marked 50 years of bullet-less border management since Indian Army's retaliation at Nathu La and Cho La in October 1967.

While Indian Army's 1967 response may have been etched in PLA's collective memory, but the hegemonic tendency of Communist Party of China (CPC)/PLA has always compelled it to constantly crawl and clutch at whatever territory wherever, whenever and how so ever much it can-again without using firearms across the long perception-based LAC, causing tension, even though it was always resolved by dialogue/discussion-most often at field commanders' levels and seldom with over-riding diplomatic parleys, or a combination of both-till May 2020.

Since 1947 till date Indian Army has never deliberately occupied any Chinese territory beyond the LAC, whereas PLA has repeatedly been haggling over it over a few metres from the LAC to chunks of territory totally amounting to over 43,000 square kms.

The LAC remains unresolved for well over seven decades/till date only because CPC- PLA have been playing their typical game of lies and deceit. The LAC cannot be resolved without China declaring its claim lines, which it does not seem to be interested in doing. Till 2014 it had managed to carry on with its 'dadagiri' (bullying) which worked with pliant Congress governments. Keeping in view the economic aims and interests of both India and China, it makes a lot of sense for resolving the LAC soon rather than letting this process take a few more decades. But China is not interested in peace as it is besotted with its plan to militarily consolidate its aims. This plan is not new but its implementation certainly got boosted during the pandemic. It involves grabbing many tracts of territory including commanding heights and tri-junctions on the Indian side of the LAC. And then there is also a focused aim of control over India's sweet water rivers, for making microprocessors.

While Indian Army's actions on 15-16 June 2020 and 29-30 August 2020, frustrated and inhibited PLA to implement its ambitious plans along the LAC, it will have to be watched hawk-like, because the possibility of it repeating/continuing such moves cannot at all be ruled out.

New Delhi must note the CPC-PLA combo's history and tendencies-chronic hegemony and lies and the weak/conciliatory stance of Nehru and the Congress party, except for Indira Gandhi's assertiveness in 1967 against China and in 1971 against Pakistan and the meaningless agreements since Panchsheel till date and evolve an assertive policy to be followed consistently, repeat, assertive and consistently, both on terrain and table.

New Delhi must be clear that the Chinese Aggression of 1962 continued bullet-less with varying intensities till 2020, when it was stepped up considerably and will continue by way of intrusions, transgressions etc, despite dozens of agreements.

India will need to be militarily very well armed and equipped and politico-diplomatically be consistently assertive towards China over its occupation of Tibet and all other Indian territories as well as its cruel suppression of Tibetans and Uighars. India must also make best use of technical surveillance from its own resources and from other friendly countries. And India must start matching the Chinese establishment in psychological warfare. It has the talent, but it needs to be channelized and developed to respond appropriately. And very important is countering China's cyber warfare which has been aimed at many countries. The book ends after about a year and a half of the Galwan clashes, the Chinese Communist Party celebrating 100 years of its existence and following the second of two disengagements of February and August 2021. Not surprisingly, there are still so-called "friction points", which really are Indian territories that Chinese grabbed/intruded into in 2020 and 2021 and have not been vacated.

Col Anil Bhat, VSM (Retd.)

Acknowledgements

The first person I thank is late Brig M.M.S. Bakshi, MVC (Retd), who was kind enough to share his experience and thoughts on his very eventful command of the Nathu La Brigade, during which period Chinese PLA opened fire many times and raised its scale of firing from small-arms to artillery and then got shocked at Indian Army's fierce fighting and retaliation with artillery in September-October 1967.

Brig Bakshi's association with me was much more than our being officers of the same Regiment, 4 Horse, also known as Hodson's Horse. Prior to his commanding the Nathu La Brigade, he commanded 4 Horse during the 1965 India-Pakistan War, during which my brother, Captain (later Brigadier) Ravi Malhotra* was the Regimental Signals Officer cum Intelligence Officer and thereby, a crew member of the Commanding Officer's / Lt Col Bakshi's tank. The entire crew of this tank had a very narrow escape, when, in an intense engagement in which they destroyed four tanks, their tank also got hit and caught fire. On bailing out of the tank they came under heavy enemy fire, but were fortunate to survive.

I would like to acknowledge and thank some veterans who participated in the skirmishes and with whom I interacted. Brigadier Rai Singh, MVC (Retd) who I met in late 2016, was in a very frail condition owing to long term aftereffects of his serious injuries during the 1967 skirmishes. I thank Col Daryao Singh Deswal (Retd) of 2 Grenadiers, who arranged for and accompanied me to meet Brigadier

---
* Brig Ravi Malhotra and I are real brothers, despite our different surnames

Rai Singh, in his Som Vihar, New Delhi residence, where he was under 24x7 close care of an Army veteran. Sadly, both Brig Rai Singh and his wife, an accomplished educationist, died one after the other some months after my visit.

The other veterans I interacted with were Colonels N.C. Gupta, Signals (then Lieutenant), Bishan Singh, Attar Singh, Himmat Singh Rathore (all of 2 Grenadiers), K.V. Chandrashekharan, N. Parulekar (both of 7/11 Gorkha Rifles) and Mr. Vijay Dagar, nephew of late Captain Prithvi Singh Dagar, VrC (Posthumous) and I thank them all for their valuable inputs. Vijay Dagar is in fact a major repository of much information about not only his late uncle, Prithvi, but also many other veterans of 2 Grenadiers and other units who participated in the Sikkim skirmishes. The dedication of Vijay and the Dagar extended family resulted in their making a small museum filled with Prithvi's photographs and memorabilia at Jafarpur Kalan, Najafgarh, Delhi.

Some more persons I would like to thank are officers of the Additional Directorate General, Public Interface (ADGPI) of Army Headquarters, Photo Section, Directorate of Public Relations, Ministry of Defence Ministry, Brig VK Saxena (JAK RIF), Lt Gen Prakash Katoch, Lt Gen VK Ahluwalia Lt Gen SL Narasimhan, Lt Gen JS Bajwa, Maj Gen Dhruv Katoch, Lt Gen DS Hooda, Lt Gen Vinod Bhatia, Lt Gen Sanjay Kulkarni, Lt Gen AK Bhatt, Lt Gen Konsam Himalay Singh, Lt Gen Amit Sharma, Lt Gen Ranjan Bakhshi (all retired), Mr. Claude Arpi, Dr Kondapalli Srikant, Dr. Swaran Singh, Mr. Iqbal Chand Malhotra, Mr. Mukul Shukla, Commodore Ranjit Rai, Vice Admiral Shekhar Sinha, Maj Gen Randhir Sinh, Late Lt Gen RM Vohra, Lt Gen PJS Pannu (all retired) and Dr. Silky Kaur. My thanks to Mr. Rajan Arya and his team at Pentagon Press LLP for all their efforts.

An acknowledgement which I received related to this book came from film maker J.P. Dutta. We first met in 1997, when I, as Defence Ministry's Army spokesperson, was part of the team previewing the movie, Border. When we happened to meet again sometime in mid-2010s, he mentioned that he was planning a film on the 1962 India-China war. I told him about what I had written on the 1967 skirmishes in Sikkim. After reading some of my articles, he thanked me for enlightening him and acknowledged that he had changed the theme of the film from 1962 to 1967. The movie he eventually made was named Paltan.

Last but certainly not least, thanks to my wife, Sucheta, my daughters, Nadiya and Mallika, my sister, Aruna Kapoor and my brother Brig Ravi Malhotra, VSM (Retd) for their support and encouragement. It was after Ravi getting commissioned from the Indian Military Academy in December 1962, six months earlier than scheduled because of the India-China War and when I had finished Class 6, that I decided to join the Army.

1
THE RUN-UP TO THE 1962 SINO-INDIAN WAR

The entire India-China, actually the India-Tibet border, 4,056 kms long, traverses a long stretch comprising the Union Territories of Jammu and Kashmir and Ladakh, Himachal Pradesh, Uttarakhand, Sikkim and Arunachal Pradesh. Since the 1962 Sino-Indian war, the demarcation was an informal cease-fire line between India and China till 1993, when it was officially accepted as the Line of Actual Control in a bilateral agreement. On the Chinese side, the line traverses the Tibet Autonomous Region. The entire Sino-Indian border can be subdivided into three sectors:

1. The Western Sector comprises of the border shared by Jammu and Kashmir, Xinjiang and Tibet. It is disputed as the Indian side has claimed that China in this division is illegally occupying an area of 43,000 sq. km.

2. The Middle Sector is the border shared by Himachal Pradesh and Uttarakhand with Tibet.

3. The Eastern Sector is the area where the Sovereignty of India is challenged by Chinese over an area of 90,000 sq. km. this area falls mostly in Arunachal Pradesh, Bum La, Lo La, Asaphi La and Tawang.[1]

Of these 4056 kms the Line of Actual Control (LAC) includes the Western Sector and the McMahon Line in the Eastern Sector. A small section in the Central Sector, which is considered to be undisputed, has been encroached by China in 2020.

Of India's many misfortunes, the first was that after many centuries of being attacked, marauded, pillaged and ruled over, Independence came with the unprecedented ordeal of Partition. Saddled with the newly formed West Pakistan and erstwhile East Pakistan, as well as a potentially hostile China, it was a time to take some hard decisions. However, that was not to be. India's top political founders made a poor start: (a) not factoring the extent of India's vast land and sea boundaries, (b) being naïve in assessing the threats and intentions of hostile neighbours, (c) failing to realise the importance of military muscle and the timely use of appropriate force, (d) spreading a phobia of military rule, and (e) propagating a warped secularism by obliterating history.

India's post-Independence history, which is still not taught in schools and colleges, exemplifies how civil-military relations can impact a country's security, integrity and standing in the world. It has been amply proved how good civil-military relations have resulted in victory in wars and vice-versa.

It is relevant here to mention the flawed decisions of India's first Prime Minister Jawaharlal Nehru and V.K. Krishna Menon, its second defence minister. While Nehru reportedly conveyed that India did not need an army—the police were sufficient, Krishna Menon believed that India's ordnance factories were better off producing pressure cookers and coffee percolators. Apart from viewing the Indian Army with suspicion, both went out of their way to not only turn down any sound advice from the Forces, but also meddle with its leadership. The result was that the Indian Army, globally acknowledged as about the best in World Wars I and II, was pitched into the 1962 Sino-Indian war, woefully under-armed (with 70 years old bolt action rifle), ill-equipped and insufficiently-clad and worst, ordered by Nehru to carry out tasks on the ground which were simply not executable. Fighting to the last man and last bullet sounds great, but it is a shame if an army is reduced to that state, as some units were in the 1962 war. Offensive use of the Indian Air Force against the Chinese would have made a great difference, but Nehru was averse to "raising the level of confrontation". The Indian Army suffered a humiliating defeat.

While dealing with Pakistan during the first war (1947-48), no aggressive use was made of the Air Force, or of the Navy. The Indian Army was quite capable of wresting the part of Kashmir grabbed by Pakistan but for Nehru's blunder of referring the matter to the United Nations.

The 1962 Sino-Indian war shamed Nehru, who had to jettison Krishna Menon, but the damage had been done. The pace had been set for India's powerful bureaucracy to keep the Armed Forces in a stranglehold. The Nehru-Krishna Menon duo allowed it, and the practice strengthened over decades of Congress rule, depriving the Forces of timely replacement of arms and equipment, upgrades in pay and status.

Till 1949, when the communist revolution was about to throw the Kuomintang regime, bilateral relationship showed no signs of stress and the organic linkages that defined the thousands of years of interactions continued via the Silk route trade across the border.

In fact, there existed an excellent understanding between both the sides during the pre-revolution times. Irrespective of the internal situation, 20th century Chinese leaders viewed India with respect, given the centuries of spiritual and cultural binds that had bound both the nations together. For instance, Chinese leader Sun Yat-sen was deeply influenced by Gandhi's struggle against British occupation of India and even expressed his support and sympathy with Mahatma Gandhi when he launched the non-cooperation movement in 1920. Gandhi's anti-imperialist ideas resonated deeply with Sen.

Further, between these two nations good diplomatic relations were formed in 1947, when China was under Chiang Kai-shek's leadership. The Asian Relations Conference, which is stated as one of the first attempts in the post-war era to chart out a vision for an Asian order was hosted by India in Match 1947, where delegates from China were also invited. Nehru had laid great emphasis on the manner in which post-colonial India would rebuild its Asia connections. At this conference Nehru declared:

[...] Asia is again finding herself ... one of the notable consequences of the European domination of Asia has been the isolation of the countries of Asia from one another.... Today this isolation is breaking down because of many reasons, political and otherwise ... This Conference is significant as an expression of that deeper urge of the mind and spirit of Asia which has persisted.... In this Conference and in this work, there are no leaders and no followers. All countries of Asia have to meet together in a common task."[2]

By early 1949, however as Red Army took over Peking the CCP declared its firm resolve to liberate Tibet. What Nehru was seeking was the friendship with China with integrity and defense of India and her vital extended linkages in Tibet. In a generous extension of the offer for friendship, India became the first non-communist nation to recognize China. At a time when China was ostracized by the international community, facing hostility especially from the US led power bloc, India stood firm by China, calling upon the leaders of the world to shun their prejudice and embrace the nation. It was the Indian leadership which was pragmatic to believe that if left alone, China could acquire the same tendencies as the once isolated German nation saw the rise of Nazism.

Nehru made it clear that China was a great country which would not be ignored no matter what resolutions were passed and what speeches were delivered in the House.

The origin of the Sino-Indian conflict goes back to the Tibetan crisis of 1950. Tibet was the first area where Chinese and Indian primary interests clashed. India had inherited from British India a moral obligation to protect Tibetan autonomy, while China claimed Tibet as a permanent province of China. India and China desired to settle the problem of Tibet peacefully and amicably. In view of security and strategic considerations, China resorted to force rather than negotiation. A favourable international situation, provided by the Korean crisis of 1950, perhaps motivated the Chinese to solve the Tibetan problem by force without awaiting the outcome of bilateral negotiations with Tibet in Beijing (formerly known as Peking). The Sino-Indian border dispute of the later 1950's and the early 1960's was another bone of contention between the two countries. China and India tried to solve the dispute peacefully and amicably, the prime methods being Zhou-Nehru personal diplomacy, summit diplomacy, bilateral negotiations between Sino-Indian officials, and international mediation. Unfortunately, all these efforts failed. The border dispute remained unnegotiated not because China and India refused to negotiate but because neither side was willing to surrender its territorial claims or make reasonable concessions, for to do so would be against the national security interests of each power.

Tibetan Settlement

It was in Tibet that the Chinese and Indian interests overlapped. All Chinese leaders, Kuomintang nationalists as well as communists, perceived Tibet as an integral province of China. After the Chinese communists came into power in 1949, Tibetan liberation became the most important issue on the agenda of liberating the Chinese territories lost in the past. India, who traditionally had viewed Tibet as an autonomous and buffer state between China and herself, was not now willing to quarrel over the issue of Tibetan liberation. The Nehru government eschewed the traditional British Indian role of maintaining Tibet as a buffer state and extending Indian influence in Lhasa, the capital. In spite of the fact that the key officials in Nehru's government disagreed with his China policy, he still showed unwillingness to fight with China over the matter. Tibet, after all, had since 1912 existed as a virtually independent entity in international relations.

Furthermore, India made it clear that she had no territorial and political ambitions in Tibet. India expressed great concern, however, about Tibetan autonomy as well as certain Indian commercial and cultural rights inherited from historical usages, traditions, and agreements. The main suggestions to Beijing were that "a settlement of the Tibetan problem should be affected by peaceful negotiations adjusting the legitimate Tibetan claim to autonomy within the framework of Chinese suzerainty."[3] To facilitate a peaceful settlement, India also urged Tibetan officials to begin negotiations with China at their earliest convenience. Beijing's response was favourable expressing a willingness to solve the issue peacefully in direct negotiation with the Tibetan government. Consequently, bilateral negotiations between Chinese and Tibetan officials began in August 1950, with the Tibetan delegations arriving in New Delhi to negotiate with the Chinese representative there. Negotiations did not go very far, however, because of the Chinese assertion that fruitful talks could not be held with Tibet on a foreign soil (India). The Chinese demanded the transfer of negotiations from Delhi to Beijing, and this was agreed to by the Tibetan delegation. Unfortunately, the Chinese, contrary to their expressed desire for peaceful and amicable negotiations, decided to liberate Tibet by force. Without waiting for the arrival of the Tibetan delegation in Beijing, the People's Liberation Army entered Tibet on October 7, 1950. Having completed a major part of its military operation on October 25, the Beijing government announced that the, "People's Army units have been ordered to advance into Tibet to free three million Tibetans from the imperialist oppression and consolidate national defense of the western border of China".[4] The Chinese gave several reasons for resorting to force. They argued that, as Tibet was an inseparable part of China, the problem thus was an internal one. They maintained that the Tibetan people were supposed to be liberated and that "regardless of whether the local authorities of Tibet wish to proceed with peaceful negotiations and whatever the results may be achieved by negotiations, the problem of Tibet is the domestic problem of the People's Republic of China and no foreign interference shall be tolerated".[5] The Chinese further added that the delay in the visit of the Tibetan delegation to Beijing for negotiation was "intentionally" caused by outside instigation.

Sardar Vallabhbhai Patel, who had a deeper insight regarding Chinese intentions and serious reservations on Nehru's China policy was also not heard. As early as 1950, following China's invasion of Tibet, he had stated: "We have to consider what new situation now faces us as a result of the disappearance of Tibet, as we knew it, and the expression of China almost up to our gates.... The Chinese interpretation of suzerainty seems to be different. We can, therefore, safely assume that very soon they will disown all the stipulations which Tibet has entered into with us in the past. That throws into the melting pot all frontier and commercial settlements with Tibet on which we have been functioning and acting during the last half a century".[6]

Being on the same page as Patel, even Syama Prasad Mukherjee alarmed the Parliament over the Chinese designs, stating that "It is no use our trying to gloss over things because these are matters which affect not only the people of Tibet but also the security of India".[7]

Panchsheel

During the visit of Premier Zhou Enlai to India, he and Nehru issued a Joint Statement on June 28, 1954 that elaborated their vision of Panchsheel as the framework, not only for relations between the two countries, but also for their relations with all other countries, so that a solid foundation could be laid for peace and security in the world. Panchsheel, as envisioned by its creators, gave substance to the voice of newly established countries who were seeking the space to consolidate their hard-won independence, as it provided an alternative ideology dedicated to peace and development of all as the basis for international interaction, whether bilateral or multilateral. At that time, the two Prime Ministers also expressed the hope in the Joint Statement that the adoption of Panchsheel, "will also help in creating an area of peace which as circumstances permit can be enlarged thus lessening the chances of war and strengthening the cause of peace all over the world."[8] The phrase "Hindi-Chini Bhai Bhai", coined by Nehru became popular, with the entire ruling leadership being held hostage to the belief that India and China could never enter into a conflict.

Meanwhile India maintained its generous gestures to keep the relationship with China on the best possible terms, and even lobbied to get it a place in the international fora, Chinese double game continued. As the Indian leadership looked elsewhere, the Tibet border showed signs of simmer from the Chinese side and by mid 1950s, though there were growing instances of incursions in Barahoti and Nelong area, part of Uttar Pradesh (now Uttarakhand), the Reakagearea on the Himachal Pradesh-Tibet border; extending across the border to Dungti, Chushul and Aksai Chin in Ladakh and also in several places in North Eastern Frontier Agency. In 1955, China began asserting more by publishing official maps, claiming 46,000 sq. miles (1,20,000 sq. km.) of Indian territory in Ladakh and NEFA (Arunachal Pradesh).

The leadership in New Delhi was also oblivious of the dangerous game that had begun in Aksai Chin. In 1957, it was reported in the Chinese papers that the highway connecting Aksai Chin and Tibet had been completed. Claude Arpi writes, quoting the report in Kuang-Ming Jih-pao newspaper, stating, "The Sinkiang-Tibet - the highest highway in the world - has been completed".[9]

Furthermore, that newspaper also reported that, "The Sinkiang-Tibet Highway... is 1,179 km long, of which 915 km are more than 4,000 metres above sea level; 130 km of it over 5,000 metres above sea level, with the highest point being 5,500 meter", something which was clear to alarm New Delhi.[10] The reporter spoke of: "Thirty heavy-duty trucks, fully loaded with road builders, maintenance equipment and fuels, running on the highway on a trial basis heading towards Tibet".[11] 12,000 square miles of territory was cut off from Jammu and Kashmir with the construction of the highway.

Months after the road opened India's then foreign secretary Subimal Dutt wrote to Prime Minister Nehru, "There seemed little doubt that the newly constructed 1,200 kilometers road connecting Gartok in Western Tibet with Yeh (Yecheng) in Sinkiang passes through Aksai Chin", suggesting Nehru that a mission be sent to check the quantum of Chinese ingress into the region.[12]

Nehru replied that, "we should send a reconnoitering party there in spring with clear instructions that they should not come into conflict with the Chinese".[13] Air reconnaissance is not desirable as it is in no way beneficial to us. Land reconnaissance will also be not beneficial to us. He also said that, "I do not see how we can possibly protest about the alignment of the road without being much surer than we are. What we might perhaps do is that in some communication with the Chinese Government in regard to the points of dispute which have to be decided, we should mention the Aksai Chin area".[14] Furthermore, "It is suggested that our maps should be sent to the Chinese. Certainly, they can be sent through our Embassy. But I think it would be better to do this rather informally".[15]

The Indian Foreign Secretary (Dutt) handed over an 'Informal Note' to the Chinese Ambassador in Delhi, which read:

> [T]he attention of the Government of India has recently been drawn to the fact that a motor road has been constructed by the

Government of the People's Republic of China across the eastern part of the Ladakh region of the Jammu Kashmir States, which is part of India. This road seems to form part of the Chinese road known as Yehchhang–Gartok or Sinkiang Tibet highway, the completion of which was announced in September 1957. The road enters Indian territory just east of Sarigh Jilgnang, runs north-west to Amtogar and striking the western bank of the Amtogar lake runs north-west through Yangpa, Khitai Dawan and Haji Langer which are all in indisputable Indian territory. Near the Amtogar Lake several branch tracks have also been made motorable".[16]

The India-China boundary in the Ladakh sector as in others is traditionally well-known and follows well marked geographical features. The territory through which the road traverses has been part of the Ladakh region of India for centuries and the, "old established frontiers' have been accepted by the Chinese in the treaty of 1842 as the International boundary. In an official communication, a Chinese member of the Boundary Commission of 1847-49 accepted the boundary as, "sufficiently and distinctly fixed so that it will be best to adhere to this ancient arrangement and it will prove far more convenient to abstain from any additional measures for fixing them".[17] Accordingly, Indian survey parties have visited the region since the nineteenth century. Travellers to the area have referred to it as part of Ladakh, and Atlases like the Johnston's Atlas of India, edition 1894, and maps published by the Survey of India show it unmistakably as part of Ladakh.

In view of the position indicated in para above, it is matter of surprise and regrets that the Chinese Government should have constructed a road through indisputably Indian territory without first obtaining the permission of the Government of India and without even informing the Government of India.

> The Government of India would like to point out that Chinese personnel, including officials and workers engaged in constructing and maintaining the road, as well as Chinese travellers traversing this road have been contravening Article V of the Agreement between the People's Republic of China and India on trade and Intercourse with Tibet concluded in 1954.[18]

According to this article, "for travelling across the border, the High Contracting Parties agree that diplomatic personnel, officials and nationals of the two countries shall hold passports issued by their own respective countries and visa by the other party"[19] except as provided in the subsequent paragraphs of the Article relating to traders, pilgrims and muleteers. No applications for visas from Chinese personnel working on the road or from Chinese travellers traversing this road have ever been received by the Government of India.

As the Chinese Government are aware, the Government of India are anxious to settle these petty frontier disputes so that the friendly relations between the two countries may not suffer. The Government of India would therefore be glad for an early reply from the Tibetan Government.[20]

In this connection the Government of India would also like to draw the attention of the Chinese Government to another fact. An Indian party consisting of three Military Officers and four soldiers together with one guide, one porter, six pony–owners and thirty-four ponies, were out on a normal patrol in this area near Shinglung in Indian territory. This patrol had been given strict instructions not to cross the border into Chinese territory. Since the end of August, however, no news of their whereabouts has been received in spite of search by air. Since there are now Chinese personnel in this part of Indian territory the Government of India would be grateful for any information that the Chinese Government may have about the party and for any assistance that they may find it possible to give to the party to return to their headquarters."

Questions followed in the Parliament, asking Prime Minister Nehru to clarify over the specific details on the dispute and the actual Chinese territorial ingress. Responding to one of such questions, Nehru replied:

> "It is rather difficult for me to answer that question. We have discussed one or two minor frontier disputes which comprise tiny tracts of territory, maybe a mile this way or a mile that way, in the high mountains where nobody lives and those are pending. We have discussed them and for the present no settlement has been arrived at".[21]

Another MP enquired about the Chinese movement on the Tibet-Uttar Pradesh (now in Uttarakhand region) border near Pithoragarh, this is what the Prime Minister had to reply:

> [I] should like to give a precise answer to such questions. I would not like to venture to give an imprecise answer. Taklakot [trijunction Nepal-Tibet-India in Pithoragarh district of today's Uttarakhand] and another place – Hoti [Barahoti in Uttarakhand] – have been places under argument and sometimes, according to our reports we have received, some Chinese have advanced a mile or two, maybe, in high mountains. It is true. We have been enquiring into it. The difficulty is that in the winter months most of these places are almost inaccessible and more inaccessible from our side than from the other side.[22]

1959–1962 Boiling Point

The failure of Mao Zedong's "great leap forward" policy in 1959, and the change in the leadership in the CPC in 1958/59, gave clear signals that things were not right in China and the government had become weak, failing to deliver on the international front as well as controlling the internal implosion, and most importantly incapable of resisting India, which had grown its pride due to several back to back strategic achievements in a very short span of time .

India was prouder than ever during that phase, as the forces had successfully liberated Goa in December 1961 of centuries long Portuguese occupation. Portugal had been a part of NATO alliance and NATO's silence on Indian action acted as a confidence booster. Nehru, with a boosted confidence began speaking openly about how India would not hesitate using force when necessary, to respond to growing Chinese incursions. Besides these, the Dalai Lama's asylum in India is understood as the tipping point, when bilateral relationship was completely rocked.

Lhasa Rebellion

Mid-1950s onwards, the Khampas were already having tense relationship with Mao regime, which had begun threatening their very existence in garb of communism. After the PLA had defeated the

Tibetan army in October 1950, Peking asked Tibetans to come to Beijing to negotiate an agreement. As a result, 17-point agreement had been signed between the Dalai Lama and Central People's Government affirming Chinese sovereignty over Tibet, in lieu of false promises offered to assuage the angry Tibetans. For instance, the fourth point mentions that "the central authorities will not alter the existing political system in Tibet. The central authorities also will not alter the established status, functions and powers of the Dalai Lama".[23] The seventh point consisted of another lie, where it was promised that, "the religious beliefs, customs and habits of the Tibetan people shall be respected and lama monasteries shall be protected".[24] The reverse took place. By 1954, more than 2.2 lakh PLA soldiers had been stationed in Tibet, further burdening the paltry agricultural base resulting in famine like conditions.

By 1956, a rebellion had broken out in in Eastern Tibet. PLA was under a severe attack by the Kham and Amdo guerrillas. Attempts by the marauding PLA soldiers to pacify the Khampas provoked such resistance, that the PLA intensified its atrocities. The PLA then began bombing monasteries, and heavily cracked down on Tibetans, arresting their nobles, monks and guerrillas. Many of them were tortured and executed in public, to convey the message to Tibetan masses that any resistance would face such horrendous consequences.

Rather than addressing the concerning issues, a Preparatory Committee for the Autonomous Region of Tibet (PCART) was inaugurated in Lhasa, headed by the Dalai Lama, another move to strengthen the Chinese occupation.

In 1956, the Dalai Lama and the Panchen Lama visited India to participate in the 2,500th anniversary commemorating Lord Buddha's parinirvana. Both were distressed and conveyed to Nehru that China had betrayed the trust of Tibetans regarding the 1951 agreement with the Dalai Lama on Tibet's autonomy, and felt unwilling to return back to Tibet. Also, present there was Enlai. Nehru had talks with Enlai regarding Tibet and he was assured that Tibet's autonomy would be taken care of by Peking. The two Lamas were persuaded and returned back. However, trust had been breached. Meanwhile, the Dalai Lama too invited Nehru to Tibet, an invitation the Prime Minister could not refuse. When time came for the visit to take place, the Maoist regime got the plan scuttled citing internal disturbances in Tibet.

In March 1959, the Chinese Military Headquarters in Lhasa invited the Dalai Lama to a drama event to be held on March 10. A day before the performance was to begin, the military authorities ordered the Dalai Lama to come alone, also putting strict conditions that Tibetan troops should not be around. This infuriated the people of Lhasa who feared that the Chinese would arrest the Dalai Lama. Since early morning on March 10, therefore, a sea of people surrounded the Dalai Lama's residence, shouting angry slogans against China. Violence had begun. Beginning from March 10, 1959, Lhasa erupted in a revolt against the ruling Chinese administration. PLA had instantly mobilized around 50000 troops with heavy artillery. Heavily outnumbered and sustained by poor weaponry, the Tibetans managed to take the Dalai Lama out safely. Dalai Lama decided to leave Tibet and in distress, wrote to Nehru:

> Ever since Tibet went under the control of Red China and the Tibetan Government lost its powers in 1951, I, my Government officers and citizens have been trying to maintain peace in Tibet, but the Chinese Government has been gradually subduing the Tibetan Government.... In this critical situation we are entering India via Tsona. I hope that you will please make necessary arrangements for us in the Indian territory. Confident of your kindness and good wishes.[25]

Amidst the difficulties, the Dalai Lama crossed into the Indian side of the border on March 31, 1959 and on April 3, Nehru spoke in the Parliament that the government of India had given asylum to the Tibetan leader.[26]

Longju and Kongka Incidents

Longju and Migyitu are the names of two villages in NEFA, or the eastern sector of the Sino-Indian border. In August 1959, the Chinese forces crossed the Thagla Ridge (read McMahon Line) in Kameng Division (then NEFA) and put up posts within Indian territory at the tri-junction point of India, Bhutan and Tibet. The Chinese military entered into Subansiri Division and surrounded Longju. Indians considered that the Tsari stream, which runs in the west to east direction south of Migyitun village, hence decided to establish a post south of the stream as the boundary alignment along these axes, given the internationally understood norm of river-based boundary demarcations. The establishment of post brought Longju within the Indian control. Indians established presence at two more places, namely Tamaden and Khinzeman.

Indian troops stationed a border post ad this forward movement put Longju, located on the other side of the valley from the Migyitun village, within Indian control. The clash took place on August 25. Indian posts were forced out of Tamaden and Khinzeman as well. In his letter dated September 7, 1959, to PM Nehru, Chou Enlai brazenly complained of this development and laid claim on a large chunk of Indian territory. Nehru immediately sent a 13-page long letter to Enlai, very well-articulated, giving a point by point rebuttal to the outrageous claims Enlai had made in his letter.

The Kongka Pass lies at an elevation of 5,171 meters is a mountain pass lying on the Chang-Chemno Range. During the summer season of the year 1959, the Government of India decided to intensify its forward policy, and in October 1959, Indian troops from the Special Border Police crossed the Kongka in a bid to set up posts on the Lanak La. As a unilateral provocation, Chinese troops detained three Indian soldiers near the Kongka Pass. The next day, the following Indian patrol, consisting of more than seventy soldiers advanced on the Chinese patrol party from two directions, trying to encircle it. During the exchange of fire, nine Indian soldiers were martyred and seven taken in custody by the Chinese. Most likely, it was the Chinese soldiers who fired on the Indian patrol. The Indian side lodged a strong protest that the Indian patrol party had been ambushed by the Chinese.

Addressing the Parliament's lower house on August 28, 1959, Nehru stated that, "this was the boundary of the old Kashmir state with Tibet and Chinese Turkestan. Nobody had marked it".[27] Secretly, he directed the cabinet on September 13, 1959. Nehru declared that any question with respect to the Aksai Chin dispute would be considered, only in the larger perspective of questions of the entire border. On October 20, a patrol of Indian troops was sent to Kongka la, resulting in a fiery clash.

The Kongka and Longju clashes are usually regarded as a prelude to the 1962 war. Unfortunately, Indian leadership still continued to believe that no further action would be forthcoming from the Chinese side. The Indian Army did not sit quietly amidst the turn of events. Voices of protest did arise within the Ministry of Defence. Institutional suffocation and Krishna Menon's dominating role in the foreign policy had begun to unravel as New Delhi failed to respond to growing Chinese provocation, with no lesson learnt a good decade after Tibet invasion. Frustrated of these policies, army chief General K S Thimayya tendered his resignation on August 31, 1959, only to be persuaded by a frantic Nehru to reconsider the decision and take back his resignation, given the delicate timing. Nothing changed however and the business continued as usual, with Thimayya being criticized by Nehru in the parliament over his decision. Literally, Nehru chided Thimayya on the floor stating the issues bothering Thimayya were trivial and inconsequential. More pliable officers were promoted to the senior most positions, the most infamous appointment being that of General Kaul as the Chief of General Staff.

The Failed Nehru-Zhou Enlai Talks

A last attempt was made by the India to defuse situation and hopes were high that Premier Enlai's visit in April, 1960 would break the ice and open avenues of dispute settlement.

Durga Das, in his seminal work, *India from Curzon to Nehru & After* has explained on this quite elaborately. Das writes, "Nehru was anxious to get China to accept the McMahon Line as the northern boundary of NEFA and Zhou was willing to do so. But in return, the Chinese Prime Minister asked for India's acceptance of Chinese presence in Aksai Chin. Nehru was not interested in Aksai Chin (where he told Parliament later, "not a blade of grass grows") and at one stage was quite agreeable to strike a deal. But premature leakage in the Press of what was going on between him and Zhou and its description of the proposed announcement as a "sell-out" on Aksai Chin blocked the agreement. The opposition in Parliament pounced on the report and extracted from an embarrassed Nehru the undertaking that "not an inch of Indian territory would be ceded or bartered away without the approval of the House." Kripalani retorted immediately: "How many miles make one inch?"[28]

Enlai later claimed that when he reached Prime Minister Nehru's residence, he was shocked to see Indira Gandhi welcoming him, wearing a Tibetan dress. Which he suspected it to be a deliberate attempt to humiliate him. Enlai also claimed that the reluctance of the Indian leaders to understand the intricacies of the dispute resulted in a failure of the negotiations. He reportedly told Morarji Desai, a senior cabinet member how China was angered by India providing asylum to the Dalai Lama.[29]

Enlai's Statement

Enlai's made a deceptive speech on his India visit, he said:

> [A]t the invitation of Prime Minister Nehru, I have paid a friendly visit in India from April 19 to 25, 1960. I am pleased to have this opportunity to visit once again the great Republic of India and extend greetings to the great Indian people. During the visit, we have been accorded a cordial welcome and hospitality by the Indian Government and Prime Minister Nehru. For this, Vice-Premier Chen Yi and I, as well as my other colleagues, wish to express our hearty thanks. The Chinese and Indian peoples are two great nations of Asia. From the remote past, there have always existed between the two people's mutual friendship and mutual sympathy, but never mutual antagonism or aggression against each other. Since our two countries successively achieved independence, particularly since we jointly initiated the Five Principles of Peaceful Coexistence, the profound friendship between the two peoples has undergone further development on a new basis.

With these sugar-coated words, he further stated that,

> [T]here is no basic conflict of interests between our two countries. Our two countries have every reason to remain friendly to each other for thousands and tens of thousands of years to come. During the past one year or two, although disputes have arisen

between the two countries on the boundary question left over by history, our two peoples have nonetheless consistently cherished the desire to be friendly to each other. We are convinced that it is entirely possible to achieve, through peaceful consultations, a fair and reasonable settlement of the boundary question between the two countries. It is precisely with this conviction that we have come here.[30]

Zhou Enlai also stated that, through the dialogues exchange he has observed that the both sides want to maintain friendly relations. Both nations also want to have common points of proximity on border issue. He stated that these common points include firstly, to acknowledge that there is an existing dispute between these two nations regarding the borders, secondly between two countries there is existence of line of actual control with respective jurisdiction area. Thirdly, in order to determine the boundary geographical principles for instance, watersheds, river valleys should be applied to all divisions of the boundary. Fourthly, national feelings of peoples on both sides should be taken into account. Fifthly, the boundary settlement should be achieved through discussions. Sixthly, to achieve tranquility on border it was important for both sides to refrain from patrolling along border.[31] With consultation both countries can eliminate the misunderstandings and distance and achievement of India-China boundary reasonable settlement.

It is clear from this sugarcoated statement how Enlai was once again able to bluff the Indian side. In 1962, Mao Zedong was convinced that it was about time to give India a dressing down, so that the road was clear to occupy the claimed territory. The Marshal of the PLA, Liu Bocheng, had been tasked with brainstorming on the invasion for almost an year, gathering strategies and resources needed for a high altitude warfare. Heavy artillery hitherto deployed at the Taiwan front was immediately transferred along the Sino-Indian frontier.

By September 1962, the situation along the Sino-Indian border in NEFA deteriorated severely. Fighting began along the border and 20 September, the PLA barged in and took the Thagla Ridge, in a bid to attack Dhola where Indian Army's brigade had been deployed. On 10 October, clashes took place at Tseng Jong (NEFA), where Indian forces gave a befitting response to the enemy, but being only 50 in strength and heavily outnumbered by 800 strong Chinese forces, they suffered heavily.

The Reaction

Reacting strongly to this development, Nehru told the Press on 12th October that the armed forces had been asked to throw out the Chinese aggressors out of NEFA. In its sharp response to Nehru's statement, a People's Daily editorial wrote the next day,

> [S]o it seems that Mr. Nehru has made up his mind to attack the Chinese frontier guards on an even bigger scale... It is high time to shout to Mr. Nehru that the heroic Chinese troops, with the glorious tradition of resisting foreign aggression, can never be cleared by anyone from their own territory... If there are still some maniacs who are reckless enough to ignore our well-intentioned advice and insist on having another try, well, let them do so. History will pronounce its inexorable verdict.[32]

And the rest which happened indeed shall go in books of history as one of most humiliating defeats a brave nation like India faced, solely due to a disinterested political leadership which not only put the international honor of the nation at stake; Aksai Chin was lost and Chinese ingress into Tawang and its unilateral withdrawal left India more vulnerable than ever. Despite having a strong army and the ablest of the officers, the incessant demoralization of the forces and the failure to consider their repeated suggestions were the key contributors to the loss.

Shiv Kunal Verma in his book *The War That Wasn't*, aptly describes the events/circumstances related to former Army Chief Gen KS Thimayya's resignation and humiliation. He stated that Nehru and Thimayya were in disagreement with each other. Thimayya held Nehru responsible for chaos of NEFA (North-East Frontier Agency), Nehru made Army responsibility of NEFA, public in Parliament. Thimayya was of the view that Nehru has "completely compromised the army".[33] Thimayya also said that Indian government has failed in providing required resources for tackling the borders by the army. As Chinese are expert in showing themselves as heroic victim Nehru has created a mess and he should find a way out of this mess in few weeks.³⁴ After Thimayya left, Nehru called Krishna Menon.

They knew that Nehru had blundered by admission in Parliament about the clashes at the border, the National Highway G219 construction across Aksai Chin, Khenzemane and Longju clashes. Parliamentarians got shocked and many of them did not understood it also. Although Thimayya wanted Nehru to undo the mistake but the question was that how Nehru can withdraw the statements he made. As Nehru and Menon were full of fear, they wanted to neutralize Thimayya, so Menon went to Thimayya and threatened Thimayya of, "possible political repercussions if the matter became public".³⁵ To this an angry Thimayya sent resignation letter. Nehru persuaded Thimayya not to resign in national interest and closed the matter. However, as Thimayya left, news of resignation was deliberately made public while latter withdrawing of resignation was not made public. On 2 September 1959, Nehru stated in Parliament that civilian authority is much better than military and Thimayya resignation was trivial and was result of temperamental differences.

The falsely propagated resignation story of Thimayya is still a secret. For general public Nehru was idealistic Prime Minister who can do nothing wrong. But the betrayed General Thimayya quietly endured humiliation and proceeded to prepare the army for Chinese confrontation when needed.³⁶

This false speculating whispering campaigning of trivial reasons for resignation was damaging for Thimayya. Temperamental differences were considered result of differences of opinion. General Thimayya was a seasoned disciplined soldier, for him national interest was most important therefore he also withdrew his resignation. After taking charges Thimayya was focussing on problems faced by Army, particularly the important civil military equation in which army was being removed strategically from making important decisions on defence issues. This resignation saga portrayed Thimayya as an "alarmist and a defeatist".³⁷ Also he was considered responsible for the weakening of the office of army chief. Therefore, Lieutenant General B.M. 'Bijji' Kaul was being considered by Prime Minister as a replacement to Thimayya. Chinese were happy because their plan was succeeding as planned. One Indian infantry was pitted against four to five times the number of Chinese troops, even then Chinese admitted 2419 casualties. The situation in which the fight was going on these results are spectacular.[38]

Brigadier L.P. (Bogey) Sen in Tawang on 22 and 23 October was also adding confusion. Sen in Tawang was doing nothing for bolstering the confidence of garrison. The meeting with Lt Gen Niranjan Prasad was on the issue of, "Nam Ka Chu rout of 7 Brigade and the immediate withdrawal from Tawang".[39] Bogey Sen opposed the withdrawal from Tawang. They were not aware of the fact that Army HQ represented by Monty Palit also wanted the same. The only difference though was that, "Prasad was planning on falling back on Bomdila with Se-la only playing the part of a delaying obstacle. Palit, on the other hand, based on the one incomplete reconnaissance made almost two years ago, had made up his mind to dig in at Se-la".[40] The Army Chief Pran Nath Thapar had tacit approval of Nehru, was made into the task of a spectator. The Thorat Plan had some discussion and plan that was being made, for instance Tawang was left and on the other hand se-la was chosen arbitrarily. Monty Palit was playing the 'cleared by cabinet'[41] card to any opposition being made. Later on, Indian military high command took more irrational decisions. Although few hours before he was admiring Prasad for his decision of pulling back from Bum-La and evacuating Tawang. But the effect of retreat was not good on the morale of Prasad and other officers. After fighting at, "Nam Ka Chu, Tsangdhar, Khenzemane, and Bum-la, all Indian units that had come into contact with the Chinese were only fighting in penny packets or withdrawing". If Tawang was to be held at all costs, then replacing Prasad would have been a good decision because by then he lost the will to fight. But taking this decision after the withdrawal order was passed increased the chaos. On 23rd October it was decided that Thapar, Palit and IB chief B.N. Mullik would fly to Tezpur to meet Bogey Sen. Thapar was not in favour of holding Se-la.

General Eric A Vas wrote in 2004 that, Nehru as a democratic leader was of the view that military force is the last option in any power struggle. He was deeply influenced by Mahatma Gandhi's beliefs of non-violence. Nehru failed to understand the importance of military or he was made to believe by Mountbatten, that not even a single Indian is capable of being the head of army. Therefore, a British officer was asked to be commander-in-chief explains his views. Initially India was occupied in celebration of newly got freedom, democracy set up and other internal problems. Admiral Mountbatten and Lord Ismay advised Nehru to,

> [O]rganise the defence structure on the council system [each of the services having a council, composed of military staff] presided over by a politician and run very much on the lines of the Railway board, with military heads as chiefs of their respective service staff or boards. Under this system, there would be no need for a bureaucratic defence secretary [whoever hears of a railway secretary?] This would require the establishment of a Chief of Defence Staff to coordinate the three services at the defence minister level. But Nehru was unwilling to do that.[42]

As Nehru was not willing to perpetuate the idea of Commander-in-Chief in India. When Nehru after becoming Prime Minister met with newly set military wing of the Cabinet Secretariat. He got stunned to see military officers wearing uniforms. He despised the presence of military officers in Cabinet Secretariat. Lord Ismay later explained to Nehru that military officers are needed. Officers were later told to always wear civilian clothes at work which is followed even today.[43]

When Nehru visited Jammu and Kashmir, he was told by IAF pilots that they are using 500 1b bombs. Nehru objected to this and said that this is a violation of the principal of 'minimum force'.[44] He later on even objected to the mark of Indian Air Force on planes. For many years' army continued to make pressure for (instituting) CDS (Chief of Defence Staff). In March 1955 Nehru announced in Parliament, "change in designation of the three service chiefs from commander-in-chief to chiefs of staff. This was nothing more than a verbal smokescreen. It is a misnomer to call our service heads chiefs of their respective service staffs without forming integrated service councils".[45]

Nehru also said that with this like in other countries India would also have defence council, it became a matter for happiness for the house, many did not even understand the issue and this ploy confused and silenced the real issue. As a result, "our irrational and inefficient system of politico-military command continues till today".[46]

Once in 1950s, negotiation for the purchase of modern guided missiles for the air force were going on with the British government in UK. When Nehru visited UK a short demonstration of the film was arranged. Nehru got enraged after watching the brief film and said that, "I will have nothing to do with these sorts of weapons" and stormed out of the room followed by his daughter Indira Gandhi.[47]

Nehru's attitude towards military officers was critical and on the other hand for bureaucrats and police officers he was very praiseworthy. Intelligence Bureau took this as opportunity to disparage military and their loyalty. The more popular and efficient officers like Thimayya and Thorat were spied more. This lowered the morale of officers.[48]

Nehru was an idealist and hoped for a world where nations would not get involved in any conflict and will settle their disputes peacefully. Nehru thought that India can lead with its idealistic and philosophical past. He also idealized United Nations. He was lacking in deep and practical thoughts on politico-military issues of India.[49]

Therefore, there is no surprise in the Jammu and Kashmir situation course we are facing today. Indian army was not allowed to take stern measures against Pakistan when it was able to do so. Also, he later ordered the Indian army to throw out the Chinese from Thagla, but by then there was no efficient senior military officer who was able to take the decision. Nehru was ignorant on military matters and his advisors were more ignorant. For instance, his defence minister Krishna Menon was more prejudiced and ignorant in military matters. Mountbatten later wrote that he urged Nehru to appoint General Thimayya to the CDS, a situation of war is coming from China. To which Nehru replied that, "there was no question of there being a war as India wished to be at peace with everybody".[50] Nehru is to be blamed for not reforming and ignoring the army after independence.

Veteran India-China relations expert and Tibetologist Claude Arpi has made meticulous efforts to highlight the archival material related to the events that took place in this time. An article of his analyzing a key CIA report on Sino-Indian crisis has been reproduced which explains how Indian consulate in Kashgar was forced shut, and gives a deeper insight into the events related to the conflict, which shows how the threat loomed large and yet Indian leadership sat on it. Claude Arpi (2017) wrote in his Blogspot that, "Post-Independence, one of the most mysterious events which occurred in the early 1950s (and perhaps earlier), is still shrouded in veils; it is the closure of the Indian Consulate in Kashgar".[51] In Parliament December 1953, Nehru stated that, "Some major changes have taken place there [Kashgar].... But when these changes, revolutionary changes took place there [we had to close our Consulate]."At that time, nobody questioned these changes.[52] Many caravans used to pass through Karakoram for trade Kashmir and Central Asia, "Delhi accepted the closure of its Kashgar consulate as a fait accompli, just because a 'revolution' had taken place".[53] The issue of Kashgar closure was never discussed, a secret note prepared for Panchsheel agreement in 1953 stated that, "We could ask the Chinese Government to restore the normal traditional trade between Sinkiang and Kashmir, which has been completely stopped now. In fact, we had to close down our Consulate General in Kashgar and all our Indian traders have returned".[54]

Some recent revelation by Central Intelligence Agency (CIA) has disclosed that in 1950s in Xinjiang, a summary of 'Treatment of Foreigners' says, "The consulates general of Pakistan and India were closed in November 1949. Shortly after the Chinese Communist Army arrived in later December 1949 and in January 1950, restrictions were placed on the movements of people".[55] But the reason for this happening before the arrival of Chinese is a secret. In the Fall of 1950, Capt. Ram Sathe the Indian Consul General was forced to leave Kashgar via Karakoram Pass. All other diplomats fled from Kashgar.

For the incidents that were happening in Xinjiang CIA on 21 March 1951 notes that, "the Chinese troops stationed in Sinkiang use systematic, disciplined violence for political reasons, ...[while] rations, ammunition and military stores are received from the USSR". The entire trade with Soviet Union and Central Asia was suddenly nationalised "and it is planned to nationalise the land. Sinkiang supplies wool, cotton and leather to the USSR, and in return receives kerosene, gasoline and old fish-plates from the USSR".⁵⁶ Hundreds of Indian traders were forced to flee Kashgar. CIA reported that all food from Sinkiang is transferred to USSR, local farmers are in abject poverty. Communist are busy in anti-American anti-British propaganda because they do not like Uyghur people. Restriction were imposed on the population and everything was done in the knowledge of communists.

The CIA further reported that,

> [B]y the end of 1952 all profitable business, including the silk industry in Khotan, was under Government control. Private business was discouraged, and almost all shops had been turned into Government owned cooperative stores. The salaries paid to shopkeepers were barely enough to cover their living expenses...any person found with gold or silver in his possession was suspected of engaging in black-market traffic in these metals, a crime, and was subjected to official interrogation concerning the manner in which he obtained it.⁵⁷

Soviets were present everywhere, but even after seventy years Han Cadre are still in control of province. CIA reposts shows the chaotic atmosphere in Xinjiang and specially in Kashgar. No detail or comment was given to Indian media or anywhere on the closure of Indian Consulate General at Kashgar.

Claude Arpi (2017) furthermore argues that, "returning to 2017, China is today keen that India should join the One Belt One Road initiative, in this case, the Indian Consulate in Kashgar should be reopened. It would be one proof of China's sincerity".⁵⁸ On the examination of the question that who started the 1962 War Hansa Malhotra (2017) writes that, "India firmly believes that it all began with the Chinese onslaught, while China insists that the war was a repercussion of India's 'forward policy' which had sought the raising of military outposts in areas claimed by the Chinese".⁵⁹

R S Kalha also stated that there are various documents and proofs that signals that "China wanted to teach India a 'lesson'".⁶⁰ He further wrote that

> [T]he then Chinese President Liu Shaoqi told the Sri Lankan leader Felix Bandaranaike that the 1962 conflict was 'to demolish India's arrogance and illusions of grandeur. China had taught

India a lesson and would do so again and again.' Mao Zedong confirmed this line of thinking when he told a Nepalese delegation in 1964 that the 'major problem between India and China was not the McMahon Line, but the Tibetan question'. In 1973, Zhou Enlai was to tell Kissinger that the conflict took place because Nehru was getting 'cocky'.[61]

NOTES

1 https://www.mapsofindia.com/my-india/politics/why-the-india-china-war-happened
2 https://icwa.in/icwa_hindi/pdfs/ptnehru.pdf
3 http://shodhganga.inflibnet.ac.in/bitstream/10603/18979/10/10_chapter%203.pdf
4 Ibid.
5 http://www.icj.org/wp-content/uploads/1959/01/Tibet-rule-of-law-report-1959-eng.pdf
6 http://www.indiandefencereview.com/spotlights/sardar-patels-letter-to-jawaharlal-nehru-on-tibet/
7 http://shodhganga.inflibnet.ac.in/bitstream/10603/63962/7/07_chapter%203.pdf
8 http://www.mea.gov.in/Uploads/PublicationDocs/191_panchsheel.pdf
9 http://www.rediff.com/news/column/nehrus-aksai-chin-blunder/20170203.htm
10 Ibid.
11 http://www.rediff.com/news/column/nehrus-aksai-chin-blunder/20170203.htm
12 Ibid.
13 http://www.indiandefencereview.com/spotlights/when-nehru-lied-in-parliament/
14 Ibid.
15 Ibid.
16 Ibid.
17 Ibid.
18 http://web.stanford.edu/group/tomzgroup/pmwiki/uploads/2093-1959-White%20Paper%201-a-HUAD.pdf
19 Ibid.
20 http://claudearpi.blogspot.com/2013/06/when-nehru-lied-in-parliament.html
21 http://www.indiandefencereview.com/spotlights/when-nehru-lied-in-parliament/
22 Ibid.
23 http://www.washingtonpost.com/wp-dyn/content/article/2008/04/09/AR2008040902367.html
24 Ibid.
25 http://www.indiandefencereview.com/spotlights/a-rare-letter-from-the-dalai-lama-to-jawaharlal-nehru/
26 Ibid.
27 http://www.claudearpi.net/wp-content/uploads/2016/12/WhitePaper2NEW.pdf
28 https://archive.org/details/indiafromcurzont00dasd
29 https://archive.org/details/indiafromcurzont00dasd/page/n495

30. http://www.indiandefencereview.com/news/a-statement-of-zhou-enlai-sixty-four-years-ago/
31. http://claudearpi.blogspot.com/2014/09/
32. https://www.nationalheraldindia.com/international/a-sino-indian-war-in-2017-will-not-be-a-repeat-of-1962
33. https://bhavanajagat.com/2016/01/27/what-is-military-intelligence-a-brave-general-not-prepared-for-1962-war/
34. Ibid.
35. Ibid.
36. Ibid.
37. Ibid.
38. Ibid.
39. Ibid.
40. Ibid.
41. https://bhavanajagat.com/2016/01/27/what-is-military-intelligence-a-brave-general-not-prepared-for-1962-war/
42. http://brighemantmahajan.blogspot.com/2015/09/nehru-indias-national-security-long-but.html
43. Ibid.
44. Ibid.
45. Ibid.
46. Ibid.
47. Ibid.
48. Ibid.
49. Ibid.
50. Ibid.
51. http://claudearpi.blogspot.com/2017/10/
52. Ibid.
53. Ibid.
54. Ibid.
55. Ibid.
56. Ibid.
57. Ibid.
58. Ibid.
59. https://www.thequint.com/news/india/facts-about-1962-india-china-war
60. Ibid.
61. Ibid.

2

THE 1967 NATHULA-CHOLA SKIRMISHES, WHICH BECAME A GAME CHANGER

It is coincidental that the Doklam incident began in June 2017 - barely four months short of completion of 50 years since the Nathu La and Cho La skirmishes of September-October 1967 and ended in August 2017 without any bullets exchanged. Kudos to the valour, albeit with great restraint, displayed by the Indian Army in responding to frequent Chinese bullying and upping the ante with not only small arms but artillery also. The Nathu La and Cho La incidents go down in the annals of history as a significant victory for India at a time when international opinion had become skeptical of India's capability to stand up to China. It also countered the likes of Neville Maxwell who were aggressively peddling propaganda not only blaming India for initiating the 1962 war, but also falsely predicting the impending disaster Indian democracy would face in the near future. It is these skirmishes which forced PLA to opt for bullet-less border management - a smart move because it never stopped its intrusions, transgressions/attempts to grab Indian territory

In 1967, Maxwell wrote a series of articles, in one of which he stated, "the great experiment of developing India within a democratic framework has failed", predicting that the 1967 general elections would be the last in India.[1] The Naxalbari uprising had made its strong repercussions felt in Siliguri[2], which was brazenly supported in the Radio Peking broadcast, hailing the incident as the "Spring Thunder"[3] revolution in India. It is in those precarious times that Nathu La was rescued by brave Indian soldiers in very few days killing almost 400 PLA soldiers and destroying a convoy of vehicles as well as many bunkers.

The 1962 war, which resulted in the Aksai Chin region going to China was also significant in another sense as the Chinese unilaterally withdrew from Tawang.[4] Key to Chinese opposition had been Beijing's non-acceptance of a colonially imposed border, which it accused India of legitimizing, even after the British had left. A newly independent and isolated China, which was still looking for acceptance by the international community, signaled that it had no intentions beyond Tibet. After a brief hiatus of five years, tensions were to ignite once again in 1967, leading to the skirmishes at Nathu La and Cho La.

In the aftermath of the 1962 debacle, as India was recuperating from the humiliation and a demoralized army, little was realized among the Indian strategic community that the occupation of Tibetan plateau was the beginning of a geopolitical game that continues to haunt Indian borders till date, all the way from Ladakh to Arunachal Pradesh. Tibet's undulating topography, in contrast to the steep sloped Indian Himalayas allowed China to make faster inroads and mobilize along their side of the border and mount incursions into the Indian territory time and again.

Nathu La (14,200 feet), on the present-day Sikkim-Tibet border, lies on the Old Silk Route used by trading caravans in the journey between Gangtok and Lhasa via Gyantse. In 1904, during Lord Curzon's tenure as Viceroy, legendary explorer Major Francis Younghusband, who was serving then as the British Commissioner to Tibet, was successful in leading a mission through Nathu La to seize Tibet. This resulted in a Convention at Lhasa, where a treaty was signed between Tibet and the British Empire. The treaty was culminated into the establishment of trading posts at Gyantse and Gartok in Tibet, with a British trade agent stationed at each post, and gave to the British the control of

Chumbi Valley in lieu of an indemnity which was put on Tibet. Next year, with the ratification of an agreement that approved the trade relations between Tibet and Sikkim, thus formation of Sikkim as an 'Indian protectorate'[5] after Indian Independence. Nathu La witnessed an influx of Tibetan refugees following China's annexation of Tibet and once again from 1959 onwards when the Tibetan uprising was brutally crushed by the Chinese forces. The Chinese were unsettled with India keeping Sikkim as a protectorate and stationing its troops in the state.

While the Nathu La and Cho La skirmishes of September-October 1967 were not much publicized then; looked at in retrospect, they are very significant, as they effectively messaged to the Chinese that they were no longer dealing with an under-strength, under-armed, under-clad, ill-equipped and politically unsupported Indian Army of 1962, but one which could retaliate firmly and fiercely.

It is in fact this chapter which is the raison d'être for this book, as the impact of these skirmishes was that for the next fifty years till October 2017 - and even beyond - the Sino-Indian border management remained bullet-less, except for a single incident on 20 October 1975, at Tulung La, when Chinese forces killed four troops of Assam Rifles, India's first and oldest paramilitary force operationally under army. But for this incident, a few thousands of transgressions and incursions by the Chinese on an almost daily basis for 50 years including the one at Doklam, which lasted for 73 days, all of them were resolved by dialogue/discussion. In fact, the Chinese very smartly incorporated the clause of no use of firearms in the peace and tranquility negotiations. In light of the above, it becomes imperative to recall history and look into the Nathu La and Cho La skirmishes of 1967.

This chapter has not been easy to put together, owing to the time lapse and some of the participants having passed away. However, it comprises personal accounts by Brigadier MMS Bakshi, MVC, the Nathu La brigade commander, Second Lieutenant (later Colonel) NC Gupta and some others as well as excerpts from published material and interactions with the author, on various actions. Brig. Bakshi's account is based on the author's exclusive interviews with him to understand the skirmishes in greater detail. While these accounts may not be in a smooth sequence they will make readers familiar with the unfolding of events and also tell the tale of the courage and bravery with which Indian Army fought and shocked the Chinese, who by then had successfully conducted nuclear tests and were expecting India as a nation with a young and newly appointed Prime Minister Indira Gandhi to cow down.

The chapter, besides recalling the stories of valour, presents a fresh historical insight by incorporating the author's detailed interview with Brigadier Bakshi, many years after his retirement, sometime in mid-2000-2010.

Brigadier MMS Bakshi's Recollections Shared with the Author

A few years ago, I had the opportunity to interact with late Brigadier MMS Bakshi, MVC (retd), who commanded the brigade in Sikkim. His recollections recorded verbatim, are informative, perceptive and indeed interesting. It is indeed an honour to have Brigadier Bakshi's valorous deeds recorded firsthand in this book.[6]

Brig. Bakshi, in his relaxed style narrated a series of operational moves and some very important and historically significant events. "In early 1967, I was promoted to the rank of Brigadier and posted to command a mountain brigade deployed to protect the Nathula Pass on the Sikkim-Tibet border at an altitude of 14,000 ft above sea level. It lies on the ancient trade route to Lhasa in Tibet".[7] Chinese occupation of Tibet is an extremely important happening in the realm of world politics. Brig Bakshi stated, "the Chinese occupation of Tibet in late fifties caused the Dalai Lama to flee to India to seek refuge. This soured the relations between the two countries. The Chinese considered it as an unfriendly act and interference in their internal affairs".[8]

The upshot of this development was that it triggered a chain of events marked by military confrontation all along the mountainous border between the two countries. China started laying claim to vast areas of Indian territory along the Himalayan border and even built a road surreptitiously through Aksai Chin, a remote and inaccessible Indian territory. This came to light much later. Thus, Brig. Bakshi recounted that, "that the entire mountainous border in the North and North East had come alive posing a serious threat to India's security.

In Sikkim, the Chinese deployed their Border Guards at the Nathu la Pass facing the Indian outpost in an eyeball to eyeball confrontation".[9] During this period of Mao Tse-tung's red revolution the Chinese had assumed a very aggressive and hostile posture towards India even to the extent of questioning India's right to be in Sikkim. Tension was built up and kept mounting to such an extent that deliberate border violations by the Chinese became the order of the day. This was intended to provoke India and to precipitate bigger armed clashes to reinforce their claims over our territory.

It eventually resulted in an invasion of India all along the border in 1962 in which India suffered a huge military set back and the Chinese Army voluntarily withdrew from most areas occupied by it. It is not intended to go into the political and military reasons for this debacle, but it does show how easily we had allowed ourselves to be lulled into the Hindi-Chini Bhai Bhai (bhai-brother) syndrome. A bitter lesson of realpolitik was learnt at a heavy cost. Again, during the 1965 war against Pakistan, China made threatening noises all along the border to tie down Indian troops in order to help Pakistan. Even at Nathula they made some aggressive moves to intimidate our troops, but the situation remained just short of open hostilities. However, it did serve their immediate purpose of tying down our troops which indirectly helped Pakistan. Brig. Bakshi narrated that,

> [t]his was the situation and the prevailing atmosphere when I as an armoured corps officer assumed command of a mountain brigade which is legitimately the domain of infantry officers. But in view of the increasing number of armour officers making the grade to the rank of Brigadier, their employment opportunities were severely limited. So, as a matter of policy it was decided to post armour officers to command infantry/ mountain brigades. This move naturally did not find favour with the infantry as the latter were not being given command of armoured brigades. It was felt that by virtue of their background and training, an infantry officer's ability to grasp the fundamentals of fast-moving mobile warfare was at a premium.[10]

Brig. Bakshi further elaborated that although, with the advent of mechanized infantry, things began to change, and more homogenous atmosphere came to be created. But this came much later. He stated that, "I was particularly unfortunate as I found myself facing very delicate and dangerous situation from the very word go. I was thus under closer scrutiny for my performance than those who were lucky enough to find themselves in more peaceful circumstances. However, we were now in a more confident mood vis-a-vis the Chinese than the days of 1962".[11]

The situation had changed drastically since then and India was now much better prepared. It had taken a strategic decision to expand the army and raise specialized divisions to fight in the mountains and to maintain its infantry divisions exclusively for war in the plains. With the American assistance it became possible to equip the mountain divisions which were soon ready to take the field. The Chinese aggression had brought about a sea change in the strategic security environment in India. The Indian army was now faced with the task of fighting on two fronts-against Pakistan in the plains and the Chinese in the mountains. Such a situation is fraught with serious consequences for any country and requires political and diplomatic skills to avoid serious involvement on both fronts simultaneously. It's a big challenge which our leadership must face squarely. Happily, of late there is a tendency, worldwide, towards solving problems between countries by peaceful means rather than by a resort to force. Our leadership must therefore persist in engaging both Pakistan and China in a dialogue to settle all outstanding issues bedeviling the mutual relations.

Brig. Bakshi further stated that,

> [w]hen I took over command of this brigade at Nathula, tensions were at their peak. The Chinese defence works and our positions were facing each other just a few feet apart and both sides were keeping each other under close surveillance. There was no formal demarcation of the border at much of the difficult Himalayan terrain separating India from China and Tibet but at the Pass it had always been fairly clearly recognized by both sides from ancient times as the trade route passed through this pass. Despite these one or two spots had somehow become disputed where the Chinese and our patrolling parties differed in their interpretation of the exact alignment even though it did not amount to a matter of more than a foot or two. It was obvious

the Chinese were using this ploy on purpose to create an atmosphere of tension and conflict to reinforce their border claims. The well-known and internationally recognized watershed principle when applied at the local ground level lends itself to conflicting interpretations-which is what the Chinese were cleverly practicing as part of a posture of intimidation.[12]

Routine patrolling on each other's home side was accepted as normal activity by both sides but to keep up the pressure, the Chinese often objected to India's right to patrol and even going to the extent of asking them to vacate Sikkim which they claimed as theirs, and which formed the theme of their daily broadcasts as well. Thus, on occasions minor scuffles would take place with neither side ready to give in to a perceived violation of the border even if it was only by inches. Many times, the confrontation would take the form of sentries kicking, shouting and yelling at each other which would bring more troops on the scene from both sides. This would result in physical use of muscle power, pushing and pulling, crossing of bayonets and the odd shot being fired in the air. It was really an absurd and potentially explosive situation. Such close proximity of opposing troops in a hostile environment could easily degenerate into a shooting match in the heat of the moment.[13]

Brig. Bakshi told that, "apart from routine patrolling of the home side of the Pass by both sides, another activity was the beaming of communist propaganda on loudspeakers aimed at subverting the loyalty and morale of our troops".[14] It had become a regular feature. From Indian side they countered it by broadcasting the virtues of our democracy and playing Hindi film songs which were secretly enjoyed by the Chinese troops. This routine eventually settled down to an unwritten understanding and both sides took turns to beam their programmes without jamming or interfering.[15]

Brig. Bakshi further recounted that,

> [C]hinese propaganda was always in Hindi and they invariably had a Hindi interpreter available with their troops. And as was the custom in all communist armies those days, at each unit and subunit level they had political commissars whose job it was to keep a watchful eye on the respective commanders to ensure

their conduct is strictly in keeping with the communist doctrine. During that period, every soldier was compulsorily required to carry a little red book of communist ideology enunciated by Mao and indoctrination was a regular feature of the daily routine of soldiers. The effect of this policy was a complete brainwashing of every soldier who became highly motivated and fiercely loyalty to the cause of communism. This attitude showed in the behaviour of the Chinese troops facing us and is clearly evident in the photographs taken by us at the time. (Reproduced in this book).

The atmosphere had become so vitiated by minor irritants that a sudden flare up was always a real possibility. However as long as the sensitive spots were not violated by either side, the Chinese garrison behaved in a correct and disciplined manner. Both sides, of course, kept strict vigil on each other and even communicated with each other occasionally through interpreters to sort out any minor problems of a purely local nature.

The underlying tension and the unresolved interpretation of the watershed however remained a cause for concern and some kind of mutual understanding brooked no delay. The need became more urgent when the Chinese attitude started becoming increasingly belligerent. Brig. Bakshi stated that,

> [E]ventually, in early Sept 1967, our higher commanders in their wisdom took a high-level decision to demarcate the border at the pass by laying a barbed wire fence along the alignment as per our understanding. In pursuance of this decision, an announcement was made to the Chinese informing them of our intention to lay a wire fence to demarcate the border in order to avoid any possibility of future misunderstanding. We made it clear that this was not meant to be a provocative step but to demonstrate our good faith. It was stressed that the prevailing hostility was not in the interest of either side who should be coexist peacefully. We gave them four days' notice to respond making it clear that at the expiry of that period, if we did not hear anything from them, we would assume that they had no objection to our proposal and at we would be free to go ahead with the fencing as scheduled.[16]

Meanwhile, Brig. Bakshi's brigade went ahead with all the preparations necessary to complete the task allotted to them. This included a detachment of Engineers who would erect the fence, dumping of stores and infantry protection for the wire laying parties. In addition, he had reinforced his troops holding the Pass from company strength to almost a battalion under the command of one of my battalion commanders. Brig. Bakshi stated that, "it is relevant to mention here that in normal times, the role of the company position at the Pass was mainly to show the flag and its defense works were not designed to withstand a full-scale attack or to stand and fight a pitched battle. Its task was to give early warning of the enemy action offer resistance and to pull back under pressure".[17]

Brig. Bakshi further elaborated that

> [T]here were also strict orders about opening of fire. Local commanders were authorized to open fire with small arms only in self defence. As for heavier weapons such as artillery even high-ranking field commanders had not been delegated the authority to employ such weapons. It transpired that this authority was vested only in the Prime Minister. Such a control has some logic of limiting a local incident from escalating into a clash of serious proportions in normal times. But in the present situation, even though the Chinese had not shown any hostile response to our fencing plan, we should not have taken it as if they had acquiesced. Certainly, the ground reality and prudence demanded that we be prepared for the worst. But sadly, our higher commanders had misread the likely Chinese reaction and in a cavalier fashion gave the orders to go ahead with the operation without taking the prudent precaution of catering for an artillery fire plan to cover the activity. In the event, such complacency cost us dear.[18]

Brig Bakshi narrated that, he left his Headquarters at the crack of dawn to be present at the Pass to oversee the operation along with his artillery commander and a signal officer. A Brigade Commander does not normally have a command post with the forward most troops in battle but in this case, their assessment of the Chinese reaction was such that they took it as a routine task. Thus, his presence as Brigade Commander at the scene of action seemed to be quite in order. So, the three of them positioned themselves behind an overhanging rock face yards away from our forward most trenches to monitor the activity.[19]

At the appointed time, the wire laying parties commenced their operation starting from both ends of the Pass while the rest of the troops were in a state of high alert manning their bunkers and trenches at the ready. The wire laying parties and their escorts totaling about one hundred men had of necessity to be out in the open to perform their task and their watchful garrison was ready to provide covering fire if required. For the first few minutes of the commencement of the wire laying operation things seemed to be going well although the Chinese were very restive and watchful, manning their battle stations at 'stand to' position. But when their troops reached the sensitive spots, a whistle was heard from the Chinese side and with that sound all hell broke loose. They opened up with all the weapons they had including their mortars and even artillery. Our troops were taken by surprise in the open and many fell in cold blood. The Commanding officer of the battalion was severely wounded by a burst of machine gun in his stomach and had to be evacuated. There was utter panic and confusion when two more officers - a captain and a major were killed as they led their troops in the open.[20] Brig. Bakshi depicted that,

> [I] was utterly dismayed as a mute witness to this disaster. I repeatedly spoke to my superior on the radio asking for permission to open up with artillery fire and also to send reinforcements urgently to enable me to restore the situation. I had to wait a long time before reinforcements started trickling in. Daylight movement of troops on foot or in vehicles is hazardous as the enemy from his vantage points is able to keep an eye on all movements under observation. As far as artillery fire was concerned, I was told that permission had to come from higher ups and till then only battalion weapons available on the spot could be used for the time being. This was already being done but was having little effect as the Chinese positions were either all underground, in bunkers or on reverse slopes. It was a desperate situation.[21]

Apparently, the Divisional Commander passed on the request for artillery fire to the Corps commander located at Siliguri who in turn asked the Army Commander in Calcutta. It so happened that the army commander (Lt Gen, later Field Marshal, SHFJ Manekshaw) was in Delhi those days standing in for the Chief of the Army Staff who had gone abroad on an official visit to France. But it was astonishing that even the Chief was helpless without the express permission from the Prime Minister who was in the Parliament at that time and could not be disturbed. Eventually, when approached she gave the go ahead instantly.[22]

Meanwhile, three crucial hours delay had taken place and the Chinese were relentlessly shelling the Indian troops and reaching out even to their rear areas. It is pertinent to say a word on the state of communications in the army prevailing at the time. Things have changed so drastically now that one can establish contact with even the remotest corner of the country in no time. But it was not so in 1967. It was an agonizing affair to communicate with old and obsolete radio and telephone equipment available in the army. And with some luck after much loud shouting one may succeed in making conversation. This was a common and frustrating experience even under normal conditions but quite a nightmare in the middle of a shooting match. Much has changed for the better since those days and today, it would not take more than a few minutes to reach even the remotest corner of the country and indeed of the world. We had to make do with an antiquated system due to apathy of the powers that be. Be that as it may,

> [w]hen we did get the permission use artillery, we went in with a vengeance and gave them as well as we got. The fire fight went on for five days in all its fury. Mercifully, neither side made any effort to make an incursion into the other side's territory and both sides began to realize the futility of this misadventure. We started getting orders to de-escalate but before that our medium guns destroyed a convoy of trucks bringing Chinese reinforcements moving up the road through Chumbi Valley to reach the Pass.[23]

Brig. Bakshi further elaborated that, that road was clearly under the observation of their artillery observation post (OP) located at a feature named Camel's Back which was the highest and the most dominating feature in the area in their possession. Their estimate was that besides the destruction of a number of enemy vehicles, at least two hundred Chinese had perished in this engagement. Clearly both sides had had enough by now and gradually the firing died down and this senseless episode came to an end but-at what price to both sides? The OP officer at Camel's back was awarded a Vir Chakra for his alertness and skill in bringing down accurate fire on the enemy at the right time. He was an emergency commissioned officer and was due to be released from Army service the next day. But, sadly in spite of Brig. Bakshi's best efforts to retain him in the Army on the strength of his sterling performance under battle conditions, he had to quit. Rules are rules-they said. A number of gallantry awards were given including two Maha Vir Chakras and three Vir Chakras.[24]

Brig. Bakshi further pointed that prudence demanded that planning for such provocative operations should be done on the basis of the worst scenario. It was naive to assume that since the Chinese had not responded to our announcement, their silence could be taken as if they had no objection. Treachery is not unknown in military history. The Chinese had demonstrated it to us in no uncertain manner in the midst of a "Hindi-Chini Bhai Bhai" (Indians and Chinese are brothers) phase of our relationship only a few years earlier. If only discretion had been used, many innocent lives could have been saved. It was a sorry state of affairs and the damage done to life and morale of troops was irreparable.[25]

However, the Corps commander looked upon this whole episode as a personal victory for his initiative in demonstrating our resolve to protect our borders regardless of the loss of life resulting from it. It was hailed as a show piece of a resurgent post 1962 Indian Army in which the Chinese had come off second best. In due course the COAS, the Prime Minister, the Deputy Prime Minister and Parliamentary delegations visited the scene of action and complimented the troops on their performance - the ugly side of which they would never know. But some good always comes out of evil. The wire fence that was erected by us became a de facto alignment of the border at the Pass - even though unofficially - and the Chinese wisely refrained from violating it.[26]

Brig. Bakshi recounted that, in 2005, he had an occasion to pay a visit to Nathu la and saw the fence still standing undisturbed. Of course, in the intervening years, the whole environment has changed drastically. Peace and amity are the order of the day all along the Northern borders and there is an ongoing dialogue in progress to solve the border dispute peacefully. The Chinese cheerfully shook hands with me across the wire and local commanders on both sides have periodic meetings in specially constructed Conference Halls in each other's territory and even enjoy each other's hospitality. This is a welcome change and a far cry from the viscous hostility during his tenure there. The latest is that Nathu la has now been transformed into a popular tourist spot where people flock to see the Chinese. A good road connects Gangtok to the Pass and a regular taxi and helicopter service is available. Soon, the route will be opened to trade for which the infrastructure is being put in place on both sides for formalities to be carried out as per norms of international trade.[27]

Nathu La Skirmish: The Beginnings

In 1965 Chinese were upset by their constant failure to capture Nathu La. They were continuously exerting pressure on India, for this they "fired on a patrol of 17 Assam Rifles, in North Sikkim, at a height of 16,000 feet, killing two men".[28]

A standard operating procedure of the PLA deployed on the Line of Actual Control (LAC) was propaganda by use of loudspeakers, classic modus of psychological warfare. At Nathu La regular broadcasts would keep playing on the distressing living conditions of Indian troops, their low salaries and lack of amenities compared to their officers living very comfortably.

This war was a type of perfect psychological warfare for Chinese and they were excellent at it, but for India it was necessary to counter it. Major General Sagat Singh, who was then GOC 17 Mountain Division had similar plan of installing loudspeakers on Indian side and playing in tape recorded Chinese language. Chinese were continuously using psychological means of war like propaganda, intimidation and other psychological means. The border was disputed and was not marked clearly, as there were certain points on the crest line which were contested, as the both sides were thinking that those points belonged to respective nations, which led to patrol causalities.

In August 1967,

[t]he 'border outposts' (BOPs) at Nathu La were occupied by 2 Grenadiers, relieving 18 Rajput. Lieutenant Colonel Rai Singh was then Commanding 2 Grenadiers. Major Bishan Singh took over as 'Tiger Nathu La', as the company commander holding the pass was generally known, with Captain P.S. Dagar as his second-in-command. The deployment at Nathu La comprised a platoon each on Camels Back, South Shoulder, Centre Bump and Sebu La. The battalion headquarters was at Gole Ghar, while the battalion 3-inch mortars were just above Sherabthang, which also had the administrative base and forward aid post. 18 Rajput took over the BOP at Yakla where they had a platoon plus. The BOPs at Cho La were occupied by a company of Jammu & Kashmir Rifles.[29]

Chinese activities were increasing simultaneously, when the Indian 2 Grenadiers were vying for taking charge of the defences at Nathu La. Gradually Chinese arrived on the crest line by 13 August and started digging trenches on the Indian side of border, adding more loudspeakers to already existing loudspeakers making it to nearly 30 to amplify their propaganda so that they can be now be heard at Changgu. Indian side on the other hand had '30-watt transistorized amplifiers with six speakers'.[30] In view of this, the Indian side's corps commander, Lieutenant General J.S. Aurora, decided that a three-strand wire fence be made alongside the border from Nathu La towards the North Shoulder. But on August 20, 1967, as the work started on the fence, angered the Chinese, who increased the level of firing at our troops erecting the fence with not only small arms but heavy mortars of their artillery.

Later on, by 1400 hours Major Bishan Singh conveyed that 75 Chinese soldiers were heading towards Nathu La. They were shouting slogans but nothing major happened at that time, Indian troops were watching and observing them. Later on, Chinese soldiers withdrew, and situation became normal. On 1st September, the corps commander along with the divisional commander went for a visit to Nathu La, they crossed the border by few steps. Seeing this Chinese Political Commissar came while shouting to specify them that they have crossed border. Again, on 4 September Major General Sagat Singh visited Nathu La, he guided that 'border from Right OP to Camels Back must be patrolled'.[31] Therefore,

> [a] patrol of two officers, one JCO and 15 OR was sent out under Major Bishan Singh'. As soon as the patrol reached the U Bump near Tekri, the Chinese surrounded them. Major Bishan Singh tried to explain to the Chinese officer that they had not crossed the border and in fact, it was the Chinese who were in Indian territory. However, the Chinese did not budge. Bishan and his men then pushed their way through the Chinese and then returned. The CO, Lieutenant Colonel Rai Singh, was watching all this from South Shoulder.[32]

Now under Major Cheema 'a platoon of 70 Field Company Engineers'[33] was assigned to support them. As the task began on 5th September, a disagreement began between Indian Colonel Rai Singh and Chinese Political Commissar regarding the border. Thus, the work was short lived for 3 hours between 0500 hours to 0800 hours. But the work on Chinese defences was continuing. Regarding North and South shoulder in night Chinese cut off one shoulder so that water discharged on other shoulder would flow within Chinese territory. Next day morning, when Indian soldiers went to rectify some wire work, few Chinese soldiers poured water on the Bump to indicate the watershed. On 7 September, the laying of the wire started again. There was hand to hand fighting with Chinese troops, but the 2 Grenadiers' Jats proved to be more physically assertive resulting in Chinese troops withdrawing and pelting stones which the 2 Grenadiers troops returned in equal measure. On 8 and 9 September there was relative peace, but Chinese were continuing to develop their defences. Seeing this the Divisional Commander Sagat getting impatient wanted the work finished before he left on leave on 12 September. On 11 September he passed instructions about expediting the task of laying the barbed wire for which he allocated additional resources. An ad-hoc force comprising of 90 men was formed to counter the situation of Chinese positions if they opened fire. Major Bishan Singh was made the in charge and Captain P.S. Dagar took the role of assistant.[34]

11th September 1967: Series of Events

On 11th September as the work began Chinese interrupted immediately. The situation was brewing with angry discussion among Chinese commander who was accompanied by Political Commissar and CO, 2 Grenadiers. Sagat knowing this in advance advised Rai Singh to stay in bunker along with Brigade Commander M.M.S. Bakshi. Rai Singh refused to comply and went ahead for facing Chinese officers openly. Unfortunately, the arguments became fiercer and more intense where both sides were not ready to budge from their ground. In this situation Chinese started firing, thus inflicting heavy casualties on the troops that were working on the wire fence. In midst of these firing unfortunately 'Colonel Rai Singh was hit by a Chinese bullet and fell down'.[35]

Grenadiers when saw the fall of their CO they became aggressive and led by Capt. P.S. Dagar instantly they the Chinese post. Major Harbhajan Singh and his company of 18 Rajput and the 'sappers and pioneers'[36] who were working on the fence were now caught in open firing and therefore suffered heavy casualties because of relentless Chinese firing. Seeing this Harbhajan Singh thought that the only way out of this is to neutralise Chinese firing through physical assault. He then started leading his men towards Chinese troops, but in this Indian troops were suffering immensely and many of them were getting 'mowed down by Chinese machine guns'[37] only few of them were able to reach the Chinese bunkers. Those who reached Chinese bunkers used their 'bayonets and accounted for many of the enemy'.[38] In this full-scale battle of six days both Harbhajan and Dagar lost their lives.

Indian Army lost 67 braves, while the Chinese lost almost 400. With China's compulsion to suppress information on many matters, truth may never be known, but it was believed by some sources to be much more. The Chinese were shocked. Indian Army's retaliation had indeed been very telling.

In an article Lessons for India and China from 1967 Nathu La clash, by Sutirtho Patranobis, Hindustan Times, from Beijing, dated July 01, 2017, states, "The current India-China standoff along the frontier in Sikkim is similar to one in 1967 that led to four days of bloody clashes between the soldiers of the two countries. The initial clashes in 1967 lasted four days. While the 1962 war was a debacle for New Delhi, the Indian Army proved more than a match for the Chinese five years later. According to an account of the clashes written by Maj Gen Sheru Thapliyal, who was posted in Sikkim at the time, the Indian side lost more than 70 soldiers while the Chinese casualties were more than 400. "We gave them a bloody nose," a former Indian diplomat told Hindustan Times. A second round of clashes erupted at Cho La on October 1, 1967, leading to more casualties. But Indian troops stood their ground and forced the Chinese soldiers to withdraw at Cho La.

Signals in Nathu La

Second Lieutenant N.C. Gupta took charge, after relieving Major R.K. Marwah. N.C. Gupta was fearless and for his achievements in Nathu La was awarded Sena Medal. He was also recommended for Maha Vir Chakra. He had a habit of maintaining diary of events. Therefore, it provides a record which is more transparent and away from myths, it also helps in correcting the regimental history written later.[39]

As the fencing was going on, all the posts and nearby areas were at full alert. Radio and cable communication were fully working. Chinese with nearly 150 troops were opposing the process of wire laying. Despite their hand to hand opposition, the plan of laying fence was getting materialized as planned. Then suddenly the number of Chinese reduced. The Chinese side began a speech of their leader Mao Tse Tung in Hindi. Their PA equipment volume was extraordinarily high and was shielding the noise of commotion. As the Indians were thinking the situation is in control suddenly the war started from Chinese side. Bunkers and guns of Chinese on North and South Shoulder started firing on Indian troops, who were laying the fence. The troops laying the fence was in front and bore maximum damage.[40]

All Indian troops were taken by surprise, through B1 net Commander started speaking to the troops on other end. It was also confirmed that the CO of 2 Grenadiers is injured. As Major Bishan Singh and Commander were in communication he instructed him to look into the causalities to H section. At 0815 there was a sound of aircraft passing but it was no aircraft, it was the sound of artillery shells that the Chinese were shooting on Indian positions. Shells were falling all around in the area of Nathu La. This information was flashed to Divisional HQ and to Army HQ. but the permission to retaliate took time from HQ. Indian firing in rear areas also caused heavy damage to Chinese. By 0930 hours Chinese fire increased and slowly the troops lost touch with the troops at North and South Shoulder. By 0945 hours, all connection was lost, creating panic. Around the same time the commander from the vantage position saw that dozens of Chinese troops were running down the slopes of South solder towards Sherabthang. This created panic, as we tried to call and observe South Shoulder but there was also no response.[41]

Then Commander asked to send someone in person to South Shoulder to restore communication. With a line party and a spare radio N.C. Gupta started moving towards South Shoulder. He reached there at around 1000 hours and was surprised to see that the post was totally abandoned. He communicated this to Commander, he saw the Chinese in their bunker across. As the fog started setting in, he was able to see few dead bodies of soldiers.[42]

From his carbine he started retaliating to intermittent firing to indicate that the post is still occupied. At 1100 hours commander informed Gupta to handle the situation as the reinforcements are on the way and reach there in around three hours. He also instructed N.C. Gupta to go 100 metres down South Shoulder where around six soldiers were sitting behind a huge rock. He went down and found all six Jawans and they all went to post and prepared themselves. As the fog intensified around 1200 hours N.C. Gupta noticed that a body was moving next to the fence which was barely 10 metres from the Chinese bunker. He went there and saw that the Major Bishan Singh in an unconscious state. By 1330 hours, Major Bishan was brought inside and the reinforcement also reached South Shoulder. On September 11, 1967, at Nathu La, Indian side lost around 70 troops in a single day. The skirmish lasted for seven days.[43]

On 11 September at around 1830 hours, with few linemen ready he decided to lay a new line to Nathu La. They reached Gole Ghar by 2000 Hours and laid the line and returned to Sherabthang. By next morning operation plan was prepared. It was decided that firstly, two patrols would patrol the area S Shoulder and North Shoulder, secondly under guidance of Capt. Daniel a platoon would assault South Shoulder to destroy or capture enemies as much they can. It was decided that as the South shoulder would fall Maj. Cheema and Capt. Rathor would go ahead to lay the wire that is left to be laid. On 12 September at around 0300 hours as they started moving towards Sherabthang, they reached there by 0430 hours and returned by 0830 hours.

On 13 September GOC reached Sherabthang to plan the next day operation. The skirmishes that started were continuing for next five days. These skirmishes left deep impression in the mind of soldiers as written by Second Lieutenant N.C. Gupta. He showed exemplary courage in saving the life of Maj. Bishan Singh, holding South Shoulder alone for few hours, with Attar Singh reoccupying the feature. Therefore N.C. Gupta was awarded a Sena Medal. General M.S. Sodhi also wrote about the Nathu La skirmishes.[44]

The account of the clash at Nathula between 2 Grenadiers and PLA on 11 September 1967, by Col. Bishan Singh, SM (retd), who participated in the action then[45] – 2 Grenadiers was earmarked to take over the front-line responsibility to hold Nathula Pass, during the month of April-May 1967. Col. Bishan Singh narrated that, "I (then Major) was given the responsibility to complete the task within a week. I carried out a detailed reconnaissance with essential personnel of my company. We spent two nights with the troops of another unit holding Nathula to understand the details of tactical layout of the Pass and the surrounding areas and to familiarize our troops with the sensitive area we were going to take over the responsibility to guard".[46]

Col. Bishan Singh recounted that,

> The physical distance between troops of both countries was very close - we were literally in eyeball to eyeball contact. The area remained generally foggy during most days of the month, specially afternoon onwards. At times there used to be deafening thunder of lightning followed by rains. Under such conditions noise of digging pits on either side remained undetected. The border generally demarcated as an imaginary line joining peak to peak distance in the mountainous area. No actual line can be drawn unless there is an understanding between both the

countries. In such conditions it becomes a problem to identify the border where the ground becomes flat and such areas were normally left undisturbed without any interference of either army, but it became a bone of contention when digging of trenches by the Chinese extended towards our side.[47]

On 7 September 1967, the JCO of Nathula right flank platoon reported early morning that he had noticed a trench dug towards the slope facing Indian territory. I immediately came down from the company HQ and reached the site of dispute at the Nathula Pass. I informed my CO, Lt Col. Rai Singh and requested him to visit the area urgently. He arrived at the sight within an hour and I briefed him in detail about the trench which the Chinese had dug on our side during the night when it was raining and with much thunder. The trench dug by the Chinese was five feet long, two feet wide and two feet deep. Although it was a minor encroachment but very meaningful if we did not take action then. We could have filled the trench and waited for the Chinese reaction subsequently.[48] But the area being super sensitive, it was obligatory and mandatory for us to inform higher HQ about this development because it had deeper implications and repercussions at the international level. Had we not taken immediate action in this matter then it was possible that the Chinese could have resorted to mass digging/encroachment later, which could have put us in an awkward situation, also reflecting negligence and lack of alertness. We both decided that the issue must be reported to higher HQ immediately.[49]

It had been decided to construct a three-strand cattle fence astride the agreed line of the border for which the pioneer platoon, defence stores and additional platoons were marshaled. The work commenced at 0400 hours on 9 September as scheduled. The Chinese commander objected to our laying of barbed wire and positioned troops with loaded weapons against us. We continued our work relentlessly in spite of objections by the Chinese and interference by way of tussling/pushing and pulling from both sides. An additional platoon of 18 Rajput and a platoon of the Division's Engineer Regiment were mustered to speed up the work. To our utter surprise the Chinese troops did not interfere and confront us as they did earlier. However, they quietly under darkness occupied dominating sites around Nathula Pass. These sites had remained unoccupied by the Chinese during peacetime. All these locations were on the Chinese side, so we could not have objected to their occupation during urgency and emergency.[50]

Our troops at Nathula Pass had been ordered to retaliate only if the Chinese opened fire. We all were organized and prepared to complete the fencing work as fast as possible and to avoid escalation. At about 0500 hours, suddenly the Chinese troops opened intense and heavy fire of small arms on our troops exposed in the open, causing casualties. I was supervising work at the proper Nathula Pass along with Capt PS Dagar. I ordered troops to take cover on the ground and fire at the enemy as directed earlier during my briefing to them. Work on the right flank of the Pass was being supervised by another officer of the unit and the company commander of 18 Rajput was managing the left flank of the Pass. The platoon of the Division Engineer Regiment and our pioneer platoons were constructing the fencing as assigned.[51]

Soon the Chinese reinforced their positions at Nathula Pass with additional troops. We were positioned and tasked to guard the troops laying the fencing and were not geared to take any further action, which in this case could have invited greater trouble at international level. We were asked to exercise restraint, keep tempers cool, but to open fire without any hesitation in case Chinese fire at us. The mist had reduced the visibility to a few feet. I and Capt. PS Dagar had taken position close by to fire at the approaching Chinese. We saw three four Chinese falling dead close to the right flank and the other Chinese crawled back to safety.[52]

Capt. P.S. Dagar was so daring that he told me that we should assault the Chinese positions located close by. I told him that we were not in an organized state to assault the Chinese positions held by almost two platoons well dug-in inside the bunkers and our troops were spread too widely. An assault would have caused heavy casualties on us in the cross firing from both sides. I told him that we should continue firing at the Chinese bunkers so that they remain pinned down in them and do not come out to assault us.[53]

In the meantime, we realized that we are exposed in the open and needed suitable cover nearby. Capt. Dagar's sten gun had developed a mechanical fault but he was so brave and courageous that unmindful of his own safety he got up and hit an approaching Chinese soldier hard on the head. Then as he was taking position behind a boulder, he was unfortunately hit by Chinese MMG bullet and fell down. I quote his last words which still ring in my memory, "Dada – I have done my assigned task as you had told me.... I am immortal – Sarvada Shakti Shali".[54]

The Chinese soldier who was hit on the head by Capt. P.S. Dagar was later shot dead by me. I crawled towards the bolder for cover but came under Chinese MMG fire and got a deep bullet wound on my left arm but I continued firing at the Chinese bunker to so that my other injured comrades could be evacuated. The CO, Lt. Col. Rai Singh got severely wounded in the stomach but despite that, he took charge of the LMG as its crew were wounded and engaged the Chinese bunker unmindful of danger to his life. Subsequently, Colonel Rai Singh and I were evacuated by helicopter to the hospital. On regaining consciousness, I learnt that our artillery and battalion mortar platoon had played havoc and inflicted heavy casualties on the Chinese troops. It is believed that over 200 Chinese were killed with the combined fire of arty, mortar and small arms. Ten to fifteen Chinese trucks carrying reinforcements came under our fire effect, again resulting in heavy casualties. Chinese also suffered some casualties while fighting from the bunkers as well. I was told that our troops kept Nathula defence positions intact by firing at the Chinese bunkers intermittently till cease fire were declared.[55]

Captain Dagar: The Hero of Nathu La[56]

While much about the skirmishes was not made public, then President Zakir Hussain, Prime Minister Indira Gandhi and Defence Minister Swaran Singh personally acknowledged the bravery of the gallantry awardees while meeting and interacting with the next of kin who came to receive the awards in the capital. Mr. Vijay Dagar, nephew of Capt. PS Dagar, Vir Chakra (Posthumous) is a repository of information about his uncle. Prithvi was a much-loved youngster in his extended Dagar family. It is from Vijay that the author has had an insight into not only the Dagar family but also personnel from other battalions which fought alongside 2 Grenadiers. Vijay also has a collection of many photographs - of Prithvi, the President, Prime Minister and Defence Minister with Capt. Dagar's father, Shri Kewal Singh and some written material, which he was kind enough to share with the author. He also arranged for the author to meet a Nathula skirmish veteran of 2 Grenadiers, Havildar Surajbhan, settled in Najafgarh, who was a young Sepoy then and an eyewitness of the Nathu la operation.[57] His account is briefed below:

> At about 0500 hours on 11 September 1967, increased Chinese activity was noticed at the Nathu La border. About 150-200 Chinese troops and 100-150 Indian soldiers were involved in a scuffle. While the Indians were laying the wire, the Chinese were continuously disrupting their work. Suddenly, the Chinese troops started retreating back and their number reduced significantly. The Indian troops intensified their work thinking the work could be finished quickly now. However, they were unaware of the intentions of the Chinese who were holed up in the bunkers in large numbers. Unexpectedly, the Chinese side opened fire on the unarmed Indian wire laying party, which had no time to cover and save themselves. There were many casualties on the both sides.[58]

Havildar Surajbhan continued narrating that,

> On hearing the firing, Capt. Dagar immediately moved with his commando platoon started moving up but were caught unawares by the Chinese assault. Dagar spotted a Chinese MMG which was causing many casualties to the Indian troops. Even though he was left with few men he made a quick decision to attack the MMG position. At about 0710 hours, he moved and selected the route to reach the MMG from the southern shoulder end. Despite the danger involved, he cautiously reached the bunker and hit the Chinese soldier with the burst of his carbine. On capturing the MMG, he turned the fire on the Chinese troops hiding in the bunker nearby killing and injuring many of them.[59]

Havildar Surajbhan recounted that after four days, Captain Koshal reached Nathu La after the ceasefire. To their surprise, four Chinese soldiers were standing near the mortal remains of Capt. Dagar. On enquiry they responded that Capt. Dagar can still stand back on his feet. Such was his fear in the heart of the enemy. The Chinese were still not willing to hand over the body and asked them to send senior officers.[60]

It was then that Major Chandershekar of 18 Rajput and, 2nd Lt. Attar Singh, 2 Grenadiers went and brought back the remains of the fallen heroes, namely Capt. Dagar, Sub. Mam Chand, Hav. Lakhmi Chand and L/Nk Harlal. Capt. Dagar and the other martyrs were cremated near Changu Lake with full military honours at 4:30 PM on 15 September 1967. After discussing these stellar accounts, we now move on to discussing the other important site of skirmishes, which is the Chola La incident, that took place only a few days after the Nathu La skirmish.[61]

September 11 became officially known as Nathu La Day.

The Cho La Incident

Cho La, another post located to the north west of Nathu La fell under 63 Mountain Brigade, then under the command of Brigadier Kundan Singh. It was occupied by 10 Jammu & Kashmir Rifles, which was being relieved by 7/11 Gorkha Rifles during the last week of September 1967. On 1st October, there was a scuffle at Point 15,450 which had been taken over by the Gorkhas the previous day. There was a boulder at the post, and Chinese and Indian sentries usually stood on opposite sides. Since the Indians were new to the post, the Chinese staked claim to the boulder, leading to a heated argument between the two post commanders. During the argument, the Gorkha JCO rested his right foot on the boulder. The Chinese kicked his foot away. The JCO then put his foot back on the boulder and challenged his Chinese counterpart.[62]

The Chinese had also decided to escalate matters and taken positions. The Chinese soldiers bayoneted the Gorkha JCO, injuring him in the arm. The Gorkhas retaliated by cutting off the arm of the Chinese with their Khukris. The Chinese opened up with all they had, with the Indians responding in like fashion. The Gorkhas charged towards the Chinese positions and there was hand-to-hand combat, with Khukris flashing repeatedly. The officiating CO, Major K.B. Joshi was on his way to Point 15,450 when the incident started. He was at Rai Gap, which was still held by 10 Jammu & Kashmir Rifles, and could see the post being annihilated. The position at Rai Gap also came under heavy fire and was attacked by the Chinese, but the Indians held on.[63]

The news of the firing was conveyed to HQ 63 Mountain Brigade by Major Nair, the second-in-command of 10 Jammu & Kashmir Rifles. Brigadier Kundan Singh, who was also officiating the divisional commander, immediately ordered the rest of the 7/11 Gorkha Rifles to move up from Tamze. He himself moved up to Twin Huts, to see things for himself, where he met Major Joshi, who requested permission to recapture Point 15,450. The attack was launched in the next morning and the position was recaptured by the Gorkhas. The battalion was awarded two Vir Chakras during the incident.[64]

Lieutenant General S.R.R. Aiyangar, who was the commanding 63 Mountain Brigade Signal Company at that time, recounts the Cho La incident in the following words:

> The Cho La incident took place barely a month after the Nathu la incident. Our Brigade 63 Mountain Brigade was operationally responsible for this Sector. On many numerous visits to this Sector, I had seen visually the close proximity of troops on either side of the LAC. I had also noticed the Chinese troops walking side by side whenever we walked across the wire obstacle we had laid after the Nathu la incident to demarcate our side of the LAC. In fact, the troops then occupying Cho La post (10 J&K RIF) often used to narrate how the Chinese troops would toss up Mao's red badge across the fence in return of any cigarette packets thrown across by our troops.[65]

Gen. S.R.R. Aiyangar further told that they had also installed a PA system similar to the one they had at Nathula. My Sig Coy-63 Mtn Bde Sig Coy had also installed from our side of the LAC beaming transmission towards the Chinese post. What was surprising that the Chinese tapes were very current catching up with their versions of happenings in the country, whereas our tapes coming from Delhi were same old propaganda stuff, what I thought at that time was very pedestrian. Also being in Chinese, one could not discern its contents objectively. In fact, I do recollect one taped message from the Chinese side which had sensed a change of guard at the post-10 JAK RIF handing over to 7/11 GR and Chinese broadcast mentioned that the Indian government was misusing the Gorkhas.[66]

On one morning (I am not able to remember the exact date now), we had frantic calls from Cho La that a heavy exchange of fire was taking place. CO of the Battalion (10 JAK RIF) was returning from leave and his 2ic was manning the fort. Reportedly at one of the forward posts where the incident of bayonet crossing as mentioned by me, a scuffle had taken place and some hand to hand combat had followed thereafter. The post was also in the process of being handed over to 7/11 GR troops. Somehow caught up in the process of handing/taking over, some vigilance from our side was not up to the mark. The Chinese started firing all across our post especially on the Bn/Coy HQ locations and generally restricting any movements in areas where they could easily see. The matter was reported to Bde Comdr (Brig Kundan Singh) and our attempt to speak to the 2ic was futile, his telephone was ringing but there was no response. His bunker was also under heavy firing from the Chinese side.

I has asked my B-1 operator, I do still remember his name - L/Nk Moga Singh, a tall young man, full of josh. I asked him to take our radio set to the 2 ic's bunker taking advantage of the lull in firing. We finally managed to speak to him on the radio set, but my own feedback from Moga Singh was that the officer was in a state of shock and the telephone was repeatedly ringing. We got some version of the event from the 2ic. Commander then decided to visit Cho La next day and wanted me to accompany him. I had done these visits on number of occasions with him and he was appreciative of our attempts to keep these communications going despite all the odds of weather and terrain etc. In fact, I do remember that after almost every visit of his to Cho La post, he would send some Rum to our boys and especially our linemen who used to maintain a tenuous WD-1 route.[67]

On reaching the Cho La post the next day, the Commander has a good idea of what had happened the previous day. We got a message across the PA system. I had mentioned earlier about Chinese wanting to hand over the dead bodies of our troops. At the appointed time the following day, our officer was sent to collect the dead bodies at the place the Chinese had indicated. I could see this process from a vantage point nearby. I could see the same Political Commissar whom I had seen at Nathu la was there, overseeing the handing over of the bodies. He was also seen having a long talk with our officer. The Chinese also asked our officer to sign a piece of paper which was written in Hindi giving all the details of bodies, weapons and small arms and ammunition. I do also recall that incident when few small arms ammunitions fell on the ground and the Chinese soldiers scooping the earth below it, spitting on it and throwing across our side of the LAC. This behaviour was indeed shocking. I also noticed that few of the bodies that were handed over bore bullet marks on the skull and the faces were very badly mutilated showing signs of some deliberate jabbing. We could not get any Chinese body. The Indian officer when debriefed by Comdr, gave the impression that the Chinese had put the blame entirely on us for transgressing the LAC and similar to what we had done a month earlier at LAC.[68]

I had put up L/Nk Moga Singh for a citation but somewhere down the line, it got lost. My Comdr did meet and congratulate him for his efforts to keep the communication going. Yes, Moga did us proud.

Cho La Skirmish 10 JAK RIF[69]

Till 25 July 1967 there was no Chinese post established at Chola. Occasionally large-scale Chinese patrols used to come to check the border area and return after a few days. On 25 July 1967, a large number of Chinese accompanied by patrol dogs took up temporary defences on the high features located on the other side of Chola, thereby indicating their doubtful intentions. Major Saroop Singh Jamwal the then Chola post commander ordered Second Lieutenant AC Chanda along with eight Jawans of 'D' Company to occupy Point 15440, the highest feature where the distance between own troops and the Chinese was eyeball to eyeball. Our troops displayed confidence and capability to prepare defence, under the cover of darkness, extreme high-altitude weather conditions and in the close vicinity of the enemy. With our confidence and competence, it was perhaps evident to the enemy that the Indian Army meant business.[70]

As for carrying out the wiring of the Chola Defence, it was decided to tackle the responsibility in a phased manner. Being about eighteen kilometers from the Battalion Headquarters, an administrative base up to jeepable road head at 'Tamze' was established. Further ahead, at the base of the Chola defences, a battalion base at Hut Area was established. Here dumping of material was completed during the road open period.[71]

Subsequently, these were independently carried through porters, ponies and troops to the individual post in a planned manner to complete the work. Each battalion of the formation had a tenure during which the assigned task was to be completed. 10 JAK RIF was assigned the initial role of establishing the administrative base, carry out dumping, carry out the wiring of the entire defences and thereafter revert back by 1st October 1967 for its Raising Day at the Chhangu Lake Battalion Headquarters. The battalion was highly motivated. The troops would volunteer to do extra work to complete the task assigned. Lieutenant Colonel Mahatam Singh was personally supervising the progress and made frequent trips. Sometimes he would stay for week or ten days at a stretch with the boys on the picquet. He would personally carry out reconnaissance of the area along which wire had to be laid or pitch a long iron picket at a spot and help the boys in holding the barbed wire along the fences. Leadership and command by personal example and participation was his style.[72]

The defences of the Chola garrison then had Point 15440, Raigap, Chola Pass and Saddle and the Hut Area as the administrative base. It was a stretch of approximately four kilometers along the crest line. The Battalion Headquarters was fifteen kilometers from the Tamze Road Head and another three kilometers to the Hut Area by mule track. It was away from the VIP (Very Important Person) visit route as it was least likely approach in the overall context and also it involved travel by 'foot' aggravated by inhospitable weather conditions like strong winds, harsh ground conditions and height problems. Work was therefore going on smoothly without interference.[73]

Major Saroop Singh Jamwal, son of Lieutenant Colonel Ajit Singh, Vir Chakra of 9 JAK RIF fame was the overall in charge of the stocking and wiring operation. He bore the brunt of responsibility, endured the initial hardship, and above all had to cater for the frequent and unannounced visits of the Commanding Officer who would prolong his stay. The Chinese at certain times were at eyeball distance and provoked our troops while they were laying out the long iron pickets. They would say "ZHE SHI MAO TSE TUNG CHINA" meaning that, it belonged to China, Saroop would very tactfully intervene and settle the issue with the Chinese Commander by physically walking and moving to the spot, where pickets were to be fixed. Loud radio music and Chinese Hindi propaganda telling them to go away from the picquet had also to be countered. To prove to the Chinese that Indian troops were a satisfied lot and were disciplined he had ordered troops to eat their high-altitude rations like eggs, meat etc. in the open on the table laid out during fair weather. The Chinese troops would watch Indian troops having a good meal while their own ration scales were meager.[74]

An interesting incident occurred during one of the visits of the Commanding Officer who stayed overnight at "Chola Post". The small post near Chola Post was frozen. Lieutenant Colonel Mahatam Singh did his morning prayer only after a bath. That day he came out of the bunker in his long kutcha and bare body. The Chinese soldiers were watching this activity with their heavy coats on. They were struck at this strange spectacle. After some time when the wiring activity commenced with Major Saroop in the lead, the political Commisar in the Chinese picquet who could speak a few broken words of Hindi, asked Saroop as to who the very important person in the post was. Saroop without hesitation replied, "Indian Mao Tse Tung"! He smiled and went back. There were no problems till the Commanding Officer stayed and smiles were exchanged. The wiring task was accomplished without an incident.[75]

For the overall performance of the assigned task with quiet efficiency, Saroop was awarded the Chief of the Army Staff Commendation Card, presently he is serving with the Jammu and Kashmir Government in the Kashmir Administrative Service.

Recalls Colonel Krishnaswami,

> During 1963-64 Saroop was a cadet at the Indian Military Academy undergoing the Emergency Course Serial No. 2. I was

on the instructional staff then. During the evening when I was going on my normal walk with my wife and young son in his stroller, Saroop with his friend was going on cycle. They paid their usual compliment by riding to attention. His friend murmured in Dogri to say that they should get down and meet us, since I was a JAK RIF officer. Saroop replied in Dogri "Chhor pare yara, kithe punishment na mili jaye".[76]

He must have thought that I did not understand his 'Dogri'. Destiny bought us closer and we served in the same unit as brother officers. He lived up to the family tradition of being a quiet, unassuming and hardworking officer, who would deliver the goods at all costs. The tradition of the JAK's must carry on father to son. The Jammu and Kashmir Government is indeed lucky to have a fine officer amongst them.[77]

The Battalion had gained the esteem of the entire formation for having carried out the task of initial dumping of stores and the difficult task of wiring the entire defences with cool efficiency and speed, in fact well ahead of time. We were geared up for celebrating the Raising Day at the Base Headquarters on 1st October 1967. The relief programme had indicated 7/11 Gorkha Rifles under Lieutenant Colonel Joshi to take over the operational responsibility by 1st October. The handing and taking over schedules were laid out. As per plan, the battalion had to pull out on the morning of 1st October after the joint stand to at the picquet.[78]

'A' Company was holding the Picquet 15440 and 'D' Company the Piquet at Chola Pass, Rai Gap and Saddle. The commanding officer after briefing Lieutenant Colonel Joshi had left on 30th September to Base Headquarters as the "Havan" at the unit Mandir was to be performed in the morning. The officiating Commanding Officer Joshi was at the base, Majors SC Dogra and Saroop Jamwal were Commanding 'A' and 'D' Companies respectively. Subedar Waryam Singh was the Platoon commander at Chola post. Lieutenant Colonel SM Joshi was to assume operational command of the Sub Sector once 10 JAK finally moved out. It was a familiar sight to see him walk with his walking stick and his pet dog every morning. On the morning of 1st October, all was quiet and peaceful. Nair was waiting to get all clear reports from the picquets to move back to the base after handing over the command to Lieutenant Colonel Joshi.[79]

Lieutenant Colonel Joshi, as usual, was on his morning constitutional walk. This time he casually chose to move towards the Chola Post. No one had known that the colonel had chosen this route. Saroop had informed that "Saddle" we handed over to the satisfaction of the new Company Commander and sought permission to proceed. The platoon at Raigap and Chola Post were being delayed for handling over of some ammunition held in the bunkers which was being again physically counted by the relieving unit. He suggested that they could pass via the Administrative Base on completion and join up with 'A' Company column to Battalion Headquarters. Major Nair gave permission and Saroop was now pulling out to proceed to the Battalion Headquarters.[80]

The Rai Gap Post Commander, Subedar Waryam Singh was not too happy at the manner in which the relieving unit Junior Commissioned Officer wanted the entire ammunition held in boxes inside the bunker to be physically counted before signing the vouchers. Waryam was not the usual high flying "qualified" Junior Commissioned Officer. He had risen the hard way with his simplicity, devotion, practical sense and personal leadership. He had the tenacity and could withstand protracted stress and strain. His post was most difficult to hold as they were virtually in eyeball to eyeball contact with the Chinese troops. He gave a few hints to the Junior Commissioned Officer on practical leadership in a picquet and how one must be ready at all times to face a combat situation and not expose oneself to danger by laying out arms/ammunition on the ground like we do in a peace area. Lieutenant Colonel Joshi was witnessing the exchange of words between the Junior Commissioned Officers without their knowledge and later appreciated the practical wisdom of this rustic 'Chib Bhau Rajput' from Jammu, dressing down his Junior Commissioned Officer. Notwithstanding the advice Waryam got the ammunition out and ordered that it be laid out.[81]

Picquet 15440 was unique, in that it could be approached easily from the Hut Area Administrative Base by beaten track and the climb was a steady steep one. The other route was along the reverse slope of the crest line route to Chola Post which was not frequented because of it being very steep and tough. At 15440 picquet complex, there was a peculiar location along the crest line which afforded clear visibility of both the Chinese and home side. It was too small a place for deployment of a body of troops. Perhaps a weapon could independently be cited here to dominate both the approaches. Both sides had agreed to leave the pace unoccupied and this was included in the handing over brief. Major Subhash Dogra had handed over his picquet to 2nd Lieutenant Rana of 7/11 Gorkha Rifles on the morning after the joint 'stand to' procedure and wished him good luck before departure. Rana assured Dogra that there was nothing to worry as they were Gorkhas. Dogra with his boys reached the Administrative Base to report to Major Nair. Nair told him about the slight delay caused by Waryam's platoon and that he could have his breakfast and they all would wait for Waryam to join. In the meantime, he could monitor the progress. He also unknowingly sent his runner to fetch Lieutenant Colonel Joshi to join them for breakfast. It was only then that he knew that Colonel Joshi was not there in his bunk.[82]

Time was around 0905 hours. Dogra heard the distinct sound of Light Machine Gun/Medium Machine Gun burst coming from the direction of his erstwhile post at 15440. Dogra at once yelled and told Nair, "My God, I hope the youngster has not provoked the Chinese". Nair came out and was watching the developments with anxiety. A very light flare was fixed from the Chinese side and that was the indication for entire sector to get alive. Firing had commenced on all the picquets. Nobody knew what had happened, who had opened the first, what was the provocation, casualties, command and control, whereabouts of Lieutenant Colonel Joshi and so on. Nair thought it fit to inform Battalion Headquarters immediately.[83]

Lieutenant Colonel Mahatam Singh, the Commanding Officer, was at the Mandir and seated beside the Panditji doing the 'Havan', when the Adjutant, Captain Parkash Chand rushed to tell him of the development. He abruptly left telling the Panditji to pray for the Unit and carry on with the Havan. He was off towards Tamze R pad Head with his radio operator and protection section. Within an hour and a half, he was well on the way to Saddle. Enroute he met Saroop and his boys and turned them back towards their old post as he thought there may be a requirement. He got in radio contact with Waryam Singh and told him to hold on and that he was coming. Waryam replied "SAAB JI TUSI PHIKAR NA KARO MAIN ITHE HI RAHNA SAB THIK HAI" (Sir, do not worry, I am here, all is well). Similarly, he got in touch with saddle and intimated them that he has 'assumed' command and that everyone will fight till the last. He could not get through to 15440. 2nd Lieutenant Rana and few boys had fallen back to the Administrative Base. He enquired of Dogra and ordered him to move towards Chola Post with his boys and be prepared to retake and reoccupy 15440. He said he was on his way.[84]

The Brigade Headquarters are frantic to know about the operational situation. Nair was making all efforts to get through to Saddle, 15440, Raigap, Chola Post to find out the progress and whereabouts of Lieutenant Colonel Joshi. Chola Post reported fierce fighting. It was virtually close quarter battle for them. They had suffered two casualties so far. Havildar Narinder and Rifleman Gagan Chand. Waryam Singh said he had killed quite a few Chinese and there was nothing to worry and he was in full command of the situation. The Gorkha troops of 15440 were trickling in towards the base, less their commander and Junior Commissioned Officer was giving confused version regarding the firing and casualties. He said Lieutenant saab was still fighting. That was not true, the troops from the post were almost there at the base. The firing had ceased. Now sporadic fire was being directed at the Hut Area also, although ineffective.[85]

The Brigade Headquarters were agog at the news of the fall of 15,440. Their query regarding Lieutenant Colonel Joshi could not be answered. Brigadier Kundan Singh gave direct orders to Nair to get him the latest about Chola, Raigap and Saddle and for him to proceed to Chola Post. Time was around 0950 hours. Nair was in a great dilemma. The command setup was so unclear. Two major posts were already handed over, only one platoon was of 10 JAK RIF and the rest of the troops were from 7/11 GORKHA RIFLES. The move from Hut Area towards Chola Post, where there was close quarter fighting taking place was not warranted, he felt. The Commanding Officer of the incoming unit, although in the defended sector was not to be traced.

The Chinese had occupied 15440 and were carrying out firing although it was ineffective.[86]

Their intentions were not known. There was a delay in his reaction to the direct order. Had he moved immediately with a platoon of 'A' Company towards Chola Post to reinforce it, then the tale would have been so different. He would have met Lieutenant Colonel Joshi enroute as he was unable to go forward/come back due to the firing by the Chinese. That was not to be. As he was preparing to go, there was a call again from the Brigade Headquarters. The Commander was on the line. Dogra picked up the phone and gave out the gist of the known information and could not satisfy the queries raised by the Commander in his stentorian voice. The Commander queied, "Is your Major Nair there?" Dogra replied "Yes, Sir". Hell was let loose "get him on the line". Dogra yelled for Nair who had gone about hundred yards away from the Hut Area. Nair came running back thinking that there were fresh orders for him.[87]

It was, a royal dressing down and a sack too!! Nair was a broken man after that. Meanwhile information came that Captain Manas Kumar Bhattacharya at Rai Gap was wounded in his thigh with Medium Machine Gun burst of the Chinese troops. He was forcibly evacuated and later moved back to Hut Area although he wanted to be at the picquet.[88]

The Brigade Commander had informed Division Headquarters/Corps Headquarters. The Divisional Artillery and Corps Artillery were placed in readiness to fire. By 1230 hours Lieutenant Colonel Mahatam Singh had reached Saddle and came on the Brigade radio link to announce that he was assuming command and would restore order. He was categorical to intimate that no artillery fire will be opened without himself asking for the same. He had wanted the situation to be "localized" and not escalate further. He was sure, he would be able to get back 15440, so he told Brigadier Kundan Singh and Major General Sagat Singh. The weather was getting cloudy and low clouds drifting provided adequate cover for troop movement. He had ordered Dogra to move towards Chola Post and he also started advancing towards it and was in direct contact with Dogra. The progress of Dogra and his boys towards their erstwhile post of 15440 was arduous and slow, as the route was such. Nevertheless, it was safe as firing was not encountered. The enemy perhaps did not know of this approach.[89]

The move was like a textbook section battle drill executed with stealth and caution. Dogra pumped in his first section on his old picquet to search the area. Time was well past 1500 hours. Dogra and his boys had re-occupied the 15440 defences by 1600 hours. Not one round was fired, not a man was lost. The lost prestige was regained for the formation. 10 JAK RIF had done it. It was a tremendous challenge. Dogra said later that he was more afraid of the Commanding Officer on his back than the Chinese in the front. The radio communications were all in chaste Dogri which must have been high grade cipher for the Chinese even if they intercepted it. Conversation like "Laaj Rakh, Izzat Bachho" goaded the men to fearlessly advance and retake their picquet.[90]

After the "Stand-to" Dogra went around the post to find 2nd Lieutenant Rana's body riddled with bullets, with the telephone set in his hand. A few more dead jawans were also found. The empty cartridges of the Chinese weapons were strewn in our picquet. All items were intact as the Chinese did not touch any of our equipment. Soon Lieutenant Colonel Mahatam Singh was on the post to congratulate the boys for their good work. He told them that they could not have celebrated the Raising Day in a better fashion. They have got themselves in the history of the battalion.[91]

Enroute to 15440, Lieutenant Colonel Mahatam Singh passed through posts of Rai gap and Chola Pass and had a pleasant meeting with Lieutenant Colonel Joshi, who was now in the picquet, complimenting Subedar Waryam Singh and his boys for their indomitable spirit, bravery, sacrifice and leadership. He was a direct witness to all the fighting at such a close range. He narrated the incident when the Verey Light of the Chinese was fired and how Waryam Singh was quick on his feet, pushed everyone to the trenches, picked up a loaded sten-gun, mowed down almost a dozen Chinese soldiers and injured quite a few before the Chinese even realized what had happened. He exercised perfect control and his personal leadership was to be seen to be believed and he had seen it. The manner in which Havildar Narinder Singh and Rifleman Gagan Chand sacrificed their lives performing their assigned duties till the very end was heroic. They gave their lives so that others could safely fight longer and hold on. They risked their lives to get the ammunition lying in the open and pulled it to the trenches. Their devotion was such that, although they were hit, they carried on relentlessly and enabled the picquet to hold on and fight with their backs to the wall. 10 JAK RIF was tested in battle that day and Lieutenant Colonel Joshi was filled with emotion when he said that the Junior Commissioned Officer and the platoon won his heart and that he would love to have Junior Commissioned Officers like Waryam Singh in his unit.[92]

The brave action of the battalion spread in the entire formation. During the evening Roll Call of the units of the formation, it was announced in clear words, "Junior Commissioned Officer ho to Waryam Singh ki tarah ho". It was a feather in our cap. The battalion was proud that the nation had recognized its action on its 4th Raising Day and covered itself with glory. Lieutenant Colonel Mahatam Singh was awarded the Mahavir Chakra and Vir Chakras were awarded to Subedar Waryam Singh, Havildar Narinder Singh (Posthumous), Rifleman Gagan Chand (Posthumous). Chief of Army Staff's Commendations went to Major Saroop Singh, Havildar Amar Nath and Riflemen Gagan Chand, Punjab Singh, Riflemen Bishan Dass, Prem Lal, Ram Krishan and Randhir Singh, all killed and ten wounded. Enemy casualties were forty-four killed, several wounded and one apprehended.[93]

The after-effect and the re-establishment of the Chola defences by 10 JAK RIF was a mixture of joy and sorrow. Joy because of the efficient and cool manner in which order was restored and sorrow because we had lost some of our brethren in the conflict and some had not performed well or well enough to rise to the occasion.[94]

After the bustle of enquiries had settled down, the battalion was relieved from operational commitments. We had joined the ranks of battle experienced and decorated units of the Indian Army and the Regiment. Letters of congratulations from many well-wishers had come. We all felt taller and walked with confidence and pride. Zorawar's descendants had avenged the dishonor of 1962.[95]

The move orders for the battalion, earmarking it for a tenure under 19 Infantry Brigade at Damana was indeed big news for all of us. It was perhaps a token recognition by the Army Headquarters Staff Duties Directorate to reward the battalion for their work and the hard stint it had gone through. They might have also known that the Commanding Officer, Lieutenant Colonel Mahatam Singh hailed from Village Damana. They perhaps rewarded him too, to enable him to command his unit in his own area. How proud the village must have been to have their son of the soil who had not only covered himself with glory but also had brought laurels to his battalion and the Regiment. Everyone in the unit considered it a privilege to be a member of this team.[96]

7/11 Gorkha Rifles: Recalling the Khukri episode

7/11 GR also taught its attackers at Chola an unforgettable lesson with khukris. A brief action of this skirmish is that the Chinese company commander and the political commissar were staking claims to a boulder at the sentry post. Naib Subedar Gyan Bahadur Limbu was having a heated argument with his counterpart at the sentry post, while he rested his right foot on the disputed boulder. The Chinese kicked his foot away. In defiance, Gyan put his foot back. The Chinese soon escalated the situation and one of the Chinese soldiers bayoneted Gyan, wounding him in his arm. The JCO responded swiftly with his khukri chopping both arms of his attacker. The Chinese then opened fire and both sides engaged in a firefight at close range. Lance Naik Krishna Bahadur, the post commander, then led a charge against the Chinese who were forming up for an assault. Although seriously injured, he continued to exhort his men forward. Rifleman Devi Prasad Limbu directly behind Krishna Bahadur, who was already engaged in a close quarter battle with the enemy, wielded his khukri and accounted for five Chinese heads, till he was felled by a direct hit. For his action he was awarded a Vir Chakra (Posthumous). Lance Naik Krishna Bahadur's body was later returned by the Chinese with full military honours. The Chinese officer, who accompanied the remains to the Indian Army, reportedly praised the performance of the Indian troops, stating that "they fought like tigers".[97]

This skirmish along with the Indian retaliation with artillery at Nathula within the same month - October - exactly five years after the humiliating defeat in 1962, owing to politico-bureaucratic ignorance and callousness compounded by some very flawed policies and decisions of then Prime Minister Nehru and Defence Minister Krishna Menon, were very significant and impactful.

In 1975 India annexed Sikkim.[98]

The brief saga of the skirmish at Chola brought the curtain down on this eventful period. Though not a major engagement, it was significant because after 1962 it represented a turn around. If the Chinese did not intervene on Pakistan's behalf in 1971, possible it was in some measure due to the Indian Army's performance in 1967.[99]

Fast-forwarding it to the ongoing developments in the eastern sector, the Chinese seem to be practicing the same intimidation again. Since China's political and military objectives against India have not changed even 50 years after the Nathu La and Cho La skirmishes, the government should not forget that this is the same army which busted the Chinese ego back then and today, it is far more prepared to face the circumstances. And if, intrusions in Sikkim or elsewhere continue, then India should seriously consider stronger options as it has been keeping firm on its stand in the prevailing situation. Despite the result of the 1967 standoff going in India's favour, its acknowledgment seems to be relatively subdued as immediately, parallels are being drawing to the 1962 embarrassment. Beijing has taken advantage of this, and deliberately attempts incursions across the LAC to exploit India's perceived vulnerabilities and unfortunately, the Chinese have been successful over the years in intimidating India in a number of instances, which left previous governments embarrassed, both due to the absence of acknowledgement of the 1967 example and also due to lack of any framework in dealing with such cases. In the end, one can only say, that helplessly watching Tibet annexed by China in good faith, with the expectation of not angering China was a grave mistake whose after-effects continue to be seen till date.[100]

NOTES

1 http://news.bbc.co.uk/2/hi/south_asia/7914229.stm

2	Read Chicken's neck region
3	https://shodhganga.inflibnet.ac.in/bitstream/10603/161480/8/08_chapter%203.pdf
4	https://idsa.in/idsacomments/WhatdidChinaGain%20attheEndoftheFighting_RSKalha_211112
5	http://veekay-militaryhistory.blogspot.com/2013/04/nathula-1967-real story.html?showComment=1382248652536
6	Bakshi, MMS. (20__, Month Date). Personal interview.
7	Ibid.
8	Ibid.
9	Ibid.
10	Ibid.
11	Ibid.
12	Ibid.
13	Ibid.
14	Ibid.
15	Ibid.
16	Ibid.
17	Ibid.
18	Ibid.
19	Ibid.
20	http://www.jottings.in/2011/11/from-todays-papers-02-nov-2011.html
21	Personal Interview with Brigadier Bakshi over a number of conversations in May-June 2009.
22	Ibid.
23	Ibid.
24	Ibid.
25	Ibid.
26	Ibid.
27	Ibid.
28	http://veekay-militaryhistory.blogspot.com/2013/04/nathula-1967-real-story.html?showComment=1382248652536
29	Ibid.
30	Ibid.
31	Ibid.
32	Ibid.
33	Ibid.
34	Ibid.
35	Ibid.
36	Ibid.
37	Ibid.
38	Ibid.
39	Ibid.
40	Ibid.

41 Ibid.
42 Ibid.
43 Ibid.
44 Ibid.
45 Personal Interview with Col. Bishan Singh dated 15 May 2017.
46 Ibid.
47 Ibid.
48 Ibid.
49 Ibid.
50 Ibid.
51 Ibid.
52 Ibid.
53 Ibid.
54 Ibid.
55 Ibid.
56 Personal Interview with Vijay Dagar dated 20 May 2017
57 Personal Interview with Havildar Surajbhan dated 20 May 2017.
58 Ibid.
59 Ibid.
60 Ibid.
61 Ibid.
62 http://veekay-militaryhistory.blogspot.com/2016/01/chapter-8-miscellaneous-operations-1947.html
63 Ibid.
64 Ibid.
65 Ibid.
66 Ibid.
67 Ibid.
68 Ibid.
69 Excerpted from Soldiers of the Sun and Snow: History of Jammu and Kashmir Rifles and Ladakh Scouts (1956-1996)
70 Ibid.
71 Ibid.
72 Ibid.
73 Ibid.
74 Ibid.
75 Ibid.
76 Ibid.
77 Ibid.
78 Ibid.
79 Ibid.
80 Ibid.
81 Ibid.
82 Ibid.

83 Ibid.
84 Ibid.
85 Ibid.
86 Ibid.
87 Ibid.
88 Ibid.
89 Ibid.
90 Ibid.
91 Ibid.
92 Ibid.
93 Ibid.
94 Ibid.
95 Ibid.
96 Ibid.
97 Ibid.
98 Ibid.
99 Ibid.
100 Ibid.

3

1967-2007: TULUNG LA AND SUMDORONG CHU - SPECIALIZING IN BULLETLESS BOUTS AND DIALOGUE

For the first time since the 1967 Nathu La-Cho La skirmishes, on October 20, 1975, PLA killed four riflemen of 5 Assam Rifles, not by bullets but by torture after capturing them. 5 Assam Rifles was the battalion which escorted the Dalai Lama after he escaped and crossed over to India in 1959. It was a lone incident of PLA killing Indian soldiers in over five decades since 1967 by sticking to the clause that the two armies should not fire at each other and resolve any border dispute issue by discussion. So technically they maintained their own initiated clause of not firing any bullets. The bodies of these four riflemen were handed over to the Commanding Officer of a Gorkha Rifles battalion, who had to negotiate a tough route and tedious procedures imposed by PLA.

After almost a decade of hiatus, diplomatic relations were restored in 1976 when ambassadorial level ties were restored and Mr. K R Narayan was appointed as the Ambassador to China, which in turn, appointed Zhen Zhao Yuan as the Ambassador to India.

Next, with the coming of the Janata Party to power in 1977, the then PM Morarji Desai gave a special emphasis on improving ties with China. China invited the external affairs minister in 1978. The impetus could have come from brewing crisis in Afghanistan which cold-war rivalry manifested in full blown manner and culminated in Soviet invasion in December 1979.

After some internal bickering within the Janta Party due to pro-Soviet faction opposing any ties with China, in February 1979, Atal Behari Vajpayee, the then minister of external affairs embarked on a visit to China. While Vajpayee was in China, the nation had intervened in the Vietnam war and he had to hastily return back. Nevertheless, Vajpayee did have wide ranging talks with senior Chinese dignitaries including Premier Hua Guofeng (1976-80) and the then Vice Premier Deng Xiaoping. However, speaking in the Parliament a few days after his return, Vajpayee conveyed India's "desire to express solidarity with the brave and valiant people of the Republic of Vietnam who [were] facing a new crisis".[1]

In April 1981, Dr. Subramanian Swamy undertook a visit to Beijing and was received by Deng Xiaoping. During the meeting, he announced that Foreign Minister Huang Hua would go to India, and also that China was considering negotiating settlement on the Sino-Indian border dispute.[2]

Huang Hua visited India in June 1981 which broke the ice of border negotiations, the first round of which began in December 1981, almost two decades after the two sides had stopped talking. Deng also conceded to Swamy's demand to re-open the Kailash-Manasarovar route in Tibet but only for Hindu pilgrims (which was China's condition).[3] He led the first delegation of pilgrims in September 1981.

However, as time progressed, the Chinese side had begun showing signs of rigidity by 1985 and even evasive on the nature of deal, without clarifying on how it wanted the LAC to be demarcated.[4] By the time seventh round of talks took place in July 1986, Chinese incursions into the Sumdorung Chu valley in Arunachal Pradesh had begun and the stage was set for a protracted standoff between both the armies. This was followed by mobilizations on both sides of the border by early 1987. Concerns about a possible military standoff over the border started growing. The incident raised temperatures in Delhi and Beijing and took a considerable time to thaw.

The Sumdorong Chu Incident

Sumdorong Chu (also known as Sangduoluo He in China) is a stream flowing north to south near the Thag La triangle, on the west of which lies the Bhutanese territory and the Thag La ridge being on its the north. It is located in the Tawang district of the Indian state of Arunachal Pradesh, north east of the confluence of the rivers, Namka Chu and Nyamjiang Chu.

On June 26, 1986, New Delhi strongly protested against incursions by Chinese troops in this territory that had occurred beginning from June 16. With its usual tactics of denying while committing the sin, Beijing stated it was unaware of any such intrusions and insisted that the Chinese troops were placed well north of the McMahon Line. Indians had found out that the Chinese troops had intruded the Macmahon Line. The transgressed territory was the Thandrong pasture on Sumdorung Chu's banks, and also the Wangdung area (located under the Zimithang circle of Tawang). Besides Indian observers, this portion of territory has been identified as lying towards the *north* of the McMahon Line by third party sources too, which have nothing to with India or China. This region lies along the old route connecting Lhasa with Tawang and even the Brahmaputra valley. Thag La ridge, lying near to Sumdorung Chu even had witnessed exchanges between both the armies during the 1962 war.

The area had been considered a neutral area by both sides since the war had finished and had not been monitored by India between 1977 and 1980, something which the Chinese side attempted to take advantage of.[5]

As infrastructure and logistics support was strengthening in the area, the Indian Army sought to reinforce and strengthen Arunachal's forward areas and patrolling was resumed in 1981. By the summer of 1984, India even established an observation post (OP) on Sumdorong Chu's banks which managed to offer a view of Chinese positions on the other side of Thag La.[6]

This post was manned by personnel of the Special Security Bureau through the summer and vacated by the time winter snow set in. In June 1986, when a 12 Assam Regiment patrol was returning to the area was shocked to discover Chinese soldiers present in larger number, busy constructing permanent structures. While the initial reports pegged the number of these troops at only forty, the number suddenly swelled up and the following reinforcements added to a total strength of about 200 men.

Statements by ministers in Parliament confirmed that the intrusion had been at most 2 kms deep inside the Indian territory.[78] The Chinese side went a step further and even constructed a helipad and began sending supplying to their troops by air, adding further to the alarming situation Indians found themselves in.

To prevent the Chinese from taking India's silence as granted, Indian Army also commenced its patrols across the Arunachal territory and other vulnerable points considered to be under potential Chinese threat. In September, as the snow was about to set in, New Delhi sought a way out to defuse the crisis by suggesting that if the Chinese withdrew in the coming winter, and India would not re-occupy the area the next summer. This offer was rejected by China and the stage was set for a long haul along the border. By September-October, an entire brigade (5th Mountain Division) was stationed at Zimithang, a helipad in close vicinity to Sumdorong Chu. The operation was codenamed "Op Falcon", involved army taking position on ridges overlooking Sumdorong Chu including the Hathung La and Langrola ridge across the Namka Chu stream, located southwards of the Thag La.[9] This was not an arbitrary plan to occupy the territory but this was the true alignment of the border as defined under the McMahon Line, which China had been opposing since the beginning of the Mao's regime.

In October, Deng Xiaoping warned Indians that if these tensions across the border persisted, China would soon teach a lesson to the Indians. Tensions between both the nations further escalated, when in December 1986, Arunachal Pradesh was given the status of a full-fledged state in the Indian Union, thus angering Beijing which claimed Arunachal as part of Southern Tibet. This drew a chorus of protests from China and New Delhi stood by its stance that any change in Arunachal's status was an internal matter, not to be reacted upon by China.

Spring onwards, in 1987 troop build-up began on both sides leading to Indian and Chinese troops being deployed eyeball to eyeball in Sumdorong Chu and raising the possibility of a serious conflict.

It was estimated that China with its large military presence in Tibet had managed to move in around 20,000 troops from the 53rd Army Corps in Chengdu and the 13th Army in Lanzhou. Even heavy artillery and helicopters had been moved into the region. China also shifted eight divisions to eastern Tibet.

Troop reinforcements by the Indian forces, which began with the commencement of Operation Falcon in 1986, further continued even in 1987 under a massive air-land move. A brainchild of the then army chief General Krishnaswamy Sunderji, this operation, codenamed Chequerboard, involved 10 divisions of the Army and several squadrons of the IAF and redeployment of troops at several places in the north-eastern states. Indian Army also placed its three divisions at strategic locations in the vicinity of Wangdung, where they were supplied and maintained solely by air support. These troop reinforcements were over and above the 50,000 troops already present across Arunachal Pradesh.

Rising tensions were slightly salvaged when N D Tiwari, the then minister of external affairs went on a visit to China in May 1987. Both the sides committed to carry on talks on the border issue and to cool things down on the heated-up border.

In August '87, Indian and Chinese troops moved their respective posts slightly apart in the S-C valley, after a meeting of the field commanders. During the 8th round of border talks on November '87, it was decided to upgrade the talks from the political level. It is at this critical juncture the young Prime Minister Rajiv Gandhi visited China.[10] Following his visit in 1988, a Joint Working Group (JWG) was set up to work harmoniously and discuss the alignment of the LAC.[11]

In 1993, the, "Agreement on the Maintenance of Peace and Tranquility along the Line of Actual Control in the India-China Border

Areas" was signed between the Indian MoS for External Affairs and China's vice-foreign minister, which paved the way for reduction of troops along the LAC.[12] The agreement was a welcome step as it was the first time, the two sides had sat together to arrive at a positive conclusion, as seen by the contents reproduced below:

> [T]he Government of the Republic of India and the Government of the People's Republic of China (hereinafter referred to as the two sides), have entered into the present Agreement in accordance with the Five Principles of mutual respect for sovereignty and territorial integrity, mutual non-aggression, non-interference in each other's internal affairs, equality and mutual benefit and peaceful coexistence and with a view to maintaining peace and tranquility in areas along the line of actual control in the India-China border areas.[13]

1. The two sides are of the view that the India-China boundary question shall be resolved through peaceful and friendly consultations. Neither side shall use or threaten to use force against the other by any means. Pending an ultimate solution to the boundary question between the two countries, the two sides shall strictly respect and observe the line of actual control between the two sides. No activities of either side shall overstep the line of actual control. In case personnel of one side cross the line of actual control, upon being cautioned by the other side, they shall immediately pull back to their own side of the line of actual control. When necessary, the two sides shall jointly check and determine the segments of the line of actual control where they have different views as to its alignment.[14]

2. Each side will keep its military forces in the areas along the line of actual control to a minimum level compatible with the friendly and good neighbourly relations between the two countries. The two sides agree to reduce their military forces along the line of actual control in conformity with the requirements of the principle of mutual and equal security to ceilings to be mutually agreed. The extent, depth, timing, and nature of reduction of military forces along the line of actual control shall be determined through mutual consultations

between the two countries. The reduction of military forces shall be carried out by stages in mutually agreed geographical locations sector-wise within the areas along the line of actual control.[15]

3. Both sides shall work out through consultations effective confidence building measures in the areas along the line of actual control. Neither side will undertake specified levels of military exercises in mutually identified zones. Each side shall give the other prior notification of military exercises of specified levels near the line of actual control permitted under this Agreement.[16]

4. In case of contingencies or other problems arising in the areas along the line of actual control, the two sides shall deal with them through meetings and friendly consultations between border personnel of the two countries. The form of such meetings and channels of communications between the border personnel shall be mutually agreed upon by the two sides.[17]

5. The two sides agree to take adequate measures to ensure that air intrusions across the line of actual control do not take place and shall undertake mutual consultations should intrusions occur. Both sides shall also consult on possible restrictions on air exercises in areas to be mutually agreed near the line of actual control.[18]

6. The two sides agree that references to the line of actual control in this Agreement do not prejudice their respective positions on the boundary question.[19]

7. The two sides shall agree through consultations on the form, method, scale and content of effective verification measures and supervision required for the reduction of military forces and the maintenance of peace and tranquility in the areas along the line of actual control under this Agreement.[20]

8. Each side of the India-China Joint Working Group on the boundary question shall appoint diplomatic and military experts to formulate, through mutual consultations, implementation measures for the present Agreement. The experts shall advise the Joint Working Group on the resolution

of differences between the two sides on the alignment of the line of actual control and address issues relating to redeployment with a view to reduction of military forces in the areas along the line of actual control. The experts shall also assist the Joint Working Group in supervision of the implementation of the Agreement, and settlement of differences that may arise in that process, based on the principle of good faith and mutual confidence.[21]

9. The present Agreement shall come into effect as of the date of signature and is subject to amendment and addition by agreement of the two sides. Signed in duplicate at Beijing on the Seventh day of September 1993 in the Hindi, Chinese and English languages, all three texts having equal validity.[22]

Evaluating Rajiv Gandhi's Efforts

Following the agreement, it was then decided to pull troops back from those check posts located in Sumdorong Chu. Following this, the Ministry of External Affairs described the prevailing ground situation as being of "close proximity", with both the sides being only 50-100 yards apart from each other. A Joint Working Group meeting was held in April 1995, India and China also agreed to withdraw troops simultaneously from the other border posts in the Sumdorong Chu. "The incident at S-C valley, viz. the establishment of an SSB post in the summer of 1985, can be considered to be a consequence of the uncertain and disputed nature of the LAC. The Indian side has been criticized by some for being the first to intrude in a neutral area, and the subsequent events characterized as a Chinese reaction to India's 'forward policy' in the early '80s".[23]

On the other hand, there is no unanimity as to the reason an isolated incident on the border should have led to such an increase in tension in early 1987. Prevailing international and domestic developments have been suggested as possible explanations. The troop reinforcements on the Indian side in the later months - during Operation Falcon, leading on to Exercise Chequerboard - have been thought by some to be an Indian reaction to growing Sino-Soviet rapprochement in 1986.[24] The Indian reactions were apparently to test the extent of normalization in relations between China and the USSR and its effect on the Indo-Soviet relations. Reiterating his analysis of the 1962 conflict, Maxwell holds India solely responsible for the escalation, claiming the incident to be Rajiv Gandhi's method of provoking a confrontation with China in order to unite the nation and facilitate the imposition of an internal emergency. Regardless of the plausibility of some the explanations offered, many observers are agreed on the effect of the robust military moves on the Indian side. It is believed that the Indian Army used the events through 1986/87 both as an effective palliative for the bitter events of 1962, and to demonstrate the difference in the ground situation since that time, to the Chinese military.[25]

On Chinese motivations behind the escalation, the consensus view seems to be that it was part of a strategy of indicating that the border issue in the Eastern sector was far from settled. While the early border talks had focused mainly on the Aksai Chin region and not on the Eastern sector, the mid-'80s saw a change in Chinese attitude. The Chinese strategy changed to linking the border issues in the Eastern and Western sector and demanding matching concessions in the Eastern sector for any Chinese withdrawals in Aksai Chin/Ladakh, in contrast to the Indian position that the two sectors be considered separately. In this view, a Chinese reluctance to react to a strong Indian military presence near or over the ML would weaken their negotiating position.[26]

While an exchange of maps of the LAC would be an essential step towards the avoidance of such incidents, and eventually to a resolution of the boundary dispute, there has been a marked Chinese reluctance to comply with this, even after several years into the multi-level border talks. There have been some reports following President Narayanan's recent visit to China, of the increasing likelihood of such an exchange, particularly in the "middle sector" (Uttar Pradesh and Himachal Pradesh). It remains to be seen if such an event comes to pass.[27]

Yang Wenchang, the President of the Chinese People's Institute of Foreign Affairs, an influential Chinese think-tank, revealed that "both sides had come close to resolving the row in the 1980s, but Rajiv Gandhi declined what many analysts saw as a reasonable offer from then Chinese 'Paramount leader' Deng Xiaoping".[28]

The offer involved mutual concessions on western and eastern sectors, Yang, then a diplomat in the Chinese Foreign Ministry, told journalists in an interaction at the CPIFA. "I personally hope the two strongmen can solve the issue," Yang said. "As a diplomat in late 1980s, I [witnessed] a chance to solve the problem with Prime Minister Rajiv and Deng, who was also a strong man". Deng said, "We do some compromise on west wing, you do some on the east wing then we can have a new border".[29] Deng even suggested renaming the contested McMahon Line in the east as a new "India-China line", Yang said.[30]

Yang only hinted at the outlines of the deal offered by Deng, which involved China making minor concessions in the western sector, where it is occupying at least 38,000 square km claimed by India, and India making similar minor concessions in the east, where China claims 90,000 square km. "We offered but Prime Minister Gandhi didn't have a response. After that I felt very sad we lost the chance," Yang added.[31]

Yang's statement that Rajiv Gandhi rejected a deal during his 1988 visit was not immediately confirmed by Indian officials, although Deng was known to have made a similar offer in the early 1980s of a deal that would see both sides more or less hold on to their respective claims in the west and east, with minor adjustments.

The Long Road to 1993 Breakthrough Agreement

A milestone in the military relationship between the two countries was the visit of Sharad Pawar, the then Defence Minister to China in July 1992. It was the first ever visit by a Defence Minister of India to China. During the visit it was agreed to develop academic, military, scientific and technological exchanges between the two countries. It is also believed that during Mr. Pawar's visit, the Chinese military leadership emphasized the importance of force reduction in the border region due to prohibitive cost. The visit fructified in the signing of the Agreement on the Maintenance of Peace and Tranquility along the Line of Actual Control (LAC) in the India-China Border area on 7th September 1993 during the visit of the then Prime Minister P.V. Narasimha Rao.[32] The Agreement was indeed a breakthrough. In view of its importance, it is worthwhile to elucidate the salient features of the Agreement in greater detail. In the first place, the Agreement affirmed the view that the India-

China boundary question shall be resolved through peaceful and friendly consultations and that neither side shall use or threaten to use force against the other by any means. Yet another important highlight of the Agreement was that it stipulated 'pending an ultimate solution of the boundary question between the two countries, the two sides shall strictly observe the LAC between the two sides and that no activities of either side shall overstep the line of actual control. In case of personnel of one side cross the line of LAC, upon being confirmed by the other side, they shall immediately pull back to their own side of the LAC. It further provided that when necessary, the two sides shall jointly check and determine the segments of the LAC when they have different views as to its alignment.[33]

Secondly, the agreement stipulated that each side will keep its military forces in the area along the LAC to a minimum level compatible with the friendly and good neighbourly relations between the two countries. It further iterated that the two sides agreed to reduce their military forces along LAC in conformity with the requirement of the principle of mutual and equal security to ceilings to be mutually agreed, and that the reduction of military forces shall be carried out by stages in mutually agreed geographical locations sector-wise within the areas along the LAC.[34]

Thirdly, as regards military exercises, the Agreement mentioned that each side shall give the other prior notification of the military exercises of specified levels near the LAC permitted under the Agreement. Fourthly, in case of contingency or other problems arising in the areas of LAC, the two sides shall deal with them through meetings and friendly consultations between border personnel of the two countries. Fifthly, the two sides also agreed in the accord to take adequate measures to ensure that air intrusions across the line of actual control do not take place and that the two sides shall undertake mutual consultation in case intrusions occur.[35]

As a follow up of this agreement, a senior level Chinese military delegation aimed at fostering CBMs between the defence forces of the two countries made a six-day goodwill visit to India in December 1993.[36]

After over three decades of eyeball to eyeball contact on the LAC, late General BC Joshi, PVSM, AVSM, VSM, ADC, became the first Army Chief to be invited to visit China. It was his idea that a large bronze bell displayed in 2nd Lancers, the Regiment he was commissioned in, should be taken by him and officially be handed over to the Chinese during his visit, as a gesture of goodwill. This action certainly had a major effect on the Chinese, who broke protocol more than once during that visit in favour of General Joshi.

This incident was personally conveyed by General Joshi to this author, who was then the Defence Ministry's Indian Army spokesperson.

A copy of Associated Press news report is reproduced:

Temple Bell Stolen 94 Years Ago is Returned

April 21, 1995

BEIJING (AP) – A gilded bronze bell stolen from China in 1901 by a British general was rehung Friday in the Temple of Heaven in Beijing.

The bell, part of a 16-bell set, was returned to its position in front of the Palace of Good Harvest at the Temple of Heaven, where Chinese emperors held annual sacrificial rites to pray for good harvests.

The 15 other bells, which date to the 1368-1644 Ming dynasty, remain missing.

The official Xinhua News Agency said the returned bell was stolen by a British general who led troops into Beijing in 1901, part of an alliance of Western nations that sought to dominate China.

The bell was given by the unidentified general to an Indian calvary unit, in which the late Gen. B.C. Joshi served before becoming chief of staff of the Indian army, Xinhua said.

Joshi returned the bell to China last July. India's ambassador to China attended Friday's ceremony reinstalling the bell.

Zhang Deqin, director of the State Bureau of Cultural Relics, said he hoped this would accelerate the return of other items taken from China.

Many Chinese artifacts and works of arts exhibited in the world's museums today were taken out of the country by Westerners in the 18th and early 19th centuries, during times of chaos in China.

After General Joshi's unfortunate death as the first Army Chief since 1947 to die in harness, a Chinese delegation came to pay tribute during the ceremony for the same.

The 1996 Agreement

After the CBMs in LAC in 1996, that is three years later, the Agreement on Maintenance of Peace and Tranquility along the LAC in India-China Border Area was followed by the Agreement Between the Government of Republic of India and the Government of the People's Republic of China on Confidence Building Measures in the military field along the LAC in the India-China Border Areas on 29th November 1996 during the visit of Chinese President Jiang Zemin to India.[37] This Agreement while reiterating and reaffirming the intent and spirit of the 1993, state agreement, inter-alias, as Confidence Building Measures, envisaged the following:[38]

1. The major categories of armament to be reduced or limited include combat tanks, infantry combat vehicles, guns (including howitzers) with 75 mm or bigger calibre, mortars with 120mm or bigger calibre, surface-to-surface missiles, surface-to-air missiles and any other weapon system.

2. The two sides shall exchange data on the military forces and armaments to be reduced or limited and decide on ceilings on military forces and armaments to be kept by each side within agreed geographically zones along the line of actual control in the India-China border. In order to maintain peace and tranquility along the line of actual control in the India-China border areas and to prevent any tensions in the border areas due to misreading by either side of the other side's intentions. Given the significance the agreement brought with it, it is imperative to analyse few articles of the 1996 agreement to understand the growing level of understanding both the sides had arrived at, almost a decade after the Sumdorung Chu affair had threatened to revive the ghosts of 1962. With regard to the agreement, both sides need to laud for the clarity noted in agreement's articles as the well as the restraint reflected in the text.

Article IV of the Agreement provided the following:
1. Both sides shall avoid holding large-scale military exercises involving more than one Division (approximately 15,000 troops) in close proximity of the line of actual control in the India-China border areas. However, if such exercises are to be conducted, the strategic direction of the main force involved shall not be towards the other side.
2. If either side conducts a major military exercise involving more than one Brigade Group (approximately 5000 troops) in close proximity of the line of actual control in the India-China border areas, it shall give the other side The two sides shall exchange data on the military forces and armaments to be reduced or limited and decide on ceilings on military forces and armaments to be kept by each side.
3. The date of completion of the exercise and de-induction of troops from the area of exercise shall be intimated to the other side within five days of completion or de -induction.
4. Each side shall be entitled to obtain timely clarification from the side undertaking the exercise in respect of date specified in Paragraph 2 of the present Article.

With a view to preventing air intrusions across the LAC in the India-China border areas and facilitating over flights and landings by military aircraft, Article V provided that:
1. Both sides shall take adequate measures to ensure that air intrusions across the line of actual control do not take place. However, if an intrusion does take place, it should cease as soon as detected and the incident shall be promptly investigated by the side operating the aircraft. The results of the investigation shall be immediately communicated, through diplomatic channels or at border personnel meetings, to the other side.
2. Subject to paragraphs 3 and 5 of this Article, combat aircraft (to include fighter, bomber, reconnaissance, military trainer, armed helicopter and other armed aircraft) shall not fly within ten kilometres of the line of actual control.

3. If either side is required to undertake flights of combat aircraft within ten kilometres from the line of actual control, it shall give the following information in advance to the other side, through diplomatic channels: a) Type and number of combat aircraft; b) Height of the proposed flight (in metres); c) Proposed duration of flights (normally not to exceed ten days); d) Proposed timing of flights; and e) Area of operations, defined in latitude and longitude. However, if an intrusion does take place, it should cease as soon as detected and the incident shall be promptly investigated by the side operating the aircraft

4. Unarmed transport aircraft, survey aircraft and helicopters shall be permitted to fly up to the line of actual control.

5. No military aircraft of either side shall fly across the line of actual control, except by prior permission. Military aircraft of either side may fly across the line of actual control or overfly the other side's airspace or land on the other side only after obtaining the latter's prior permission after providing the latter with detailed information on the flight in accordance with the international practice in this regard. Notwithstanding the above stipulation, each side has the sovereign right to specify additional conditions, including at short notice, for flights or landings of military aircraft of the other side on its side of the line of actual control or through its airspace.

6. In order to ensure flight safety in emergency situations, the authorities designated by the two sides may contact each other by the quickest means of communications available. Similarly, with a view to preventing dangerous military activities along the line of actual control in the India-China border areas.

Article VI stipulates that:

1. Neither side shall open fire, cause biodegradation, use hazardous chemicals, conduct blast operations or hunt with guns or explosive within two kilometres from the line of actual control. This prohibition shall not apply to routine firing activities in small arms firing ranges.

2. If there is a need to conduct blast operations within two

kilometres of the line of actual control as part of developmental activities, the other side shall be informed through diplomatic channels or by convening a border personnel meeting, preferably five days in advance.

3. While conducting exercises with live ammunition in areas close to the line of actual control, precaution shall be taken to ensure that a bullet or a missile does not accidentally fall on the other side across the line of actual control and cause harm to the personnel or property of the other side.

4. If the border personnel of the two sides come in a face-to-face situation due to differences on the alignment of the line of actual control of any other Neither side shall open fire, cause bio-degradation, use hazardous chemicals, conduct blast operations or hunt with guns or explosive within two kilometres from the line of actual control.

Article VII of the agreement envisaged the following:

1. To maintain and expand the regime of scheduled and flag meetings between their border representatives at designated places along the line of actual control;

2. To maintain and expand telecommunication links between the border meeting points at designated places along the line of actual control; and c. To establish step-by-step medium and high-level contacts between the border authorities of the two sides.

Article VIII of the Agreement provides the following guidelines:

1. Should the personnel of one side cross the line of actual control and enter the other side because of unavoidable circumstances like natural disasters, the other side shall extend all possible assistance to them and inform their side, as soon as possible regarding the forced or inadvertent entry across the line of actual control. The modalities of return of the concerned personnel to their own side shall be settled through mutual consultations.

2. The two sides shall provide each other, at the earliest possible, with information pertaining to natural disasters and epidemic

diseases in contiguous border areas which might affect the other side. The exchange of information shall take place either through diplomatic channels or at border personnel meetings.

Article X mentions following provisions:

1. Recognizing that the full implementation of some of the provisions of the present Agreement will depend on the two sides arriving at a common understanding of the alignment of the line of actual control in the India-China border areas, the two sides agree to speed up the process clarification and confirmation of the line of actual control. As an initial step in this process, they are clarifying the alignment of the line of actual control in those segments where they have different perceptions. They also agree to exchange maps indicating their respective perceptions of the entire alignment of the line of actual control as soon as possible.

2. Pending the completion of the process of clarification and confirmation of the line of actual control, the two sides shall work out modalities for implementing confidence-building measures envisaged under his Agreement on an interim basis, without prejudice to their respective positions on the alignment of the line of actual control as well as on the boundary question.[39]

Thus, it can be seen from various provisions of different agreements and accords signed between India and China that every conceivable aspect of military contingency has been thoughtfully anticipated and ways and means to deftly handle them without precipitating the matter have been envisaged. It was against this backdrop of signing of various agreements providing for CBMs that a slew of visits at various levels between the two countries were given further impetus.[40]

The most significant of the visit was that of the then Defence Minister, George Fernandes to China in April 2003.[41] The visit of Mr. Fernandes took place after the gap of more than one decade and also helped ease the post Pokhran tension. Defence cooperation and military engagement between the two countries further received a boost during the visit of the then Prime Minister Atal Behari Vajpayee to China in June 2003.[42]

The joint declaration between the two countries signed on 23 June 2003, inter alia, mentioned that "...they agreed on the need to broaden and deepen defence exchanges between the two countries, which will help enhance and deepen mutual understanding and trust between the two-armed forces. They confirmed that the exchange of visits by their Defence Ministers and of military officials at various levels should be strengthened".[43]

2003 Visit Declaration

Both sides affirmed that they would abide by the following principles, promote a long-term constructive and cooperative partnership and, on this basis, build a qualitatively new relationship:[44]

Both sides are committed to developing their long-term constructive and cooperative partnership on the basis of the principles of Panchsheel, mutual respect and sensitivity for each other's concerns and equality;

As two major developing countries, India and China have a broad mutual interest in the maintenance of peace, stability and prosperity in Asia and the world, and a mutual desire in developing wider and closer cooperation and understanding in regional and international affairs;

The common interests of the two sides outweigh their differences. The two countries are not a threat to each other. Neither side shall use or threaten to use force against the other; and

Both sides agree to qualitatively enhancing the bilateral relationship at all levels and in all areas while addressing differences through peaceful means in a fair, reasonable and mutually acceptable manner. The differences should not be allowed to affect the overall development of bilateral relations.

Both sides agreed to hold regular high-level exchanges between the two countries. This will greatly enhance mutual understanding and expand bilateral relations. With a view to deepening their coordination and dialogues on bilateral, regional and international issues, both sides agreed on the need for annual meetings between Foreign Ministers of the two countries. They also agreed that personnel exchanges and friendly contacts between ministries, parliaments and political parties of the two countries should be further enhanced.[45]

The two sides welcomed the positive momentum of bilateral trade and economic cooperation in recent years and shared the belief that continued expansion and intensification of India-China economic cooperation is essential for strengthening bilateral relations.

Both sides shared the view that existing complementarities between their two economies provide an important foundation and offer broad prospects for further enhancing their economic relations. In order to promote trade and economic cooperation, both sides will take necessary measures consistent with their national laws and rules and international obligations to remove impediments to bilateral trade and investment. They reaffirmed the importance of the ministerial meeting of the Joint Economic Group (JEG) and agreed to hold the next (seventh) JEG meeting within the year.[46]

The two sides decided to set up a compact Joint Study Group (JSG) composed of officials and economists to examine the potential complementarities between the two countries in expanded trade and economic cooperation. The JSG would also draw up a programme for the development of India-China trade and economic cooperation for the next five years, aimed at encouraging greater cooperation between the business communities of both sides. The Group would present a study report and recommendations to the two Governments on measures for comprehensive trade and economic cooperation by the end of June 2004.[47]

The two sides exchanged views on the India-China boundary question and expounded their respective positions. They reiterated their readiness to seek a fair, reasonable and mutually acceptable solution through consultations on an equal footing. The two sides agreed that pending an ultimate solution, they should work together to maintain peace and tranquility in the border areas and reiterated their commitment to continue implementation of the agreements signed for this purpose, including the clarification of the Line of Actual Control.[48]

The two sides agreed to each appoint a Special Representative to explore from the political perspective of the overall bilateral relationship the framework of a boundary settlement.[49]

Yet despite such diplomatic niceties and even compromises from the Indian side, Chinese coercive tactics continued and the usual Chinese practice of keeping the LAC heated up – even at a time when the two sides discussed potential breakthroughs and avenues for a stronger economic ties – demonstrated that somewhere down the line, Beijing was not committed to honoring India's efforts to extend its arms for the cause of peaceful borders. This pattern has been a consistent Chinese policy and has been repeated time and again, as the book shall discuss in the following pages. This is despite that fact that India had given up not only its organic relationship with Xinjiang, with the closing of the Ladakh silk route branch by the Communist regime after it assumed power, and all its ties with Tibet with the surrender of all transactional and spiritual links India enjoyed with Tibet.

Today, the Indian side recognizes that the Tibet Autonomous Region is part of the territory of the People's Republic of China and reiterates that it does not allow Tibetans to engage in anti-China political activities in India. The Chinese side expresses its appreciation for the Indian position and reiterates that it is firmly opposed to any attempt and action aimed at splitting China and bringing about "independence of Tibet".[50]

A ubiquitous achievement of the Vajpayee's visit was the translation of CBMs into the decision to open the Nathu La for trade, which was opened in 2006. Nathu La was a significant breakthrough not because due to the trade factor as the volume would not be huge, but due to the fact that it was opened after more than four decades (the pass was closed in 1962). It was a great symbolic victory as it marked the first attempts of cooperation on disputed borders. The 4000 km long LAC, which was otherwise seen as a tense territory, was for the first time viewed with hopes of a peace. Second, China even recognized India's sovereignty over Sikkim, almost three decades after Sikkim's inclusion in the Indian union in 1975.

Year 2004 was also landmark phase as bilateral trade crossed $10 billion value for the first time.[51]

Protocols on CBM's along the LAC, 2005

The upward swing of defence cooperation and military engagement between the two countries was given a further impetus during the visit of Chinese Premier Wen Jiabao in April 2005.[52] The result of the visit was the signing of protocol between the Government of the Republic of India and the Government of the People's Republic of China on The Political Parameters and guidelines for Resolving the Boundary Question which signed on 11 April.[53]

This protocol can be seen as building up on what the two nations negotiated in the 1996 confidence building accord while reiterating verbatim of some of the bilateral commitments in the accord. Some of the amplified provisions which merits attentions are as under: Every conceivable aspects of military contingency have been thoughtfully anticipated and ways and means to deftly handle them without precipitating the matter have been envisaged.

Article III of the Protocol envisages the following provisions:

 a. In the event of an alleged air intrusion of its controlled air space by the military aircraft of the other side, either side may seek a Flag Meeting within 48 hours of the alleged air intrusion in order to seek a clarification. The investigation shall be completed by the other side and its results communicated through a Flag Meeting within a period of four weeks.

 b. If a military aircraft of either side is required to fly across the Line of Actual Control or to overfly the airspace of the other side, prior permission shall be sought from the other side according to procedures and formats to be mutually agreed upon.

 c. If a military or civilian aircraft of either side is required to fly across the Line of Actual Control or to land on the other side of the Line of the LAC in an emergency situation, the two sides will ensure flight safety in such a situation by adhering to procedures to be mutually agreed upon.[54]

Article V provides the following:

 a. Both sides shall hold two additional border meetings each year at Spanggur Gap in the Western Sector, Nathula Pass in the

Sikkim Sector and Bum La in the Easter Sector respectively in celebration of the National Day or Army Day of either side. Specific arrangements shall be decided through consultation between the border forces of the two sides.

b. Both sides are in principle to expand the mechanism of border meeting points to include Kibithu-Damai in the Eastern Sector and Lipulekh Pass/Qiang La in the Middle Sector. The precise locations of these border meetings points will be decided through mutual consultations.

c. Both sides shall conduct exchanges between the relevant Military Regions of China and Army Commands of India. Specific arrangements shall be decided upon through mutual consultations between the relevant agencies under the Ministries of Defence of the two sides.

d. Both sides shall strengthen exchanges between institutions of training of the two-armed forces, and conduct exchanges between institutions of sports and culture of the two-armed forces. Specific arrangements shall be decided upon through mutual consultations between the relevant agencies under the Ministries of Defence of the two sides. If a military aircraft of either side is required to fly across the Line of Actual Control or to overfly the airspace of the other side, prior permission shall be sought India-China Defence Cooperation and Military Engagement.[55]

Besides the growing understanding seen in defence and the strategic aspect in the protocol, Wen Jiabao's visit was also aimed at strengthening the bilateral economic relationship which both sides were keen to exploit, since the talk of 21st century being the Asian century of development had already gaining ground, and that India and China were the two engines on which the Asian growth story would rest. Being India's technology hub, Wen's visit to the Bangalore signaled that both the nations would welcome the new millennium in the spirit of the most advanced levels of cooperation. Calling upon both the nations to cooperate, Wen described 21st century as the "Asian century of the IT industry". Another achievement which followed was China's induction in SAARC regional group as an observer. The message was clear that after years of fear, India had finally felt comfortable in partnering with China in developing the nations of the Indian subcontinent through regional institutions.

Defence Minister Pranab Mukherjee's Visit to China

It was against this background of what may be called the heightened engagement between the two countries that the then Defence Minister Pranab Mukherjee visited China on a five-day visit in May/June 2006 and held wide ranging talks with Chinese leaders including Chinese Premier Wen Jiabao and his Chinese counterpart General Cao Gangchuan.[56] The high point of the visit was the signing of the Memorandum of Understanding (MOU) which is first ever of its kind between the two countries. The MOU envisages for the establishment of a mechanism to ensure frequent and regular exchanges between leaders and officials of the Defence Ministries and the armed forces of the two countries in addition to developing an annual calendar for holding regular joint military exercises and training programmes.[57] In the past few years, the two countries had conducted joint naval manoeuvres, but the interaction between the ground forces has been limited to border meetings and mountaineering expeditions and there had been no interaction between the air forces of the countries. Prior to this the MOU signed between the two countries, thus, aimed at addressing these imperatives. The Defence Minister also visited the sensitive Lanzhou Military Area Command which controls the largest physical area of China's seven military regions. The region holding the nuclear research and missile testing facilities in the Chinese west comes under the Command of this area. Mr. Mukherjee's visit to the headquarters of the Lanzhou Military Command was a significant step in the process of building bilateral trust and confidence on part of China. These gains were further consolidated during the visit of Chinese President Hu Jintao to India in November 2006. In the Joint Declaration signed between the two countries on 21st November, it was mentioned that 'the exchange of visits in the field of defence has resulted in the building of mutual trust and enhancement of mutual understanding between the defence establishments of the two countries. Both sides shall fully implement the provisions of the

Memorandum of Understanding for exchanges and cooperation in the field of defence signed on 29 May 2006, which provides a sound foundation and institutional framework for further development of defence cooperation. In the past few years, the two countries had conducted joint naval manoeuvres, but the interaction between the ground forces has been limited to border meetings and mountaineering expeditions and there had been no interaction between the air forces of the countries.

Certain concrete steps were taken as a follow-up of the CBM's. For example, Armed Forces of India and China held a warm meeting at a new border point in Arunachal Pradesh, on 18th November 2006, on the eve of President Hu Jintao's visit to India.[58] The two sides met at Kibithu in Anjaw district of Arunachal Pradesh, and discussed modalities for the conduct of troops along the border.

An official press release claimed, "The meeting and exchanges were characterised by great warmth and bonhomie. It marks another milestone in the growing relationship and military exchanges between the armed forces of the two countries."[59] Border meetings between personnel of the armed forces of the two countries have traditionally been held at Chusul in Ladakh, Nathu La in Sikkim, and Bum La in Kameng district of Arunachal Pradesh.

Unfortunately, these nominal gains were to change in the coming years as by 2008, the world faced the global economic meltdown, which saw a relative decline in America's hold over the world economy. China, by the virtue of holding American debt was confident that its time had arrived and thus began a serious of global blackmail whether neither India, nor China's smaller neighbours and not even the Americans were spared of the Chinese aggressions. The next chapter will examine, how 2008-9 onwards, New Delhi was witness to a more aggressive China which seemed bent on undoing all the nascent gains that has been achieved over the past decades, and how the following decade would set the stage for the confrontation at Doklam.

NOTES

1   https://www.dailypioneer.com/2017/sunday-edition/vajpayees-calibrated-outreach-to-china.html

2. https://www.thehindu.com/news/national/Subramanian-Swamy-meets-President-ahead-of-China-visit/article14344281.ece
3. Ibid.
4. http://www.indiandefencereview.com/the-sumdorong-chu-incident-a-strong-indian-stand/
5. https://www.bharat-rakshak.com/ARMY/history/siachen/286-Sumdorong-Incident.html
6. http://www.indiandefencereview.com/the-sumdorong-chu-incident-a-strong-indian-stand/
7. https://www.bharat-rakshak.com/ARMY/history/siachen/286-Sumdorong-Incident.html
8. https://www.indiatoday.in/magazine/neighbours/story/19860831-after-initial-hullaballoo-india-plays-down-chinese-intrusion-into-arunachal-pradesh-801177-1986-08-31
9. https://www.orfonline.org/research/operation-falcon-when-general-sundarji-took-the-chinese-by-surprise/
10. https://www.indiatoday.in/magazine/cover-story/story/19890115-prime-minister-rajiv-gandhi-visit-to-china-marks-a-new-beginning-in-bilateral-relations-815628-1989-01-15
11. https://www.tandfonline.com/doi/abs/10.1080/00358530410001679602
12. https://www.stimson.org/agreement-on-the-maintenance-of-peace-along-the-line-of-actual-control-in-t
13. Ibid.
14. Ibid.
15. Ibid.
16. Ibid.
17. Ibid.
18. Ibid.
19. Ibid.
20. Ibid.
21. Ibid.
22. Ibid.
23. https://www.bharat-rakshak.com/ARMY/history/siachen/286-Sumdorong-Incident.html
24. Ibid.
25. Ibid.
26. Ibid.
27. Ibid.
28. https://www.businesstoday.in/current/economy-politics/china-hopes-pm-narendra-modi-will-end-border-dispute/story/218135.html
29. https://www.indiatoday.in/world/story/rajiv-china-border-deal-modi-xi-jinping-248316-2015-04-13
30. https://www.businesstoday.in/current/economy-politics/china-hopes-pm-narendra-modi-will-end-border-dispute/story/218135.html
31. Ibid.

32 https://idsa.in/system/files/jds_4_4_rndas.pdf
33 Ibid.
34 Ibid.
35 Ibid.
36 Ibid.
37 https://peacemaker.un.org/sites/peacemaker.un.org/files/CN%20IN_961129_Agreement%20between%20China%20and%20India.pdf
38 Ibid
39 Ibid.
40 https://idsa.in/system/files/jds_4_4_rndas.pdf
41 https://www.indiatoday.in/india/story/doklam-standoff-india-china-threat-george-fernandes-1025404-2017-07-20
42 https://idsa.in/system/files/jds_4_4_rndas.pdf
43 https://www.thehindu.com/2003/06/25/stories/2003062505701200.htm
44 https://www.thehindu.com/2003/06/25/stories/2003062505701200.htm
45 https://www.mea.gov.in/in-focus-article.htm?7679/Declaration+on+ Principles +for+Relations+and+Comprehensive+Cooperation+Between+the+Republic+of+India+and+the+Peoples+Republic+of+China
46 Ibid.
47 Ibid.
48 Ibid.
49 Ibid.
50 https://www.tribuneindia.com/2003/20030626/main13.htm
51 https://www.thehindubusinessline.com/2004/12/03/stories/2004120302760600.htm
52 http://www.rediff.com/news/2005/apr/11wen3.htm
53 https://www.mea.gov.in/bilateral-documents.htm?dtl/6539/Protocol+between+the+Government+of+the+Repu
54 https://www.mea.gov.in/incoming-visit-detail.htm?6539/Protocol+between+the+Government+of+the+Republic+of+India+and+the+ Government+of+the+Peoples+Republic+of +China+on +Modalities+for+the+Implementation+of+Confidence+Building+Measures+in+the +Military+Field+Along+the+Line+ of+Actual+ Control+in+the+IndiaChina+Border+Areas
55 Ibid.
56 https://www.oneindia.com/2006/06/02/china-visit-highly-successful-pranab.html
57 https://www.dnaindia.com/india/report-indian-china-sign-mou-to-enhance-military-relations-1032054
58 http://www.rediff.com/news/2006/nov/18chinachat.htm
59 https://idsa.in/system/files/jds_4_4_rndas.pdf

4
2007-2017: Intrusions Galore and Dra'goon' Diplomacy

The visit of Chinese president Hu Jintao to India in 2006 once again generated high expectations that relations between both the states were on the way towards course correction. The highlight of the visit was Jintao's speech, in which he gave his five-point proposal for strengthening Sino-India relations, focusing on "increasing political trust, business cooperation, cultural and social exchanges, boundary issues and multilateral cooperation".[1] Both the leaders (President Jintao and PM Singh) stated, "The special Representatives shall complete at an early date the task of finalizing an appropriate framework for a final package settlement covering all sectors of the India-China boundary".[2] However, despite all the good talking, the excitement was short-lived and by the time 2007 arrived, the Chinese posture had been completely changed.

In May 2007, BJP MP Kiren Rijiju from Arunachal Pradesh made a startling claim that China had moved 20 kilometers into the Indian Territory, amounting to 9000 square kms. "It has been continuing for a long time.... I have written to Government of India and raised the issue in the Parliament. The government of India is not accepting the incursion openly. But defence personnel do acknowledge that this is happening and that the Chinese are occupying our land." said Rijiju and claimed that Ministry of External Affairs had admitted to Chinese occupation of Arunachal Pradesh.[3] 140 incursions reportedly occurred in 2007. The Indian Government, then led by the Congress Party depended on outside support from the Communist Parties of India which had in the past conflicts openly supported China instead of India. Thus, the Government was forced to follow indirect orders from pro-China Communists and go soft on its policy vis-a-vis China', India Defence stated.[4]

Despite this, India still attempted to stop the ties from deteriorating and in January 2008, PM Manmohan Singh visited China and signed a document titled "Shared Vision for the 21st Century" which envisaged a common path for both the nations aimed at promoting global prosperity under the guidance of Panchsheel principles. Unfortunately, the situation was to change in the coming months as India once again found herself caught by Chinese deception.

In early June 2008, even as China reeled from the severe earthquake and its aftershocks and accepted substantial Indian relief material, it piped up a claim on the Northern tip of Sikkim, referred to as the "Finger". The boundary here is demarcated by stone cairns, which the Chinese have objected to. India has told China that it will not allow Chinese troops into the area and that it would mean a breach of the treaty to maintain peace along the border.[5]

Wen Jiabao not meeting him, even if Vice President Xi Jinping did, it was only to warn India against supporting the Tibetan cause and linking Sikkim once again to the border dispute, means that this visit was nothing but a snub for India. No Chinese leader stated that the issue was settled.[6]

June 16 onwards, a few days after Mukherjee's visit, it emerged from various media reports that Chinese People's Liberation Army's (PLA) vehicle-mounted patrols and persons in plain clothes intruded at least one km across the Line of Actual Control (LAC) to the Finger area 60 to 72 times over the past six months.[7]

Further, the Chinese foreign ministry challenged a statement made by Mukherjee saying that Arunachal was an integral part of India. "We deeply regret the Indian side's remarks that take no regard of the historical facts. China and India have never officially settled demarcation of borders, and China's stance on the eastern section of China-India borders is consistent and clear-cut,"[8] foreign ministry spokesman Qin Gang at a press conference.

Qin's statement is in direct contrast with the views of Indian officials including foreign secretary Shiv Shankar Menon, who maintained that the issue of Tawang, leave aside the whole of Arunachal Pradesh, is out of the range of border negotiations. With the Chinese government challenging Mukherjee's stance on Arunachal, it was apparent that years of effort at resolving the border problem had come under a cloud.

The Chinese hegemonic pattern against India has usually been cartographic and diplomatic, followed by tactical incursions on ground. In 2008, Prime Minister Manmohan Singh's visit to Arunachal Pradesh calling it, "India's land of the rising sun" and announcing a long overdue development package, preceded and followed again by Defence Minister A K Antony's - the latter one to Tawang - provoked a prolonged reaction from China[9], which had already been smarting after the high level India-US Exercise Malabar-7, with ships from India, Australia, Japan, Singapore, and the US joining up in Bay of Bengal to practice inter-operability procedures.

China's aggressive posturing vis-a-vis India and its aggressive militarization and infrastructure modernization in Tibetan plateau all along the LAC prompted India, in 2008 to reactivate the famous Daulat Beg Oldi (DBO) airstrip in northern Ladakh overlooking the strategically significant Karakoram Pass, lying merely few kilometers away south of Aksai Chin. This was intended to send a send a strong message to China, whose troops had been regularly undertaking incursions into the Indian side of the LAC.[10]

In view of the above and China's hegemonic mindset, voracious appetite for territory, sustained modernisation and enhancement of offensive capability and now stepping into J&K, where its old friend Pakistan has been busy, India has been continually facing twin threat on its northern frontier.[11]

Chinese checkers has been described as a game in which players try to be first to race their pieces across the hexagram-shaped gameboard to the opposite corner using single-step moves or moves which jump over other pieces. Redux means 'brought back' or 'resurgent'.[12]

By the end of August 2009 there were at least twenty-six violations of Indian air space in the Eastern Ladakh part of Jammu and Kashmir (J&K) by Chinese helicopters including two air-dropping canned food, as PLA soldiers painted their country's name on rocks in Indian territory.[13]

That these happened in August 2009, a month packed with negotiations in New Delhi and Beijing, was not surprising but ominous. It must be recalled that the Chinese build-up and incursions in this region in 1954, which were brought to the notice of the then Prime Minister Jawaharlal Nehru by Indian Army's top brass, were trashed by him.[14]

Both the air and land intrusions have been in South East J&K, in the general area of the barren land at Chumar, East of the picturesque Morari Tso (lake), Zulung La (pass) and the 22, 420 feet high Mount Gya – meaning "fair princess of snow" – located at the tri-junction of Ladakh in Jammu and Kashmir, Spiti in Himachal Pradesh, and Tibet. Indian Army border troops reported on 31 July 2009 that Chinese troops had entered nearly 1.5 kilometres into the Indian territory and panted "China" in Chinese script on various rocks and boulders along the Zulung La.[15]

These intrusions happening in August 2009, a month packed with Sino-Indian negotiations at New Delhi, followed by former Indian Army Chief General V.K. Singh, then GOC-in-C Eastern Command, visiting Beijing and even Lhasa, capital of Tibet, was not surprising, but the fact that they were in J&K, where Pakistan has been brewing trouble for 62 years, was a new development which raised some worrisome questions.[16]

Apart from dropping or landing stores, helicopters are also ideal platforms for observing the adversary's deployment, patrols or to detect movements of larger bodies of troops/heavy weapons/equipment, which google maps or old satellite images cannot cover. In this case, the disappearance of Indian troops' fuel containers, painting of rocks and Chinese helicopters dropping supplies are indicative of PLA troops having infiltrated and camping thereabouts. And this may well be in response to India finally waking up to Chinese border build-ups over the years by reactivating old airfields like Daulat Beg Oldi and Chushul in this sector.[17]

Indian Government's official stand was that there was no increase of incursions; they are basically due to differences in perception of the LAC - at places it crosses each other's delineated boundary - which could have been avoided had there been a common perception. Foreign Minister S. M. Krishna stated that on road construction projects in East Ladakh under NREGA were halted in absence of centre's approval and not under Chinese pressure.

The main cause of worry is construction of airfields, roads, railway lines and strategic link up of Kashghar, in Pakistan with Havelian in Pakistan Occupied Kashmir (POK) and ultimately with Tibet's Medog region bordering Arunachal. Also worrying are China's efforts to bolster surveillance capability by constructing border out posts (BOPs), which at places, can also be used for directing precision guided munitions (tv guided cruise missiles, terrain guided missiles eg - KH59 mk II, which has a range of over 1200 kms) - all of which have the potential to alter the strategic balance in favour of China.[18]

Government's written reply in Rajya Sabha to the question stated there is no cause for alarm as any violations are regularly taken up with Chinese side through the established mechanism that includes joint working group, expert border personnel and flag meetings as well as diplomatic channels. Nevertheless, number of violations increased when compared to 2009 - from 28 to 19 in January and from 38 to 65 in February 2010.

It is quite typical of China to often punctuate its diplomatic dialogue "in an atmosphere of warmth etcetera...", but with intrusions into India or aggressive cross-border actions. Former Prime Minister AB Vajpayee's visit to Beijing in 2003 was timed with a Chinese patrol coming at least 16 kms inside India and intimidating an Indian detachment. Another act PLA is famous for is creating tension during normal deployment on the border without any incursion, but by sparking off a dispute over just a few feet of territory. In 2000, Arunachal Pradesh Chief Minister Mukut Mithi accused China of violating the

LAC and crossing into Indian territory. Mithi said Chinese-built mule tracks had been discovered by Indian Army soldiers near the Kyela Pass in the state's Dibang Valley district, bordering Tibet. "They come in the guise of hunters, cross the LAC and at times even claim that parts of Arunachal belong to them", he had said.[19]

The same year, Chinese embassy in New Delhi began issuing visas to Indians residing in Jammu and Kashmir on a separate sheet of paper. The paper was not stamped in their passports as the norm goes. Furthermore, in an interview to *The Hindu*, a Chinese embassy official brazenly justified China's stance and did not admit to the fact that Chinese ambitions on J&K were beginning to unravel. "This kind of visa is one category of Chinese visa. It is valid. This has been practised for many years. Upon the implementation of this, a note was sent to your immigration authorities. All the visa holders of this kind have not met any problem in the past in your custom/border control", the official stated.

Following the unusual and disturbing kind of intrusion by Chinese border forces from 15 April 2013 in eastern Ladakh, Jammu and Kashmir (J&K), which got solved after an impasse of three weeks, External Affairs Minister Salman Khurshid went to China soon after and returned with a rosy picture of his two-day visit. Noting that China had given a proposal for Border Defence Cooperation Agreement (BDCA), the minister said India had also given a counter proposal and both countries were examining these proposals. Declining to give details of the Indian proposal, he also clarified that the proposals were not meant to replace any existing ones. While the Chinese reportedly expressed no regret for their intrusion into south-eastern Ladakh, Mr. Khurshid gushed to his hosts that he would "love to live in Beijing." Shortly after Chinese troops were persuaded to withdraw from the intruded area, Mr. Khurshid was quoted saying that he "did not do a postmortem or apportion blame", that he saw no reason to go into "details of hair splitting" and asserted that he "raised and flagged it and we said that we both need to do analysis of why it happened.... On the problem on the Line of Actual Control (LAC), both countries are on the same page.... We don't have prickly issues of significant difference." On the need to expand or set up a separate mechanism to deal with issues pertaining to trans-border rivers, Mr. Khurshid claimed that for the first time, India has seen some "movement" with China assuring that China was committed to ensuring that India's rights were "not harmed".

Very shortly later, Chinese prime minister, Li Keqiang, arrived in New Delhi on his first foreign trip since assuming office in March and found himself traversing roads mostly empty, thanks to the super security cover provided for him, leaving millions of the capital's commuters stuck in endless traffic jams miserable and cursing. Leading a large delegation of Chinese business leaders, including bankers and executives from two Chinese telecommunications giants, Huawei and ZTE, Li was to keep the three-day trip focused on economic ties between China and India, which have grown rapidly over the past decade. The Chinese Ministry of Commerce said last week that bilateral trade reached $66 billion in 2012, setting a goal of $100 billion by 2015.

While it may sound hunky-dory that China has become India's biggest trading partner, the trade so far has been highly in China's favor, which is another source of concern for India.

While Prime Minister Manmohan Singh, External Affairs Minister Khurshid and the diplomats involved in the negotiations may well have addressed all the contentious issues and the Chinese government-controlled media going to town cheering this meet as very successful-what with eight agreements signed-statements like premier Li's: "India and China have differences, but our shared interests outweigh them", have to be taken with a spoonful of salt. No doubt, Mr. Li has been on a great charm offensive, but all that he has said on this trip can only be assessed once implementation begins and remains sustained. With his next stop being Pakistan, it remains to be seen how the strategic/border issues, particularly those of eastern Ladakh will be played out. And Premier Li's repeated reference to India as a "strategic" partner is indeed quite ironic.

China's possession of nuclear weapons targetable to any part of India, its nuclear cooperation with Pakistan resulting in swelling of Pakistan's nuclear arsenal, boosting nuclear proliferation in South Asia; China supporting Pakistan in supplying conventional weapons and never checking Pakistan for its anti-India activities; China supporting/

supplying arms to India's north east and Left Wing Extremists; China competing for resources in third countries; China's efforts to strengthen its relations with other countries in the Indian Ocean region; the China-India 'perception-based' border dispute, which keeps propelling its army/border troops to cross the LAC and intrude into India. China has kept the 3477 kms long LAC (3477 kms plus 1580 kms of undisputed border, totals 4957 kms) live with incursions, albeit without firing any bullets. The stepping up was beginning with Finger, the northern-most point as named by the Indian Army in, Sikkim, by May 2010, motorised foot and amphibious armed patrols of the PLA intruded into the strategic Trig Heights and Pangong lake in eastern Ladakh, bringing the figure of transgressions to 30 in Trig Heights itself, thereby signifying a quantum jump up of 52 per cent from 27 per cent in 2009. Then there was a spree of painting 'China' on rocks in Mandarin and numerous air space violations also in the same area. While whatever intrusions there may have been in the Central and Eastern segments of the LAC, the same in the Western segment including Jammu & Kashmir's Ladakh region are particularly worrisome for very obvious reasons. This should be particularly seen in the light of decades-old anti-India-based China-Pakistan relationship and joint military exercises, like Stride 2009, conducted in China's northwest Ningxia Hui Autonomous Region, at an unprecedented level of 50,000 troops and aiming to test its long-distance mobility; 'Sympathizing' with India on water issues with assurances of not adversely affecting India's water resources while relentlessly pursuing its own projects of building dams is a mockery. In 2011 China said that it was constructing a hydropower project at Zangmu and that there will be four more on the Brahmaputra, which would be all inside Chinese territory and being a run-of-the-river project, it would not involve storage of water. China also made it clear that it did not really have to share its plans with India but was doing it out of a sense of "trust". The 510 MW project, worth $1.2 billion, is being built by Gezhouba, one of China's biggest dam-building companies.

Governments, particularly of countries with multiple threats, must never play the ostrich in matters of national security. And in democracies like India, where control over the Armed Forces degenerated into total dominance coupled with contempt for them by the politico-bureaucratic establishment, national security has suffered great setbacks as valuable recommendations and advice on strategic matters was either not sought or, if sought or offered, it was disregarded.

The working arrangement for guarding land and sea borders of India has generally been that undisputed international boundaries are guarded by Border Security Force (BSF)/Ladakh Scouts/Assam Rifles (AR) under command of the Army and Coast Guard under Indian Navy. In fact, for Coast Guard, it was decided at the outset itself that it would be under Ministry of Defence, unlike BSF, AR, which are under Ministry of Home Affairs (MHA). Of the two disputed borders, the Line of Control (LoC) with Pakistan and the Line of Actual Control (LAC) with China, while both should be directly manned by the Army, with BSF/AR or the Indo-Tibetan Border Police (ITBP) in situ being under Army's command and control, the LoC is being guarded by Army. However, in the case of the LAC, it is not known as to why any part of it has been allotted for guarding to ITBP and that too under direct control of MHA and not the Army, as in the case of South East Ladakh, where both major Chinese incursions of 2008-9 in the general area of the barren land at Chumar, East of the picturesque Morari Tso (lake), Zulung La (pass) and the 22,420 feet high Mount Gya and the April 2013 one in Daulat Beg Oldi occurred.

Interacting with this writer, Lt Gen JS Bajwa (R), author of *Modernisation of the PLA: Gauging its Latent Future Potential* (Lancer) and Maj Gen Dhruv Katoch (R), Director, Centre for Land War Studies (CLAWS) have both reiterated what they succinctly wrote about the drawbacks and disadvantages of deploying ITBP on the LAC in recent articles written for Indian Defence Review and the CLAWS website respectively. While Bajwa has gone into details about various aspects of ITBP's lack of suitability for guarding the LAC, Katoch strongly recommends that Army must replace ITBP on the LAC and the latter be deployed against Left Wing Extremists (LWE), instead of requesting for Army's assistance, which the Defence Minister has correctly declined.

Five battalions of the lightly armed ITBP are deployed in Eastern

Ladakh including those on the Line of Actual Control (LAC) do not have the kind of integrated intelligence set-up, which is very essential in that scenario. The DIG Headquarter controlling these forces is located at Srinagar, 258 kms by air and 418 kms by road from Leh. Zoji La, on the Himalayan Range, and located on the main highway from Srinagar to Leh, is closed to road traffic from November to end May. Considering the separation of the Headquarter from the units, an adhoc Headquarter is functional under the Deputy at Leh. ITBP's basically High Frequency radio communications are vulnerable to interception and being jammed. ITBP under MHA is a police force, whereas Chinese Border Defence Units deployed and garrisoned along the entire LAC are directly under the PLA, which is surely not mere "policing" duties. The Chinese have been very active on the LAC and those who camped in Depsang required more than a "police "force response. Deploying ITBP on the LAC sends the wrong message to the Chinese who interpret it as a tacit acceptance of the Indian Government that the LAC is not active or live and as such does not need to be guarded by Army.

Bajwa states: "MHA's reluctance to place the ITBP under the Army is indicative of the underlying resistance of the IPS lobby to serve under any commander from the Army. IPS as seen from the factual ground realities considers itself as an "administrative cadre" akin to IAS. They loathe the notion of leading from the front as field commanders. The direct entry ITBP young officers endorse the requirement of operating under the Army".

New Delhi must not repeat the Himalayan blunders of trashing Army's inputs and recommendations which led to avoidable humiliation in 1962. India's political leadership and External Affairs Ministry must study many incidents on the LAC post-1962, particularly India's retaliation at Sikkim in 1967 and the upping of ante in Sumdorong Chu in the 1980s. This recent intrusion is far out of the ordinary and must neither be taken lightly nor lull us into complacence after Mr. Li's visit and particularly his hype. Because Sino-Indian history of the recent decades is replete with China proceeding with what and how it is benefited in trade, culture etc, while it actively pursues its predatory instincts on the ground. However, it has proved that it understands the language of strength and the will to use it.

Dealing with Dra'goon' Diplomacy

Addressing personnel of the Indo Tibetan Border Police (ITBP) on its 53rd Raising Day, on 24 October 2014, Union Home Minister Rajnath Singh announced the setting up of 54 new border outposts to cover some gaps along the Line of Actual Control (LAC) in Arunachal Pradesh, along with a package of Rs. 175 crores. The announcement is significant as China has been objecting to India's long overdue infrastructural development in this state.

Almost three weeks after major face-offs on the disputed Sino-Indian Line of Actual Control (LAC) in Eastern Ladakh, during Chinese president Xi Jinping's maiden visit to India, the Working Mechanism for Consultation and Coordination on India-China Border Affairs (WMCC) met in New Delhi. Both sides were reported to have reached a broad consensus on measures to maintain peace on the LAC. According to Chinese foreign ministry spokesperson Hua Chunying, both sides have agreed to establish regular meeting mechanism between the two-military headquarters of neighbouring military areas and border troops. They also agreed to set up new border meeting posts and decided to set up hotlines between military headquarters of the two countries. She further said, 'We also believe these measures will help to build communication and connections between the two militaries especially the border troops of the two countries and will help the two sides to properly deal with border affairs.' It remains to be seen how meaningful this meeting/discussion/agreement will be.

Hopes and expectations of a new page in Sino-Indian relations had been building up in the days preceding People's Republic of China's president Xi Jinping's maiden, visit to India from 17-19 of September 2014. President Xi Jinping's timing of the visit intended to cover Prime Minister Narendra Modi's birthday and that too with Ahmedabad preceding New Delhi, as the arrival destination, seemed to be further catalysts to give an unprecedented boost to the troublesome relationship between India and China/economic bonanza for both. Ranging from exotic settings of Xi Jingping and his wife Peng Liyuan swaying on a Sankheda swing at the Sabarmati waterfront, the cultural delights to the delectable Gujarati cuisine, Mr. Modi and the government left no stone unturned in extending warmth, hospitality, diplomatic decorum etc. However, that was not so as the Chinese response turned out to be a bad mix of its culinary formula of sweet and sour-with the sourness far exceeding the sweetness.

To some of us analysts, not without our share of cynicism based on China's track record of border transgressions punctuating tours/talks, the announced itinerary and thirteen agreements planned to be inked sounded rather too good to be true. This visit could have been the springboard for meaningfully giving a much-needed fillip to the complex Sino-Indian relationship. But by the time the two leaders were sitting together to enunciate their presentations at Hyderabad House, New Delhi, the tension caused by two major intrusions by Chinese forces was quite visible. While Mr. Modi calmly conveyed India's concerns to Xi Jinping saying that "peace and stability in our relations and along our borders are essential for us to realise the enormous potential in our relations," the manner, extent and duration of the intrusions which exceeded two weeks left no doubt about Chinese intentions.

Through the maze of media reports what emerged was that Chinese workers constructing a road on their side of the Line of Actual Control (LAC), entered into the Indian side to continue the construction. There are at least two versions of when these intrusions began-before Xi Jinping's arrival in India or with it. When objected to by the Indian side, Chinese workers asserted that they had instructions to build a road up to Tible, five kilometres deep into Indian territory. Indian army asked the Chinese workers to leave as otherwise they would face prosecution under Indian laws of entering into the country illegally. However, on night 21-22 September, nearly 100 Indian soldiers were reported to have been encircled by 300 Chinese PLA men after which a face-off started. Reinforcements were rushed to the area preventing Chinese troops to proceed further and also asking them to retreat to their side.

Three flag meetings failed to convince the Chinese to withdraw from the areas they had encroached into. The request for a fourth flag meeting came from the Chinese PLA. Indian Army did not respond to it for two days. Eventually the Chinese agreed to retreat taking almost a week to do so.

Another version reported in media subsequently was that in addition to the Demchok–Chumar intrusions, Chinese were building two more roads into Indian territory - one in Sikkim and another in Ladakh several kilometres away from Chumar.

Both these roads were reportedly destroyed by Indian forces upon discovery and a confrontation, which arose, was resolved without another standoff, even when Indian and China forces were eyeball to eyeball in Chumar for over a fortnight in September, 2014. When the Chinese objected to Indian forces destroying this road claiming it was well within their territory, it led to a long process of going through various records to convince them that it was indeed Indian territory and a standoff was averted.

Timed after his India visit Xi, considered China's most powerful leader after Deng Xiaoping, who succeeded Mao, directed the People's Liberation Army (PLA) to be combat ready to win a "regional war" and make sure that all decisions from the central leadership are strictly followed.

In April 1974, Deng Xiaoping, in a special address to the UN General Assembly, declared that "China is not a superpower, nor will she ever seek to be one. If one day China should change her color and turn into a superpower, if she too should play the tyrant in the world, and everywhere subject others to her bullying, aggression and exploitation, the people of the world should identify her as social-imperialism, expose it, oppose it and work together with the Chinese people to overthrow it."

The 2010s decade was marked by China's feverish military modernization and euphoria of its perceived economic progress making it only more belligerent and nuisance/threat to not only its land neighbours but also those in the South China sea region. Its only close friends now seem to be Pakistan and North Korea.

The economic package of $ 20 billion in 5 years falls far below what India expected and also just over half of Japan's recent package of $ 33.6 billion. Of course, India's recent strides in ties with Japan and Vietnam, it's long overdue infrastructural works as well as President Pranab Mukherjee's visit to Vietnam just preceding Xi's to India would certainly be major factors.

A minor consolation is that while the UPA government's responses to repeated violations in Eastern Ladakh from 2007 till 2013, were too soft, the Modi government has shown at least some assertiveness. First, the government swiftly withdrew the "political clearance" granted to a high-profile Chinese media delegation to attend a conference in the capital. Second, while Indian forces encircled the Chinese in sufficient strength from dominating positions at Demchok and Chumar, Indian Army did not respond to the Chinese request for a flag meeting for at least 48 hours till 25 September 2014.

If China claims to be a civilization it must also conduct diplomatic relations in a civilised manner and not in a goon-bully mode. Indian diplomacy must work towards convincing China that there is much to be gained by both nations by China not becoming periodically hyper on the borders and that there is a limit to Indian troops patiently/restrainedly resolving border confrontations by verbal requests to pushing with hands. India must also convey to China in no uncertain terms that in view of China's nuclear and conventional arsenal, its deployment/strategic reach, India will exercise its right to build its own arsenal and infrastructure.

China Pakistan Economic Corridor

In April 2015, when President Xi Jinping was en-route to Pakistan, his plane was escorted by eight JF-17 Thunder fighter jets. His arrival signaled a new era in Sino-Pak strategic relationship as both sides unveiled $46 billion China Pakistan Economic Corridor, a transnational corridor consisting of seamless highways, power plants and upscale infrastructure projects linking Balochistan's strategic port of Gwadar with Xinjiang's Kashgar. With time, the amount pledged has grown from $46 billion to $62 billion. The corridor enters Pakistani territory through Gilgit-Baltistan, which India has been claiming since the 1947, when the region was snatched away from India following a coup by the British officer Major Brown, then commanding the Gilgit Scouts (the fall of Baltistan followed soon once Gilgit was captured). Despite repeated protests by the Government of India, China has disregarded India's concerns and gone ahead with the project. In a way, China's growing inroads into Gilgit-Baltistan are increasingly making the region both strategically and economically dependent on China.

In May 2017, prominent Pakistan daily *Dawn* exclusively accessed China's CPEC masterplan. More than investments, the masterplan, for the first-time revealed China's long-term ambitions, not only to dominate the Pakistani economy, but gradually convert Pakistan into in an extended satellite state, whose sole purpose would be to play a subservient role to the Chinese economy. Specifically, the plan put out in detail what Chinese intentions and priorities were for fifteen years.

The three pillars on which the long term plan is based are:

1. Leasing out thousands of acres of agricultural land to Chinese enterprises to set up "demonstration projects" in areas like seed development and working on irrigation technology.
2. Complete monitoring and surveillance in cities from Peshawar to Karachi, with 24 hour video recordings on roads and marketplaces to maintain law and order.
3. A nationwide fiber optic backbone for the country for internet traffic as well as terrestrial distribution of broadcast Television, which, interestingly will cooperate with Chinese media in the "dissemination of Chinese culture".[20]

According to *Dawn*, "the plan envisages a deep and broad-based penetration of most sectors of Pakistan's economy as well as its society by Chinese enterprises and culture. Its scope has no precedent in Pakistan's history in terms of how far it opens up the domestic economy to participation by foreign enterprises".[21]

The plan exquisitely states that the corridor "spans Xinjiang Uygur Autonomous Region and whole Pakistan in spatial range" with the larger aim to link Xinjiang with Pakistan. It is divided into a "core area" and "radiation zones", that is, those areas that shall absorb the spillover effects from the investment and economic initiatives being undertaken in the core area.[22] The *Dawn* report further defines core area as including "Kashgar, Tumshuq, Atushi and Akto of Kizilsu Kirghiz of Xinjiang" from China, and "most of Islamabad's Capital territory, Punjab, and Sindh, and some areas of Gilgit-Baltistan, Khyber Pukhtunkhwa, and Balochistan" from Pakistan.[23] It has "one belt, three passages, and two axes and five functional zones", where the belt is "the strip area formed by important arterial traffic in China and Pakistan". The Long-Term

Plan's details, as discussed by the Dawn report are reproduced as below with quotations and minor modifications.[24]

Agriculture

In the domain of agriculture, the plan outlines an engagement that more or less completes an entire supply chain including "provision of seeds and other inputs, like fertiliser, credit and pesticides", since Chinese enterprises are supposed to also operate their own farms. In tandem, Logistics companies would be running large storage and transportation systems for managing the agricultural produce.[25]

The plan identifies opportunities for "entry by Chinese enterprises in the myriad dysfunctions that afflict Pakistan's agriculture sector". For instance, "due to lack of cold-chain logistics and processing facilities, 50% of agricultural products go bad during harvesting and transport", it notes.[26] Hence, rather than introspecting and putting checks and balances on the policy failures that are responsible for the poor state of Pakistan's agriculture, Pakistan seems to have comfortably delegated its agricultural sector to Chinese firms.

Companies entering agriculture will be given high levels of assistance from Chinese government. The plan encourages these enterprises to "make the most of the free capital and loans" from various ministries of the Chinese government as well as the China Development Bank. The plan also offers to maintain a mechanism that will "help Chinese agricultural enterprises to contact the senior representatives of the Government of Pakistan and China".[27]

Further, China will "actively strive to utilize the national special funds as the discount interest for the loans of agricultural foreign investment". In the longer term the financial risk will be spread out, through "new types of financing such as consortium loans, joint private equity and joint debt issuance, raise funds via multiple channels and decentralize financing risks".[28]

The plan proposes to "harness the work of the Xinjiang Production and Construction Corps to bring mechanization as well as scientific technique in livestock breeding, development of hybrid varieties and precision irrigation to Pakistan". The plan envisages this opportunity to prop up the laggard economy of Kashgar, which suffers from a high poverty rate of 50 per cent. Added to this, the region lying to the China's landlocked west makes it difficult to connect to larger markets and integrate it seamlessly in the larger network of supply chains.[29]

However, for the Chinese, this is the main driving force behind investing in Pakistan's agriculture, in addition to the many profitable opportunities that can open up for their enterprises from operating in the local market. The plan makes some reference to export of agriculture goods from the ports, but the bulk of its emphasis is focused on the opportunities for the Kashgar Prefecture and Xinjiang Production Corps, coupled with the opportunities for profitable engagement in the domestic market.[30]

The plan shows great interest in the textiles industry in particular, but the interest is focused largely on yarn and coarse cloth. Meat processing plants in Sukkur are planned with annual output of 200,000 tons per year, and two demonstration plants processing 200,000 tons of milk per year. In crops, demonstration projects of more than 6,500 acres will be set up for high yield seeds and irrigation, mostly in Punjab. In transport and storage, the plan aims to build "a nationwide logistics network, and enlarge the warehousing and distribution network between major cities of Pakistan" with a focus on grains, vegetables and fruits. Storage bases will be built first in Islamabad and Gwadar in the first phase, then Karachi, Lahore and another in Gwadar in the second phase, and between 2026-2030, Karachi, Lahore and Peshawar will each see another storage base.[31]

Asadabad, Islamabad, Lahore and Gwadar will see a vegetable processing plant, with annual output of 20,000 tons, fruit juice and jam plant of 10,000 tons and grain processing of 1 million tons. A cotton processing plant is also planned initially, with output of 100,000 tons per year. "We will impart advanced planting and breeding techniques to peasant households or farmers by means of land acquisition by the government, renting to China-invested enterprises and building planting and breeding bases" it says about the plan to source superior seeds.[32]

In each field, Chinese enterprises will play the lead role. "China-invested enterprises will establish factories to produce fertilizers, pesticides, vaccines and feedstuffs" it says about the production of agricultural materials. "China-invested enterprises will, in the form of joint ventures, shareholding or acquisition, cooperate with local enterprises of Pakistan to build a three-level warehousing system (purchase & storage warehouse, transit warehouse and port warehouse)" it says about warehousing.[33]

One of the most intriguing chapters in the plan speaks of a long belt of coastal enjoyment industry that includes yacht wharfs, cruise homeports, nightlife, city parks, public squares, theaters, golf courses and spas, hot spring hotels and water sports. Then it talks about trade. "We will actively embark on cultivating surrounding countries in order to improve import and export potential of Pakistani agricultural products and accelerate the trade of agricultural products. In the early stages, we will gradually create a favorable industry image and reputation for Pakistan by relying on domestic demand."[34]

In places the plan appears to be addressing investors in China. It says Chinese enterprises should seek "coordinated cooperation with Pakistani enterprises" and "maintain orderly competition and mutual coordination." It advises them to make an effort "seeking for powerful strategic partners for bundling interest in Pakistan."[35]

As security measures, enterprises will be advised "to respect the religions and customs of the local people, treat people as equals and live in harmony". They will also be advised to "increase local employment and contribute to local society by means of subcontracting and consortiums." In the final sentence of the chapter on agriculture, the plan says the government of China will "[s]trengthen the safety cooperation with key countries, regions and international organizations, jointly prevent and crack down on terrorist acts that endanger the safety of Chinese overseas enterprises and their staff."[36]

Industry

For industry, the plan trifurcates the country into three zones: western and northwestern, central and southern. Each zone is marked to receive specific industries in designated industrial parks, of which only a few are actually mentioned. The western and northwestern zone, covering most of Balochistan and KP province, is marked for mineral extraction, with potential in chrome ore, "gold reserves hold a considerable potential, but are still at the exploration stage", and diamonds. One big mineral product that the plan discusses is marble. Already, China is Pakistan's largest buyer of processed marble, at almost 80,000 tons per year. The plan looks to set up 12 marble and granite processing sites in locations ranging from Gilgit and Kohistan in the north, to Khuzdar in the south.[37]

The central zone is marked for textiles, household appliances and cement. Four separate locations are pointed out for future cement clusters: Daudkhel, Khushab, Esakhel and Mianwali. The case of cement is interesting, because the plan notes that Pakistan is surplus in cement capacity, then goes on to say that "in the future, there is a larger space of cooperation for China to invest in the cement process transformation".[38]

"There is a plan to build a pilot safe city in Peshawar, which faces a fairly severe security situation in northwestern Pakistan". For the southern zone, the plan recommends that "Pakistan develop petrochemical, iron and steel, harbor industry, engineering machinery, trade processing and auto and auto parts (assembly)" due to the proximity of Karachi and its ports. This is the only part in the report where the auto industry is mentioned in any substantive way, which is a little surprising because the industry is one of the fastest growing in the country. The silence could be due to lack of interest on the part of the Chinese to acquire stakes, or to diplomatic prudence since the sector is, at the moment, entirely dominated by Japanese companies (Toyota, Honda and Suzuki).[39]

One of the CPEC transport routes. Gwadar, also in the southern zone, "is positioned as the direct hinterland connecting Balochistan and Afghanistan." As a CPEC entreport, the plan recommends that it be built into "a base of heavy and chemical industries, such as iron and steel/petrochemical". It notes that "some Chinese enterprises have started investment and construction in Gwadar" taking advantage of its "superior geographical position and cheap shipping costs to import crude oil from the Middle East, iron ore and coking coal resources from South Africa and New Zealand" for onward supply to the local market "as well as South Asia and Middle East after processing at port."[40]

The plan shows great interest in the textiles industry in particular, but the interest is focused largely on yarn and coarse cloth. The reason, as the plan lays out, is that in Xinjiang the textile industry has already attained higher levels of productivity. Therefore, "China can make the most of the Pakistani market in cheap raw materials to develop the textiles & garments industry and help soak up surplus labor forces in Kashgar". The ensuing strategy is described cryptically as the principle of "introducing foreign capital and establishing domestic connections as a crossover of West and East".[41]

Preferential policies will be necessary to attract enterprises to come to the newly built industrial parks envisioned under the plan. The areas where such preferences need to be extended are listed in the plan as "land, tax, logistics and services" as well as land price, "enterprise income tax, tariff reduction and exemption and sales tax rate."[42]

Fibreoptics and Surveillance

One of the oldest priorities for the Chinese government since talks on CPEC began is fibreoptic connectivity between China and Pakistan. An MoU for such a link was signed in July 2013, at a time when CPEC appeared to be little more than a road link between Kashgar and Gwadar. But the plan reveals that the link goes far beyond a simple fibreoptic set up.[43]

China has various reasons for wanting a terrestrial fibreoptic link with Pakistan, including its own limited number of submarine landing stations and international gateway exchanges which can serve as a bottleneck to future growth of internet traffic. This is especially true for the western provinces. "Moreover, China's telecom services to Africa need to be transferred in Europe, so there is certain hidden danger of the overall security" says the plan. Pakistan has four submarine cables to handle its internet traffic, but only one landing station, which raises security risks as well.[44] So the plan envisages a terrestrial cable across the Khunjerab pass to Islamabad, and a submarine landing station in Gwadar, linked to Sukkur. From there, the backbone will link the two in Islamabad, as well as all major cities in Pakistan.[45]

The expanded bandwidth that will open up will enable terrestrial broadcast of digital HD television, called Digital Television Terrestrial Multimedia Broadcasting (DTMB). This is envisioned as more than just a technological contribution. It is a "cultural transmission carrier. The future cooperation between Chinese and Pakistani media will be beneficial to disseminating Chinese culture in Pakistan, further enhancing mutual understanding between the two peoples and the traditional friendship between the two countries." The plan says nothing about how the system will be used to control the content of broadcast media, nor does it say anything more about "the future cooperation between Chinese and Pakistani media".[46]

Judging from their conversations with the government, it appears that the Pakistanis are pushing the Chinese to begin work on the Gwadar International Airport, whereas the Chinese are pushing for early completion of the Eastbay Expressway. It also seeks to create an electronic monitoring and control system for the border in Khunjerab, as well as run a "safe cities" project. The safe city project will deploy explosive detectors and scanners to "cover major roads, case-prone areas and crowded places...in urban areas to conduct real-time monitoring and 24-hour video recording." Signals gathered from the surveillance system will be transmitted to a command centre, but the plan says nothing about who will staff the command centre, what sort of signs they will look for, and who will provide the response.[47]

Tourism and Recreation

One of the most intriguing chapters in the plan is the one that talks about the development of a "coastal tourism" industry. It speaks of a long belt of coastal enjoyment industry that includes yacht wharfs, cruise homeports, nightlife, city parks, public squares, theaters, golf courses and spas, hot spring hotels and water sports. The belt will run from Keti Bunder to Jiwani, the last habitation before the Iranian border. Then, somewhat disappointingly, it adds that "more work needs to be done" before this vision can be realized.[48]

The plans are laid out in surprising detail. For instance, Gwadar will feature international cruise clubs that "provide marine tourists private rooms that would feel as though they were 'living in the ocean'." And just as the feeling sinks in, it goes on to say that "[f]or the development of coastal vacation products, Islamic culture, historical culture, folk culture and marine culture shall all be integrated."[49] Apparently more work needs to be done here too.

For Ormara, the plan recommends building "unique recreational activities" that would also encourage "the natural, exciting, participatory, sultry, and tempting characteristics" to come through. For Keti Bunder it recommends wildlife sanctuaries, an aquarium and a botanical garden. For Sonmiani, on the eastern edge of Karachi, "projects like a coastal beach, extended greenway, coastal villa, car camp, SPA, beach playground and a seafood street can be developed."[50]

It is an expansive vision that the plan lays out, and towards the end, it asks for the following: "Make the visa-free tourism possible with China to provide more convenient policy support for Chinese tourists to Pakistan."[51] There is no mention of a reciprocal arrangement for Pakistani nationals visiting China.[52]

Finance and Risk

In any plan, the question of financial resources is always crucial. The long term plan drawn up by the China Development Bank is at its sharpest when discussing Pakistan's financial sector, government debt market, depth of commercial banking and the overall health of the financial system. It is at its most unsentimental when drawing up the risks faced by long term investments in Pakistan's economy.[53]

The chief risk the plan identifies is politics and security. "There are various factors affecting Pakistani politics, such as competing parties, religion, tribes, terrorists, and Western intervention" the authors write. "The security situation is the worst in recent years". The next big risk, surprisingly, is inflation, which the plan says has averaged 11.6 per cent over the past 6 years. "A high inflation rate means a rise of project-related costs and a decline in profits."[54]

Efforts will be made, says the plan, to furnish "free and low interest loans to Pakistan" once the costs of the corridor begin to come in. But this is no free ride, it emphasizes. "Pakistan's federal and involved local governments should also bear part of the responsibility for financing through issuing sovereign guarantee bonds, meanwhile protecting and improving the proportion and scale of the government funds invested in corridor construction in the financial budget."[55]

It asks for financial guarantees "to provide credit enhancement support for the financing of major infrastructure projects, enhance the financing capacity, and protect the interests of creditors." Relying on the assessments of the IMF, World Bank and the ADB, it notes that Pakistan's economy cannot absorb FDI much above $2 billion per year without giving rise to stresses in its economy. "It is recommended that China's maximum annual direct investment in Pakistan should be around US$1 billion."[56] Likewise, it concludes that Pakistan's ceiling for preferential loans should be $1 billion, and for non-preferential loans no more than $1.5 billion per year.

It advises its own enterprises to take precautions to protect their own investments. "International business cooperation with Pakistan should be conducted mainly with the government as a support, the banks as intermediary agents and enterprises as the mainstay."[57] Nor is the growing engagement some sort of brotherly involvement. "The cooperation with Pakistan in the monetary and financial areas aims to serve China's diplomatic strategy."[58]

The other big risk the plan refers to is exchange rate risk, after noting the severe weakness in Pakistan's ability to earn foreign exchange. To mitigate this, the plan proposes tripling the size of the swap mechanism between the RMB and the Pakistani rupee to 30 billion Yuan, diversifying power purchase payments beyond the dollar into RMB and rupee basket, tapping the Hong Kong market for RMB bonds, and diversifying enterprise.

Militarizing CPEC

It would not have mattered even if China's ambitions regarding Pakistan would have remained limited to the economic realm only. Rather, as events unfold, CPEC is turning into a military corridor running all the way from Gwadar to Kashgar. Rather than debating on the feasibility of projects (many of which are being increasingly questioned by Pakistan's own economists), especially those of coal and hydropower, which constitute a major chunk of CPEC investments, the establishment (read Army) has diverted the narrative towards sensitizing Pakistanis about the "threats" India poses to CPEC. While India continues to oppose CPEC by the virtue of its alignment passing through PoK, this in no way means India has been involved in sabotaging a project, which naturally poses risks to Pakistan's sovereignty, given the conditional loans, high interest rates and a looming presence of the Chinese government, which leaves very little independence on part of the Pakistani decision-makers. The army, via its spokespersons and the ISPR propaganda machine has been continuously blaming India as a threat to CPEC's survival. This means that any failures to successfully be attributed to India's hidden hand and the army would take credit for any project that becomes successful.

This construction of threat has justified Pakistani army's additional militarization of the CPEC. As a result, decks were cleared to set up a Special Security Division (SSD) headquartered in Gilgit to protect CPEC against external threats. Approximately 15000 troops have been mobilized to serve in the SSD, which would be headed by a Major General Rank officer. A Gwadar Maritime Task force has been set up to protect the CPEC's maritime domain. The creation of the maritime task force has been justified by the establishment as guarding against threats from India. Last year, Pakistani agencies had accused India of sending its submarine in Pakistani waters to spy on the developments around Gwadar. The agencies also claimed to have successfully chased the submarine. This became a justification to set up the maritime task force. Furthermore, Pakistani media had also reported that Pakistan and China had been mulling over setting a joint counter terrorism unit to guard against the CPEC after disenchantment in Balochistan has led to Chinese workers being targeted by Baloch nationalist organizations.

The militarization of CPEC, with clear sanctions from China should not go unregistered by India's security agencies as the corridor is more about tying mutual security interests of both the nations together. Pakistan has for long been falsely accusing India of stoking fire in its frontier zones by promoting separatism among Baloch and Pashtuns. By getting the Chinese to invest in Balochistan's troubled regions, any threat on Chinese workers operating in these regions would prompt

Pakistan to directly put the blame of India. This would readily lead to deterioration of ties between India and China and initial signs of this dangerous games have been visible when Chinese workers were attacked in Balochistan recently. Before any investigation could fix accountability, Pakistani authorities quickly blamed Indian agencies behind the attack on Chinese. Therefore, in crux, the construction of Indian threat, CPEC's militarization and putting the blame for instabilities in Balochistan on India act as ready ingredients into this threat multiplier, which risks deteriorating the already vulnerable strategic balance in South Asia.

The CPEC challenge is being accompanied by growing Chinese presence along the LAC, as a continuation of Beijing's long standing policy of keeping the borders ignited. The nature of Chinese intrusions has been discussed in the earlier of this chapter and this leads us to understand how India has been responding in far more assertive manner. Several developments became more visible starting from last year, which have angered the Chinese substantially. Speeding up the construction of the strategic Indo-China border roads, an initiative continuing from 2005, setting up a tank brigade in Ladakh and the deployment of BrahMos and India's recent test of Agni-V has really irked the Chinese. This posturing, which is being carried by use of tactful diplomacy like inviting the Dalai Lama to Tawang and deepening ties with Myanmar, Vietnam and ASEAN block has taken as challenge by the Chinese.

Strengthening Posture along the LAC: Tank Brigade, Brahmos and the Agni-V Challenge

By 2016, an armoured brigade was deployed in Eastern Ladakh. Besides this, efforts were undertaken to ensure faster repairing/completion of old and construction of new advanced landing grounds. Also, India announced deployment of Brahmos missile and additional Sukhoi jets in the Eastern Sector of the LAC. Sure enough, it generated a negative reaction from the state-controlled Chinese media. The message had been sent that that erstwhile perception of northeast India being dependent on the vulnerable "Chicken's neck" or the Siliguri Corridor was no longer valid.

India's successful test launch of the 5000 plus km range Agni-V missile from a canister based launcher in December 2016 was the final nail in the coffin, which caused huge furore among the Chinese strategic circles. The fact that India was now capable of striking major Chinese cities that too from flexible canister launchers have unsettled the balance of power equation between both the nations.

This change in strategic posturing was further augmented by inviting the Dalai Lama to Tawang, despite repeated Chinese warnings, which India did not bow down to. Chinese media, especially *Global Times*, went ballistic, throwing a volley of rhetoric's warning New Delhi of dire consequences.

India has realized that with strong economy and strong military capabilities, it has to brace herself to face the China challenge sooner or later. There have been no signs of any thaw from the Chinese side, both in the geostrategic challenge it poses via propping up Pakistan, as well as diplomatically sidelining India by refusing to acknowledge Masood Azhar as a terrorist and by repeatedly blocking India's legitimate and long pending entry into the Nuclear Suppliers Group.

Another opportunity to mend ties came in February 2017 when both sides organized the first ever India-China strategic dialogue in Beijing. The dialogue was jointly chaired by Foreign Secretary S. Jaishankar and China's vice-foreign minister Zhang Yesui. India raised her legitimate demands on myriad issues like the NSG membership, China's continuing support of Masood Azhar, mounting trade balance and CPEC's illegal crossover from PoK. Indian foreign secretary's approach on the need for a strategic dialogue was indeed pragmatic, where he stated that, "The international strategic situation is in flux...one thing that we could do together was a more stable, substantive, forward looking India-China relationship which would inject a greater amount of predictability into the international system".[59]

As expected, the Chinese yielded nothing and neither Beijing showed even the slightest signs of sensitivity to Indian concerns. On the issue of Azhar, India was snubbed by the brazen response that India needed to furnish more proof to strengthen the case against Azhar and convince the Chinese. Similarly, nothing was forthcoming from the Chinese side even in the case of the growing trade imbalance.

Responding to this disregard, India refused to participate in China's formal inauguration of the OBOR in May, 2017, that is, the Belt and Road Forum. To allay India's concerns, the Chinese ambassador to India Luo Zhaohui even offered to rename CPEC but later, his statement was quietly omitted from Chinese embassy's website.

Conclusion: The Way Forward

The purpose to deliberately highlight the dangers of fragile peace on the LAC, CPEC and Pakistan's role in the same chapter is to get a thorough understanding on how China has made its intentions clearer that its hitherto policy of making gradual inroads into India's periphery is no longer valid. Notwithstanding the vulnerable LAC, which has faced recurring episodes of brinkmanship from time to time, the Chinese taking advantage of Pakistan's ailing economy, their aggressive ambitions, as mentioned in the Dawn report, and continuing militarization of CPEC have also proven the fear of India's strategists to be true. CPEC is not merely an OBOR economic venture as projected by China, but a blueprint of the Chinese statecraft with direct connotations on India's security fabric. The old policy of engaging India at two-and a half fronts does show signs of maturing as Sino-Pak nexus deepens with time. A resurgent China, buoyed by a manipulated exchange rate and a growing industry of reverse-engineered weapons is increasingly challenging its neighbors both along its territorial as well as maritime borders. A calculated strategy of keeping the East China Sea, South China Sea and the Himalayan frontier on the boil clearly depicts a pattern of how rising imperialist powers attempt to destabilize their neighborhood when their global ambitions begin to become less and less subtle. Being the sole challenger to Dragon's might, the prospects of protracted conflict with China too have risen and India finds itself being challenged by a economically superior neighbor which also happens to command a geo-strategically favorable ground vis-à-vis India.

The most unfortunate result of this rivalry has been the strategic flux India finds itself into. As suggested repeatedly by several renowned scholars, China wants to limit India's ambitions to South Asia and be tied down to a perpetual Indo-Pak rivalry in which India tires itself combating the deadly sub-conventional warfare and engaging in an nuclear arms race with Pakistan. While China could sustain Pakistan's nuclear program without any impunity, India would exhaust herself battling the international nuclear norms and diverting the much needed resources away from crucial economic initiatives. Moreover, in absence of a sophisticated defence industrial base, India would be more concerned with arms purchases to meet immediate threats, thereby relegating serious efforts to embark on a long-term plan to develop strong defence manufacturing base.

By tying down India with its rogue western neighbour, the path is clear for China to divert its resources solely on a fast economic growth and single-handedly focus on working towards achieving a strategic parity with the US.

India needs to brace up to face the joint challenge from China and Pakistan. While in the short run, India needs to face the immediate challenge of dealing with border instabilities which China and Pakistan attempt on a frequent basis. Today, borders have become more sensitive than ever and India faces a burning Kashmir valley and ceasefire violation on its western frontier, and continuing intrusions by the PLA on its north. On the international level, India's attempts to balance externally against China by forging deeper alliances with Japan and USA too have drawn ire from Beijing, which in turn continues to question India's intentions, since the strong potential of a Indo-Japan-US trilateral relationship could swing the Asian balance of power in favour of India not only in geostrategic domain, but also in the economic domain, if India is able to utilize the economic partnership forthcoming from Tokyo and Washington DC.

Cogitating on opportunities for strengthening economic ties should be fast-tracked among India, US and Japan, in addition to their existing respective mutual cooperation mechanisms and dialogues in the economic and commercial spheres.

NOTES

1 http://en.people.cn/200611/23/print20061123_324370.html
2 https://www.mea.gov.in/bilateral-documents.htm?dtl/6363/Joint+Declaration+by+the+Republic+of+India+an

3   http://kanglaonline.com/2013/05/chinese-checkers-redux-with-five-tents/
4   http://www.claws.in/77/claiming-sikkim-%E2%80%93-chinas-incursions-into-indian-territory-col-anil-bhat-retd.html
5   Ibid.
6   Ibid.
7   Ibid.
8   http://www.china.org.cn/international/foreign_ministry/2008-11/11/content_16748195.htm
9   http://tradingexpertx.blogspot.com/2009/09/
10 http://timesofindia.indiatimes.com/India/After_43_yrs_IAF_plans_ to_reactivate_Ladakh_airstrip/articleshow/2964674.cms
11 http://himalayanaffairs.org/article.aspx?id=206
12 http://kanglaonline.com/2013/05/chinese-checkers-redux-with-five-tents/
13 Ibid.
14 http://www.millenniumpost.in/chinese-chequers-redux-with-tents-27711?NID=28123
15 http://himalayanaffairs.org/article.asp?r=63.3732407517485&svr=54&lang=en_us&x?id=199
16 Ibid.
17 Ibid.
18 http://www.jottings.in/2012/01/from-todays-papers-05-jan-2012.html
19 http://himalayanaffairs.org/article.aspx?id=199
20 https://economictimes.indiatimes.com/news/defence/cpec-could-destroy-pakistan-economy-and-society/articleshow/58722033.cms?from=mdr
21 https://www.outlookindia.com/website/story/secret-china-pakistan-economic-corridor-document-reveals-beijing-is-the-new-east/298919
22 https://www.outlookindia.com/newsscroll/master-plan-of-cpec-revealed/1051026
23 https://www.dawn.com/news/1378963
24 https://www.dawn.com/news/1333101
25 https://www.dawn.com/news/1333101
26 https://www.dawn.com/news/1333101
27 Ibid
28 Ibid.
29 Ibid.
30 Ibid.
31 Ibid.
32 Ibid.
33 Ibid.
34 Ibid.
35 Ibid.
36 Ibid.
37 Ibid.
38 Ibid.
39 Ibid.
40 Ibid.

41 Ibid.
42 Ibid.
43 Ibid.
44 Ibid.
45 Ibid.
46 Ibid.
47 Ibid.
48 https://www.dawn.com/news/1333101
49 https://www.uyghurcongress.org/en/exclusive-cpec-master-plan-revealed/
50 https://www.dawn.com/news/1333101
51 https://www.dawn.com/news/1333101
52 Ibid.
53 Ibid.
54 https://rava.pk/slider-articles/cpec-exclusive-master-plan-revealed/amp
55 https://thediplomat.com/2017/05/understanding-chinas-master-plan-for-pakistan/
56 https://thediplomat.com/2017/05/understanding-chinas-master-plan-for-pakistan/
57 https://books.google.co.in/books?id=NcmGDwAAQBAJ&pg=PA102&lpg=PA102&dq=Inte rnational+business+cooperation+with+Pakistan+should+be+conducted+ mainly+ with+ the+ government+ as+a+support,+th e+banks+as+ inter mediary +agents+and+enterprises+as+the+mainstay&source=bl&ots= 8fVlWJdb UI&sig=ACfU3U1wuQxL5h8HoptjgwUr-d3j1MJPWA&hl=en&sa=X&v ed=2ahUKEwj79cfprtjnAhVTU30KHaOqBnoQ6AEwAHoECAgQAQ#v=on epage&q=International%20business%20cooperation%20with%20Pakistan%20should %20be%20conducted%20mainly%20with%20the%20government%20as%20a%20support %2C%20the%20banks%20as%20intermediary%20agents %20and%20enterprises %20 as%20the%20mainstay&f=false
58 https://usiofindia.org/publication/usi-journal/china-pakistan-economic-corridor-connecting-the-dots/
59 https://www.livemint.com/Opinion/TtuTsD7Cwbo1nLKDeLDJ4K/The-reality-of-the-IndiaChina-strategic-dialogue.html

5
Doklam

Following PLA upping the ante with not only small arms but artillery also and a fierce retaliation by Indian Army at Sikkim in 1967, the 4057 kms long complex and perception-based Line of Actual Control (LAC), has been managed by both armies without pulling the trigger for the fifty third year (barring Tulung La on October 20, 1975-which was also bulletless, because the Assam Rifles riflemen they were killed by torture) now. And that is despite very frequent incursions/transgressions mainly/much more by China's People's Liberation Army (PLA), many of which resulted in unarmed grappling by troops of both armies, but always ended with negotiations by field commanders and/or diplomatic dialogue.[1]

However, PLA's transgression beginning on 08 June 2017 into Bhutan's Doklam plateau (also known as Doka La by India and claimed as Donglang by China), at the tri-junction of India's Sikkim, Bhutan and China-held Tibet, actually amounts to aggression and has resulted in a dangerous stand-off, continuing for 72 days. On the very next day, 09 June, when the Prime Minister Narendra Modi and President Xi Jinping met for the Shanghai Cooperation Organisation's summit at Astana, Kazakhstan, it was reported: "There was an understanding that where we have differences, it is important that differences should not become disputes."² But PLA's actions on the ground belies such a spirit. First, it demolished two bunkers and then began constructing a road towards Doka La. The Royal Bhutan Army (RBA) tried to intervene but were pushed back. RBA then sought assistance of the Indian troops, who moved down the ridge and obstructed the construction work, leading to the standoff. Visuals on TV news networks of Indian soldiers relentlessly grappling with their PLA counterparts leave no doubt about their determination and great restraint.³

India expediting the building of hollow block bunkers along the LAC, India's refusal to take part in the One Belt, One Road summit organized by China and PM Modi's visits to the US and Israel, have all peeved China. Since then, Beijing has issued a warning over India's strategic infrastructure development along/near the LAC, especially in the north-east region. China opposed the infrastructure development issue several times. It is certainly not happy about India raising a mountain corps with two divisions already and the construction of bunkers particularly, has been a flashpoint in Sino-India ties.⁴

Former foreign secretary and also former Indian ambassador to China, Nirupama Rao is reported to have stated the last few months have exposed the fragilities and strains in the India-China relationship. The equilibrium is already pitched at a low level. There has been no visible attempt to defuse tensions as the temperature has risen steadily. India has some genuine grievances which China has shown little understanding of. The Chinese handling of the China-Pakistan Economic Corridor issue is one example. The dispute in the Doklam area is known. It is not a new phenomenon. But China's road construction is a deliberate move to trigger a response from Bhutan and from India. Through its actions, China seeks to impose its own definition of the tri-junction point of the boundary between Bhutan, China and India (Sikkim). The move has serious security ramifications for both Bhutan and India's defence interests. Bhutan and India enjoy the closest relationship of mutual trust and confidence and enduring friendship. There is absolutely no controversy about military-to-military cooperation and understanding between our two countries. India holds Bhutanese sovereignty as sacred and inviolable.⁵

The chapter analyses the events leading up to Doklam crisis in light of the events taking place in the trijunction region as well as by taking into consideration the long-term Chinese strategy at play.

The Run-up to Doklam

As has been argued by several strategists, Doklam should not been seen as an isolated event in the Sino-Indian standoff. That is, clubbing Doklam with the hundreds of scuffles which have taken across the LAC shall risk missing out the Chinese grand strategy at play.[6] While there had been growing signs of provocation in the recent years, it is indispensable to analyse the PLA military reforms which have preceded this new era of conflict. 2015 onwards, PLA embarked on military reforms, reorganizing itself into theatre commands.

In fact, in May, 2016, *The Global Times* also ran an editorial highlighting the importance of Tibetan Military District of the WTC, especially in its role against India.[7] In the larger framework, these reforms consolidated Xi's power over the armed forces. The reforms aim at augmenting China's capability to undertake joint operations by crossing service lines.

The Western Theater Command (WTC) is geographically the largest among these commands, which has been constituted after merging Chengdu and Lanzhou Military Regions. The troop levels in the WTC were reduced by two group armies in 2016. The terrain in WTC comprising of high-altitude permafrost zones as well as desert regions (Xinjiang and Tibet) could also be compared to the border region with India which it is responsible for. Ladakh's desert and jagged peaks and the Himalayan belt across the LAC is an apt topography suited for the WTC operations.

The immediate impetus seems to have come from a couple of events preceding the standoff. The previous year onwards, when strengthening of defences along through LAC was proceeding at a swift pace, India played diplomatic masterstrokes to legitimize its claim on Tawang. In October 2016, American ambassador to India Richard Verma paid a visit to Tawang, making it the first instance of such a visit. This move came as a response China's reluctance to support India's NSG membership and blocking attempts at the UNSC to declare Masood Azhar as a terrorist. "The intervention of any third party will only complicate the issue and is highly irresponsible," Chinese foreign ministry told the Press Trust of India.[8]

In April, the Dalai Lama too paid a visit, with the event attracting strong criticism from China. China's foreign ministry was quick to threaten India, stating that "India in disregard to China's concerns obstinately arranged the Dalai Lama's visit to the disputed part of the eastern part of China-India border, causing serious damage to China's interests and China-India relations".[9]

In May 2017, when China organized the Belt and Road Forum, India not only refused to take part in the event. India's stance generated consternation in Beijing which had been expecting cooperation from India.

On 26th May, barely three weeks before the standoff, when the Dhola-Sadiya bridge was inaugurated by the Prime Minister, a clear signal that northeast India would no longer remain vulnerable from mainland Indian landmass. Another symbolism associated with the presence of Prime Minister in the inauguration ceremony is fact that the bridge the country's longest road bridge. The 9.15 km-long Dhola-Sadiya bridge on Assam's Lohit river will vastly improve connectivity with Arunachal Pradesh. Besides the geostrategic significance, the bridge is also capable of allowing the Army's 60-tonne Arjun and T-72 main battle tanks. Around the same time, Home Minister had chaired a meeting of Himalayan states to fasten the development of infrastructure along the LAC.

On June 16, 100 PLA soldiers shifted earthmoving units and 4-5 bulldozers to Doklam and began building a road towards Che La. Noticing the blatant territorial aggression by the Chinese, the Royal Bhutan Army tried to intervene from Jamperei but they were pushed back so the latter approached the Indian troops. According to Indian Express, the Chinese troops are from the PLA's 6 Border Defence regiment (Unit-77649).

Indian troops, resultantly moved to the site and stopped the Chinese from proceeding with the construction and pitched their tents, thus leading to a standoff. Unlike other cases of border tensions which usually got resolved with border meetings, Doklam spiraled into a diplomatic standoff between the two nations even with the threat of an armed confrontation not being ruled out.

The Chinese Ministry of Foreign Affairs, as confirmed by the Indian Foreign Office made a statement on 26 June 2017 alleging that "Indian border troops crossed the boundary line in the Sikkim sector of the China-India boundary and entered Chinese territory. This has been reiterated since then in other Chinese official briefings".[10]

The strategically located Siliguri Corridor, which is even less than 20 km wide at its narrowest stretch, besides being the sole link connection the northeast with the rest of India, is naturally the sole link feeding the military formations located in the NER.

The description of the events leading to the Doklam stand-off, as stated by the MEA is as follows:

"The facts of the matter are as follows:

(i) On 16 June, a PLA construction party entered the Doklam area and attempted to construct a road. It is our understanding that a Royal Bhutan Army patrol attempted to dissuade them from this unilateral activity. The Ambassador of the Royal Government of Bhutan (RGOB) has publicly stated that it lodged a protest with the Chinese Government through their Embassy in New Delhi on 20 June.

(ii) The Foreign Ministry of Bhutan has also issued a statement underlining that the construction of the road inside Bhutanese territory is a direct violation of the 1988 and 1998 agreements between Bhutan and China and affects the process of demarcating the boundary between these two countries. They have urged a return to the status quo as before 16 June 2017.

(iii) In keeping with their tradition of maintaining close consultation on matters of mutual interest, RGOB and the Government of India have been in continuous contact through the unfolding of these developments.

(iv) In coordination with the RGOB, Indian personnel, who were present at general area Doka La, approached the Chinese construction party and urged them to desist from changing the status quo."[11]

There is need to clear the air regarding the incorrect cartographic depiction of Doklam by numerous media channels. The site of the standoff Doklam (or Dolam) is different from the Doklam Plateau which lies 30 km to the north east to the former and lies in close vicinity to the northern end of the Chumbi Valley. Veteran journalist Manoj Joshi has aptly described the situation in his Indian Express article:

> "The Bhutanese believe the tri-junction is at a place called Doka La, where the so-called intrusion is believed to have taken place. The Chinese believe the tri-junction is located at a place called Gamochen, about 15 kms south of Dhoka La, and are building a road in this direction – which the Bhutanese are objecting to, saying Beijing is intruding into its territory. While India says the tri-junction is located at Batang La, about 6.5 km north of Gamochen."[12]

1890 Treaty

That treaty, called the "Convention between Great Britain and China relating to Sikkim and Tibet", essentially paved the way for the colonial power to annex the small state of Sikkim. The treaty's first article has been particularly highlighted by Chinese officials.

"The boundary of Sikkim and Tibet shall be the crest of the mountain range separating the waters flowing into the Sikkim Teesta and its affluents from the waters flowing into the Tibetan Mochu and northwards into other rivers of Tibet. The line commences at Mount Gipmochi, on the Bhutan frontier, and follows the above-mentioned water-parting to the point where it meets Nepal territory," Article 1 states.[13]

"Where the boundary in the Sikkim sector is concerned, India and China had reached an understanding also in 2012 reconfirming their mutual agreement on the 'basis of the alignment'. Further discussions regarding finalisation of the boundary have been taking place under the Special Representatives framework," the external affairs ministry said in a statement on Friday. China's double standards are evident from the fact that on one hand, China has consistently opposed any settlement of the border dispute based on a colonially imposed border and on the other hand, its claim on Doklam based on the 1890 treaty appears to treat the treaty as a sacrosanct text over which it is in no mood of negotiating.

The issue also came up during Sino-Indian negotiations which preceded the 1962 war. A fortnight after the standoff began, the spokesperson of Chinese foreign office Geng Shuang cited a letter written by Nehru to Zhou on March 22, 1959. Geng blatantly lied Nehru's letter accepted that Sikkim-China border demarcation as stated by the 1890 convention as well the 1895 demarcation. In the letter, India only accepted the agreement regarding northern Sikkim. An excerpt from Nehru's letter is stated,

> [T]his Convention of 1890 also defined the boundary between Sikkim and Tibet; and the boundary was later, in 1895, demarcated. There is thus no dispute regarding the boundary of Sikkim with the Tibet region. This clearly refers to northern Sikkim and not to the tri-junction which needed to be discussed with Bhutan and Sikkim and which is today the contentious area. And once more, let us not forget that the 1890 Treaty was an unequal treaty as Tibet, Sikkim and Bhutan were not involved.[14]

Bhutan Issues Demarche

After the standoff broke out, Bhutan accused China of violating the 1998 agreement in which both sides agreed to avoid altering the status quo by signing peace agreement for the first time, in which both sides promised to 'Maintain Peace and Tranquility on the Bhutan-China Border Areas.' This was a significant breakthrough because China for the first-time acknowledged Bhutan as a sovereign nation and declared its respect for 'the territorial integrity and independence of Bhutan.' Requesting China to honour this two-decade old agreement, Bhutan issued a demarche to China over the construction of a road towards its Army camp in Jampheri area of Doklam and asked Beijing to restore status quo by stopping the work immediately.

"We have issued a demarche to China through its diplomatic mission here. Recently, the Chinese army (People's Liberation Army) started construction of a road towards Bhutanese Army camp at Zomphiri in Doklam area which is in violation of an agreement between the two countries," Ambassador of Bhutan to India Vetsop

Namgyel told PTI.[15] Doklam is a disputed territory and Bhutan has a written agreement with China that pending the final resolution of the boundary issue, peace and tranquility should be maintained in the area," said Namgyel.[16]

In reality, Chinese consternation stems from Bhutan's refusal to agree to a border agreement proposed by China where it wants Bhutan to give up claim on the strategically located Doklam plateau in lieu of China giving up claim on two valleys on Bhutan's northern boundaries. In 1996, when China offered Bhutan a deal, proposing to exchange Pasamlung and Jakarlung valleys (495 sq. km) with the pastureland of Doklam, Sinchulung, Dramana and Shakhatoe (269 sq.). Sensitive to the threat Doklam may pose once handed over to China, Bhutan has evaded Chinese pressure. Till date, there have been 24 rounds of border talks between Bhutan and China and Beijing seems to have been frustrated after the Bhutanese failed to yield to their demands.

Live Fire Drills: Escalating the Threat

Doklam has become a tough test to assess the extent of India's restraint as Beijing is leaving no opportunity to drag India into a conflict. Besides threats emanating from official as well as media circles, the PLA has also been upping the ante against India to elicit the latter's strategy. A psychological war has been in the making and live wire drills held in early August were among the key arsenals of this strategy. In the first week of August, China Central Television ran a video showing a PLA unit carrying out live-fire firing exercises in Tibet.

"China has made it clear that there is no room for negotiation and the only solution is the unconditional and immediate withdrawal of Indian troops from the region.... If China backs down now, India may be emboldened to make more trouble in the future" said a commentary in Xinhua in the backdrop of these drills.[17] In addition, the statement by Chinese defense ministry spokesman added fuel to the fire. "No country should underestimate the Chinese forces' confidence and capability to safeguard peace and their resolve and willpower to defend national sovereignty, security and development interests", it said, indirectly threatening India.[18]

General Malik's Warning

In a speech delivered by General (Retd) V.P. Malik on the issue of Doklam and the nation's military preparedness he highlighted some crucial facts which New Delhi needed to look into with utmost urgency. As the chief of the Army during the Kargil War, none other veteran would be second to General Malik in commenting on the need to focus on and address the external threats by sound internal structure of the decision-making processes. General Malik highlighted the shortage of arms and even alluded to the persisting bureaucratic red tape that prevented the swift introduction of arms. Skirmish or not, the general stated that mobilization would still be the foremost policy response which needed adequate arsenal in place. The neglect of borders runs the risk of gravely compromising the nation's national security. The same vulnerabilities which were faced by the forces during the Kargil conflict continue to persist till date. It is worth mentioning an excerpt of what General Malik said in context of the standoff:

> [W]e have reached the stage where there is a requirement to seriously review our policies toward China, not just diplomatically, economically, militarily also.... The military part, there is no doubt we must review. We have to improve our border roads and military capability in the mountains as long as we continue to have an unresolved boundary with China. Lately, the frequency of such confrontations along the LAC (Line of Actual Control) has been increasing. The cycles are getting shorter. The decibel level of threats and warnings has gone up. Under these circumstances, the military has to be prepared for all eventualities. Sound defence is a part of sound foreign policy. India is not interested in picking a fight, but when your national interests are jeopardised, like in this case, diplomacy without adequate military backing cannot succeed. Your risk-taking ability in negotiations gets enhanced when you know that you can defend yourself on the border. We don't want a war, but when you are faced with such a situation, you don't want to leave your diplomacy and political initiatives without any backing. It's nothing new to say that globally, diplomacy feels more comfortable in negotiations when they know that there is a strong military to defend the country. India had operational advantage at Doklam, but it has to be prepared for skirmishes in

any part of the Line of Actual Control—from Ladakh to Arunachal Pradesh.... We do not have enough helicopters, light artillery and other equipment which can be fielded more easily in the mountains. We will require considerable amount of logistics and high-altitude conditioning of troops and equipment. Our troops are quite capable of going through that. But it will definitely have its financial and some health costs.[19]

"The mindset in the government," he said, "has never recognised that we can have a serious confrontation with China sometime or the other. Otherwise why should our infrastructure on the northern border be so weak? We have been talking about infrastructure on the northern border from the time I was Army chief, that is nearly two decades ago. Plans were made but they remain on paper mostly."

"Even though the budget as a percentage of GDP has been going down every year, we are often unable to spend the capital side. We have been surrendering part of the budget so often."[20] Recalling his controversial statement at the time of the Kargil War that "we will fight with what we have", Malik said the situation was no better now. "Same kind of problems, attitudes that we faced in my time, the present lot [in the Army] seems to be facing," he said.[21]

Japan Issues Statement

Besides growing diplomatic and economic ties, the realization of a common threat from China has brought India and Japan closer than ever in recent times and the recently concluded nuclear deal with India is a proof of this. That a nation which has been highly reluctant of entering into nuclear ties with a non-NPT signatory India and even critical of India at times revised its policy to negotiate shows how deeply both nations value each other at this moment. Further, the mutual capacity of India and Japan to influence US, Australia and ASEAN nations in aspiring for stronger economic ties and in tackling the Chinese threat has been a bone of contention of China, which has traditionally prevented its smaller neighbors from uniting to address their border disputes. Nations like India, Japan and even Vietnam have stood up to China and a combined pressure and a collective recognition of the Chinese threat is something China had always feared. China's fears came true when Japan was learnt to have conveyed its displeasure to China regarding the Doklam standoff.

"As far as India's role is concerned, we understand that India is involved in this incident based on bilateral agreements with Bhutan. Former External Affairs Minister Sushma Swaraj had made it clear that India would continue to engage with dialogue through diplomatic channels with China to find a mutually acceptable solution. We consider this attitude towards peaceful resolution important," the Japanese ambassador to India and Bhutan Kenji Hiramatsu said.[22]

What's important in disputed areas is that all parties involved do not resort to unilateral attempts to change the status quo by force, and resolve the dispute in a peaceful manner", he went on further.[23] A rattled China was quick to react, subtly warning Japan to stay out of this matter. "I have seen the Japanese Ambassador in India really wants to support India. I want to remind him not to randomly make comments before clarifying relevant facts," said the Chinese foreign office spokesperson.

Foreign Minister's Balancing Act

Despite the rising tensions, then External Affairs Minister took the opportunity to address the parliament over the crisis. Her statement, which was a clear offer for reconciliation failed to break ice with Beijing, which seems in no mood of lowering the vicious rhetoric. Swaraj went a mile ahead to acknowledge China's positive contributions to Indian economy, yet her efforts went in vain.

Speaking in the upper house (Rajya Sabha), in her reply to a discussion on India's foreign policy, Swaraj said: "Hamari jo aarthik kshamta badh rahi hai, usme China ka yogdaan hai...unka yahan bahut zyada risk, stake hai...kitne zyada contract unhe diye huye hain (China has contributed to our growing economic strength. For them, there's a lot at stake, risk here. They have been awarded many contracts)."[24] She requested for maintaining "patience" and "restraint", and also "restraint in statements", in light of the bitter war of words emanating from Chinese media.

The maturity of Indian side is evident from her balanced statement, where she said that Indians "will continue to engage with the Chinese side through diplomatic channels to find a mutually acceptable solution on the basis of the Astana Consensus between our leaders. I note the sense of the House is supportive in this regard. In keeping the traditional friendship with Bhutan, we will also continue to maintain close consultation and coordination with the Royal Government of Bhutan."[25] Unfortunately, such a civilized approach has been taken for granted time and again by China, which always misunderstands New Delhi's humility as India's weakness.

Specifically, her statement that India's concerns "emanate from Chinese action on the ground which have implications for the determination of the tri-junction boundary point between India, China and Bhutan and the alignment of India-China boundary in the Sikkim sector" did not go down well with Beijing.[26]

Global Times' Vitiated Response

As soon as the Doklam issue began, there was constant flurry of media attacks on government of India. Chief among these is the state-run *Global Times*, the international face of *People's Daily*. Every week, the paper ran several editorials threatening India of dire consequences. These editorials not only commented on Sino-Indian ties but spread propaganda against India's mistreatment of its smaller South Asian neighbours. A couple of editorials are analysed below to show the venom the paper has been spewing. Rather than analyzing the issue in light of legality or international law, the paper stooped down to mudslinging, name-calling and even threatening India of another invasion if its army did not withdraw.

"India made constant provocations at the China-India border in 1962. The government of Jawaharlal Nehru at that time firmly believed China would not strike back. China had just undergone domestic turmoil and natural disasters; Beijing and Washington were engaged in hostility and China's relations with the Soviet Union had begun to chill.... Fifty-five years have passed, but the Indian government is as naïve as it ever was," the editorial said.[27]

Global Times wrote that, "She (Sushma Swaraj) was lying to the parliament."[28] "First, India's invasion of Chinese territory is a plain fact. New Delhi's impetuous action stuns the international community.

No other country will support India's aggression. Second, India's military strength is far behind that of China. If the conflict between China and India escalates to the intensity where their row has to be resolved through military means, India will surely lose."

"India should abandon the fantasy of a long-term standoff at Doklam. China will by no means agree to the withdrawal of troops from both sides in order for talks to be held. Doklam is Chinese territory. The withdrawal of Indian troops must be a precondition for talks and China will not compromise on this stance."[29] In what could be called a warning to New Delhi, it further said that "If Indian troops continue trespassing into China's territory, what Beijing may do next is to get prepared for a military confrontation and resolve the conflict through non-diplomatic means."[30]

Now that the PLA has moved in on the China-India border, they will definitely not call back troops unless they recover the Chinese territory. "China cannot afford to lose an inch of territory. If New Delhi remains stubborn, India should get prepared for all possibilities from a potentially grave escalation of tension in the future."[31]

Talking tough on delay in withdrawing the Indian troops, it wrote: "That the later India withdraws troops, the greater the risk that it will face from a military counteraction and the more clout it will lose politically. China's military pressure on India will increase every day and India will end up losing face and be totally disgraced."[32]

In August alone close to two hundred articles had occurred on Doklam issue in Chinese papers.

Xinhua's Attacks

Accusing India of committing "seven sins" in the two-month long Doklam standoff near Sikkim, a three-minute video, produced by the government mouthpiece *Xinhua*, China's official news agency, ridiculed India and Indians. The video called Narendra Modi's administration "asleep" and "thick-skinned. The video, an edition of Xinhua's new "Spark" show, features anchor Dier Wang accusing India of "sins" that include "trespassing, confusing right and wrong, putting the blame on the victim, hijacking a small neighbour and sticking to a mistake knowingly.... Do you negotiate with a robber who had just broken into your house.... You just call 911 or just fight him back, right?"[33]

What was shocking about the video was its racist nature. The anchor appeared dressed up in a turban and fake brown beard and a long moustache mocking Indians. The incident was criticized the media world over. However, after the global backlash to this video, Xinhua came out with another toned-down version after a few days. Threats were still issues, albeit in a sober manner. Highlighting that India and China were not born rivals, the anchor said that India must "unconditionally withdraw all troops from the Chinese territory".

The anchor warned that India must "remain sober and guard against any future poor judgment" and added that "co-existing harmoniously and peacefully only stands to benefit their combined 2.7 billion people. Any spiral into some kind of hostile rivalry could be disastrous."[34]

Ladakh Standoff

Incursions in eastern Ladakh are not new phenomenon but have been taking place on and off. However, there have been instances when these incursions have coincided with important events in Sino-Indian relationship, which point to deep underpinnings of the Chinese statecraft. For instance, in 2014, Xi Jinping's visit to India was coincided by incursions in Ladakh and Prime Minister Modi was believed to have personally told the Chinese leader to look into the matter in spirit of bilateral ties.

On Independence Day 2017, Indian troops stationed at Pangong Tso (one third of which is under India's control and remaining under China) were confronted by PLA soldiers near Finger Four and Finger Five areas near the Lake. Finger Four is almost 5 km into Indian territory from the Line of Actual Control (LAC), manned by the Indo-Tibetan Border Police. "If this has indeed happened in Pangong Tso, it is a fallout of the Doklam standoff," former northern army commander Lieutenant General BS Jaswal said when interviewed by Hindustan Times.[35]

Days after these reports a video was released by Lieutenant General

(Retd) Prakash Katoch showing the scuffle between Indian and Chinese troops where they both the sides are seen dealing blows, kicks and throwing stones. When contacted by The Hindu Newspaper, Gen. Katoch told that "the visuals clearly showed that it was the Chinese who started to push around Indian soldiers and they also started throwing stones". "They started it all; our chaps only responded," he said.[36]

Ladakh incident closely followed a statement by a prominent Chinese strategist, a PLA Navy officer named Senior Captain Zhang He, who threatened that just like India intervened in Doklam on Bhutan's behalf, China could use the same strategy to intervene in Kashmir on Pakistan's behalf. "As a third party of the Sino-Bhutan border dispute, does the Indian military have the right to trespass across the Sino-Indian established border to stop China's road construction? If yes, it would be very dangerous, for under India's logic, if Pakistan requests, a third country's army can enter the area disputed by India and Pakistan, including India-controlled Kashmir", Zhang threatened.[37]

This confirms India's persisting fear about the possibility of a two-front war in Kashmir. Ladakh remains sandwiched between Pakistan occupied Gilgit Baltistan and Xinjiang-Tibet from the Chinese side, hence the possibility of a joint attack has never been ruled out. The strategic Karakoram Highway cuts from Gilgit into Xinjiang and it has been notorious for secret transfer of missile batteries and weapons ever from China to Pakistan. The post-Burhan Wani wave of violence in the Kashmir valley has added another dimension to the prevailing threat, which prompted General Rawat to declare India's readiness for a "Two and a half front war", with half pointing towards Indian Army's anti-terrorist operations in the valley.

Launching Multiple Incursions

As expected, and stated in the beginning of the chapter, the Doklam affair has been a lynchpin of multi-pronged contest China has attempted to launch against India. The first step the PLA undertook was to heat up the entire LAC.

The Ladakh scuffle has already been discussed in the last paragraphs. A few days before NSA Ajit Doval was scheduled to visit

Beijing in the last week of July, Chinese soldiers entered one km into Uttarakhand's Barahoti in Chamoli, located along the LAC, which has long been kept disputed by the Chinese.

Further, China has been attempting to deteriorate India-Nepal relations by prompting Nepalese politicians and journalists to raise the Lipulekh tri-junction and other issue of Kalapani on Uttarakhand-Nepal border.

The Thaw

After two months of the strong diplomatic exchanges and armies of both the sides staring eye to eye, the last week of August finally arrived with the positive news that both the sides had decided to disengage mutually. "In recent weeks, India and China have maintained diplomatic communication in respect of the incident at Doklam. During these communications, we were able to express our views and convey our concerns and interests," an Indian foreign ministry statement on Monday said.[38] "On this basis, expeditious disengagement of border personnel at the face-off site at Doklam has been agreed to and is ongoing," it added.[39]

The *Indian Express* reported from the ground situation that "this disengagement—wherein both sets of soldiers, along with their tents and road construction equipment, moved away from the faceoff site on Dolam plateau but only by a distance of around 150 metres each— is fully in accordance with the two statements issued by the Ministry of External Affairs (MEA) on August 28".[40] After almost 10 weeks of sustained negotiations between top-level Indian and Chinese officials, the MEA on Monday said "expeditious disengagement of border personnel at the face-off site at Doklam has been agreed to and is ongoing."[41]

Well Crafted Response

What was noticeable was that the Indian diplomats, politicians and statements from the army officers perfectly complementing each other. Unanimity in response.

The negotiations were conducted at various levels – first, during the visit by NSA Ajit Doval to China in July, where he held discussions with his counterpart Yang Jiechi. Next, the then foreign secretary S Jaishankar led the diplomatic talks with the Chinese side, helped by India's ambassador to China Vijay Gokhale, who worked with the Chinese government over couple of months to achieve an outcome that would be acceptable to both sides.

At 1430 or so on August 28, India withdrew its personnel and equipment to the Indian side of the border line.[42] China's Foreign Ministry spokeswoman Hua Chunying said "that the Chinese army's patrols in Doklam will continue, and also said China would make necessary adjustments and deployments according to the changes," without elaborating what the adjustments would be.

"China will continue to exercise sovereignty rights to protect territorial sovereignty in accordance with the rules of the historical boundary," Hua was quoted as saying by *Reuters*. "China hopes India respects the historical boundary and works with China to protect peace along the border on the basis of mutual respect of each other's sovereignty," she added.[43]

MP Shashi Tharoor lauded Narendra Modi government for the way it dealt with the recent Doklam issue. "Now that Chinese withdrawal seems to be confirmed, it looks like a victory for @Indian diplomacy. Congratulations MEA & @PMO India! (sic)" Tharoor wrote on Twitter.

Following the Doklam standoff, the Indo Tibetan Border Police (ITBP) has decided to make it compulsory for new recruits to learn Chinese language – both Mandarin and the version of the language that is spoken in Tibet. From this year onwards "We are a force fully deployed on the border with China. It is only prudent that every person should know the language. We interact with Chinese soldiers almost on a daily basis. A good knowledge of their language may help avoid misunderstandings and lead to better resolution of confrontations that arise out of ground zero developments," said the officer.[44] "As far as our northern adversary is concerned, flexing of muscles has started. Salami slicing, taking over territory in a very gradual manner, testing our limits of the threshold is something we have to be wary of and remain prepared for such situations, which could gradually emerge into conflict," Rawat had said in New Delhi, referring to China.[45] Reacting to General Bipin Rawat's remarks that India should be prepared for a two-front war, Chinese Foreign Ministry spokesperson Geng Shuang said: "We don't know if he was authorised to speak those words or if it was his spontaneous words and whether his remarks represented the position of the Indian government."[46]

Jolted by the military face-off in the Doklam plateau, India and China are rebooting their ties, by opening new channels of official communication to address points of friction before they develop into full-blown crises. China's apparent policy shift on international terrorism, as reflected in the BRICS statement, will be tested when the United Nations 1267 committee meets in October to discuss designation of Masood Azhar, the head of the Pakistan-based Jaish-e-Mohammad, as an international terrorist.

In the larger strategic backdrop, Doklam had strategic implication of fate of Xi Jinping and his position in the Communist leadership. The episode was a tactfully timed move taking place just before the 19th Communist Party Congress about to take place, where Xi was expected to further strengthen his position. China's Communist Party on Tuesday elevated President Xi Jinping to the same exalted status as the nation's founding father, Mao Zedong, by writing his name and ideas into the party constitution, something which even the great Chinese leader Deng Xiaoping attained posthumously. His thought "Xi Jinping Thought on Socialism with Chinese Characteristics for a New Era" was duly added to the Chinese constitution.[47]

Chinese muscle flexing during the run up to the Doklam crises played a major role in this affair. Hence, Doklam has indeed been a master move by Jinping to win over the military and demonstrate his power to the Chinese people. And this is the reason why Beijing has continued to stir up the crises even after both the sides disengaged respectfully. Months after Indian and Chinese troops disengaged, the Chinese side was found to be constructing a military complex within the disputed region in Northern Doklam. In response, the Chinese side brazenly justified these activities terming them "legitimate" and "aimed at improving the lives of its troops and the people living on its own territory."

When asked about reports of satellite images of a Chinese military complex in the northern Doklam, Chinese Foreign Ministry spokesman

Lu Kang said: "I have also noted the relevant report. I don't know who offered such kind of photos.... In order to patrol the border and improve the production and lives of border troops and residents, China has constructed infrastructure including roads in the Donglong (Doklam) area".[48]

Unfortunately, rather than coming out with strong unified response, officials from the Indian side have somewhat contradictory statements. It is not clear whether why the Army and the Foreign Office came out with contradicting statements on such a sensitive issue.

In the month of January, the army chief confirmed the presence of Chinese infrastructure twice within a span of one week. The first acknowledgement was on 12th January, which was a press conference the army had organized prior to the Army Day. This was followed by another statement at ORF's Raisina Dialogue where he said that "they have carried out some infrastructure development, most of it is temporary in nature. But while their troops may have returned and the infrastructure remains, it is anybody's guess whether they would come back there, or it is because of the winter they could not take their equipment away that."[49]

A different kind of a statement came from the Foreign Office the next day. "Our attention has been drawn to some reports that question the accuracy of the position stated by the Government in respect to the situation in Doklam. Subsequently, in response to repeated questions about any change in the status quo at the face-off site, Government had stated that there was no basis for such imputations", Raveesh Kumar, the official spokesperson of the MEA, said in a statement.[50] "Government would once again reiterate that the status quo at the face-off site has not been altered. Any suggestion to the contrary is inaccurate and mischievous", he continued.[51]

Another interesting finding has been of Colonel (Retd) Vinayak Bhat, a satellite imagery expert, who made public revealing imagery of the Chinese infrastructure in Doklam. Images he shared indicated that China took control of the northern side of Doklam region. Satellite images revealed "concrete Chinese posts, helipads, new trenches and several dozen armoured vehicles close to the point where the Indian Army and the People's Liberation Army (PLA) troops were locked in a 72-day standoff last year. Artillery guns are not visible in these images but there are points which are dug out and look like gun emplacements."[52] This finding came only a few days after discovery comes days after General Bipin Rawat had stated that China continues to have troops in North Doklam, hence complements the general's statement.

The Bumpy Road to Wuhan

As Sino-Indian politics revolved around Doklam, new developments have been taking place since the appointment of the new foreign secretary Vijay Gokhale, who has been undoing some old structural determinants of Sino-Indian ties with some revolutionary measures. The first move was seen in March when an event marking 60 years of his exile in India were cancelled, following a note circulated by the foreign and home secretary directing the government officials not to celebrate such events and keep distance from the Dalai Lama, a move seen as sign of accommodation to China. Parallelly, senior members of the ruling BJP did participate in their unofficial capacities in these events, later shifted to Dharamshala, in an effort to signal that there was space for unofficial support if China's old attitude was to persist. New Delhi also reduced the public rhetoric over BRI, which it had been doing especially in 2017, following the BRI conference last May. Together, this signaled thawing of the erstwhile hawkish stance New Delhi had continuously maintained.

April onwards, a series of high-profile visits by the NSA, Defence Minister, External Affairs Minister paved the way for Prime Minister Modi's visit to the city of Wuhan, also known as informal summit. The idea has been to look at Sino-Indian ties from a different prism, other than the structural manner, otherwise characterized by border dispute and regional contest in South Asian neighbourhood. The fact that global cooperation offered far more benefits and even the opportunity to shape the global economic order became the motivation behind the summit. The personal bonhomie shared between Modi and Xi in those two days also stated a willingness on part of the two leaders to approach bilateral ties with more understanding and amity. While issues of global importance dominated bilateral discussions, the border issue was given due concern and it was decided that both the leaders would give "strategic guidance to their respective militaries to strengthen communication in order to build trust and mutual understanding and enhance predictability and effectiveness in the management of border affairs".[53]

Rather than adding new methods, it was decided that only the existing mechanisms in place would be used to solve the border dispute. Unlike Xi's 2014 visit, when Chinese troops encroached into the Indian territory, no such disturbances were reported this time, which even points towards the seriousness both the leaders approached the summit. The summit ended on a successful note, with high hopes and the vow to not repeat Doklam type instances, given the benefits of cooperation and the horrors a war could revive. While the summit cannot be stated as a guarantee for better ties, but it was a much-needed breakthrough both the sides want for long. In this regard, it could be concluded that Doklam could have been a blessing in disguise for Sino-Indian ties in this regard.

However, eventually Doklam got compromised because the Chinese, as brought out by Lt Gen P.G. Kamath in his article, *China Lies and India Believes: The Road Ahead*, "Look at Doklam Plateau; though we have not allowed them to build a road from Batang La to Gyemochen, Chinese have occupied the whole of the Bhutanese plateau of 89 sq km and have built an alternative road further east of the road that we had stopped. India can keep thumping its chest but the Chinese have stolen a march and are closer to the plains of India." (https://www.linkedin.com/pulse/china-lies-india-believes-road-ahead-lt-gen-p-g-kamath/)

NOTES

1. http://www.millenniumpost.in/sundaypost/beacon/chinas-doklam-transgression-endangers-50-years-of-bullet-less-border-management-254991
2. https://timesofindia.indiatimes.com/india/differences-should-not-become-disputes-sitharaman-tells-chinese-defence-minister/articleshow/63899297.cms
3. https://www.aninews.in/news/national/politics/china-endangering-50-years-of-bullet-less-border-management/
4. Ibid.
5. Ibid.

6. https://www.foreignaffairs.com/articles/asia/2017-09-07/what-were-chinas-objectives-doklam-dispute
7. http://www.globaltimes.cn/content/982843.shtml
8. http://www.thehindu.com/news/international/us-envoys-arunachal-is-part-of-india-remark-irks-china/article8556158.ece
9. http://www.thehindu.com/news/international/us-envoys-arunachal-is-part-of-india-remark-irks-china/article8556158.ece
10. http://www.mea.gov.in/press-releases.htm?dtl/28572/Recent_ Developments _ in_Doklam_Area
11. http://www.mea.gov.in/press-releases.htm?dtl/28572/Recent+ Developments+ in +Doklam+Area
12. http://indianexpress.com/article/opinion/india-china-standoff-bhutan-clash-trijunction-eyeball-to-eyeball-in-the-himalayas-region-4728629/
13. https://www.livemint.com/Opinion/kfpkmisQLSnGho2e2oo2rO/China-is-wrong-on-SikkimTibet-boundary.html
14. http://www.xinhuanet.com/english/2017-08/02/c_136494625_7.htm
15. http://indianexpress.com/article/world/bhutan-issues-demarche-to-china-over-its-armys-road-construction-4726615/
16. http://indianexpress.com/article/world/bhutan-issues-demarche-to-china-over-its-armys-road-construction-4726615/
17. http://www.globaltimes.cn/content/1059645.shtml
18. https://www.hindustantimes.com/india-news/china-warns-india-says-its-restraint-over-doklam-standoff-has-a-bottom-line/story-iCSnqBjQXJ8KKDwf7K4V8K.html
19. http://indianexpress.com/article/india/gen-v-p-malik-calls-for-full-review-of-ties-with-china-diplomatically-economically-militarily-4801780/
20. Ibid.
21. Ibid.
22. http://timesofindia.indiatimes.com/india/doklam-stand-off-japan-backs-india-says-no-one-should-try-to-change-status-quo-by-force/quickstirshow/60111396.cms
23. Ibid.
24. http://indianexpress.com/article/india/doklam-not-only-issue-with-china-solution-will-emerge-through-dialogue-sushma-swaraj-4781525/
25. http://indianexpress.com/article/india/doklam-not-only-issue-with-china-solution-will-emerge-through-dialogue-sushma-swaraj-4781525/
26. https://economictimes.indiatimes.com/news/defence/dokalam-standoff-no-easy-answers-as-china-quotes-1890-india-2012-pact/articleshow/59921533.cms
27. http://www.globaltimes.cn/content/1060128.shtml
28. Ibid.
29. http://www.globaltimes.cn/content/1057440.shtml
30. Ibid.
31. Ibid.
32. Ibid.
33. http://www.business-standard.com/article/current-affairs/china-starts-video-war-117081800042_1.html

34 Ibid.
35 https://www.hindustantimes.com/india-news/indian-troops-foil-china-s-incursion-attempt-in-ladakh-minor-injuries-on-both-sides-after-stone-pelting/story-U4kLwjt70U8bXwED3e9noM.html
36 http://www.thehindu.com/news/national/video-shows-troops-trading-kicks-punches-in-ladakh/article19526068.ece
37 http://www.globaltimes.cn/content/1058378.shtml
38 https://www.financialexpress.com/india-news/doklam-standoff-ends-india-china-agree-to-withdraw-says-mea/828903/
39 https://www.financialexpress.com/india-news/doklam-standoff-ends-india-china-agree-to-withdraw-says-mea/828903/
40 http://indianexpress.com/article/india/disengagement-at-doklam-troops-stepped-back-150-metres-each-side-remain-on-plateau-4832252/
41 http://indianexpress.com/article/india/disengagement-at-doklam-troops-stepped-back-150-metres-each-side-remain-on-plateau-4832252/
42 https://www.reuters.com/article/us-india-china/india-and-china-agree-to-end-border-standoff-idUSKCN1B80II
43 https://www.reuters.com/article/us-india-china/india-and-china-agree-to-end-border-standoff-idUSKCN1B80II
44 http://indianexpress.com/article/india/mandarin-made-a-must-for-itbp-recruits-indo-tibetan-border-police-chinese-language-4818401/
45 https://www.livemint.com/Politics/k5KLT816ETjFdMX8ynP8II/Pointing-to-China-Army-chief-Bipin-Rawat-says-India-must-be.html
46 https://www.livemint.com/Politics/QPMLQq7AzuUGtnbRaMBtkK/Bipin-Rawats-remarks-contrary-to-views-expressed-by-Xi-Jinp.html
47 http://www.xinhuanet.com/english/2018-02/25/c_136999028.htm
48 https://www.livemint.com/Politics/cZgraaRn8WS5ZAY9qiM1KJ/China-says-infrastructure-in-Doklam-aimed-at-improving-lives.html
49 https://www.hindustantimes.com/india-news/china-builds-up-presence-at-doklam-army-chief-gen-rawat-says-it-is-temporary/story-JGgSsdQk3hbSuGUEigdWoI.html
50 Our attention has been drawn to some reports that question the accuracy of the position stated
51 Ibid.
52 http://www.india.com/news/world/china-builds-military-complex-in-doklam-occupies-northern-side-of-disputed-plateau-reports-2848735/
53 https://www.outlookindia.com/newsscroll/modi-xi-agree-to-issue-strategic-guidance-to-their-militaries-to-build-trust-eds-updates-with-more-details-quotes/1296987

6

WUHAN AND MAMALLAPURAM SUMMITS FOLLOWED BY THE WUHAN VIRUS

When PM Narendra Modi attended the Wuhan Summit, little did the world know that a virus originating from there will contaminate 214 countries and territories globally, ruin their economies and be followed by China flexing its military muscles. This included China bullying some nations, projecting its power in the South China Sea region and major acts of aggression and bloodshed against Indian Army across a disputed border with the aim of changing the status quo unilaterally.

There is no doubt that the posturing of the Indian forces at Doklam increased India's geostrategic footing in the region.[1] A clear support from Japan and behind the scenes support by South east Asian nations on India's stand exposed the regional mood on the aggressive Chinese ambitions.[2] After the intense months of 2017, signs of re-engagement were visible by the early 2018 when both sides began moving. As the months following the thaw still did not give few reasons to believe all was well between both the nations, a positive development came in March 2018, when a special envoy from China paid a visit to India. Song Tao, the chief of CCP's International Relations department visited New Delhi and given his closeness with Xi Jinping, the visit was significant. That this came after Foreign Secretary Vijay Gokhale visiting China a month before Song's visit gave all the signals of India and China pursuing normalization of relations seriously on a fast track basis.

On March 24, 2018, India's ambassador to China, Gautam Bambawale, reportedly denied reports of Chinese military stepping up the infrastructure in the disputed area of Doklam and added that the status quo in the area did not change. On the issue of the standoff, he said that it happened because Beijing tried to alter the status-quo. However, on March 26, 2018, Chinese Foreign Ministry spokesperson Hua Chunying said that Doklam belongs to China and India should have learned lessons from the stand-off last year. The Chinese republic also claimed that its activities in the area are within its sovereign rights and there is no such thing as changing status quo. Then came the "informal" summit of Narendra Modi and Xi Jinping in Wuhan, which was expected to stabilise the two nations' relationship.[3]

From the Chinese side, on April 26, 2018, China's military spokesman, Col. Wu Qian told the media in Beijing, "It is the common expectation of both peoples to stabilise relations between the Chinese and Indian armed forces and maintain peace and tranquility at the border areas." The entire international community was shocked with the surprise announcement of Modi-Xi meeting in Wuhan during the last week of April. While the dialogue was informal, the understanding showed high degree of convergence, even though it can be argued to have appeared on surface. As the MEA website shows, a large number of confidence building measures were discussed during the meeting. On the border issue it was agreed that the two leaders would issue "strategic guidance to their respective militaries to strengthen communication in order to build trust and mutual understanding".[4] They even "expressed their support for the work of the Special Representatives on the India China Boundary Question and urged them to intensify their efforts to seek a fair, reasonable and mutually acceptable settlement."[5] On issues of global and regional interest, "they agreed on their need to strengthen strategic communication through greater consultation on all matters of common interest."[6] A significant development was the decision to cooperate on a joint project in

Afghanistan, which would indeed be a path breaking development not only from the perspective of how India saw international cooperation in Afghanistan, Also, both nations cooperating in a country Pakistan considers as its strategic backyard would be interesting to watch, especially with regard to its impact on the Sino-Pak alliance.

India's Foreign Secretary Vijay Keshav Gokhale, addressing media on the summit reportedly stated:

> [•]Four of the meetings were one-to-one. • There were no agreements for announcements. There were discussions between Messrs. Modi and Xi on bilateral issues of global importance, trade, bilateral issues and strategic military relations. • Mr. Modi discussed the importance of bilateral trade, and also ways to promote cultural, and people-to-people relations. • Proposals included moving ahead on spirituality, terms on building ties in films, environment etc. • Also discussed were sports and performances on the international level and how to strengthen tourism and holistic health between India and China.[7]

Mr. Xi shared his appreciation on the preservation of Yangtze river, on the banks of which in Wuhan, the world was able to watch the two leaders interacting. If the unprecedented Narendra Modi-Xi Jinping conclave at Wuhan made waves, it is because it was approached and organized/implemented differently compared to any previous Sino-Indian summits. While wish lists of both India and China on what all should happen or should not happen, some basic essentials that India considers most important are peace on the Line of Actual Control (LAC), without the almost daily border dispute issues, fair trade ties, ruffle-free politico-diplomatic relations and good/social, business, cultural and educational exchanges.[8]

In retrospect, the Wuhan meet leaves doubts about China's and India's serious intent. It is also just as well that its content was controlled, in that, there were just a few official disclosures from officials. And what was also good news was that there were no reports of any untoward incident on the LAC, unlike during almost all earlier state visits or diplomatic events, when China's PLA crossed it in some form or the other.[9]

Not surprisingly, what escaped public notice and in official circles taken for granted/not made much of was that Doklam marked the completion of fifty years of bullet-less border management, i.e. since the bloody skirmishes at Nathula and Chola, in Sikkim, in September –October 1967 (except for a single incident in 1975 of PLA ambushing an Assam Rifles patrol and killing four Riflemen). And while the 73 days long Doklam stand-off also ended without any bullets, there were reports of resumption of Chinese PLA's construction/occupation related activities.[10]

Yet another development viewed as a step in strengthening the consensus reached at Wuhan was the visit of China's State Councilor and Defence Minister Gen. Wei Fenghe to India from 21-24 August 2018, which was marked by extensive discussions between him and Defence Minister Nirmala Sitharaman as well as Defence ministry and Army officials. The statement by the Indian defence ministry read that two countries decided to increase the "engagement between their armed forces relating to training, joint exercises and other professional interactions".[11] As a result, "India and China agreed to boost interaction between their armed forces and operationalise a hotline to step up strategic communication."[12] Reaffirming his faith in the recently achieved understanding, Wei stated that "his visit will deepen our bilateral military exchanges and cooperation on security, enhance mutual trust and push forward the new development of our military ties to protect peace on the border", while PM Modi spoke of the bilateral ties dating back to thousands of years.[13]

Considering the Chinese renewal of activity in at least North Doklam and intrusions in other sectors like Demchok, it remained to be seen if the August Defence Ministers' meet would have any meaningful effect. A Defence Ministry press release stated that the two Ministers covered bilateral defence related engagement as well as regional and international developments in a "free, frank and constructive manner". They welcomed recent exchanges between both countries' Armed Forces "which had enhanced mutual trust and understanding to implement the consensus reached between Prime Minister Narendra Modi and President Xi Jinping at the Informal Sumit in Wuhan."[14]

It was decided that engagement between both countries' Armed Forces relating to training, joint exercises and other professional interactions would be expanded and followed up with a new bilateral MoU on Defence Exchanges and Cooperation to replace the earlier MoU signed in 2006. Discussing issues related to border areas, the Ministers agreed to work towards "full implementation of ongoing confidence building measures" as well as greater interactions at the working level to ensure the maintenance of peace and tranquility, including expediting the of the hotline between the relevant departments of their Armed Forces.[15]

During his visit, there were also reports about Mrs. Sitharaman having raised the issue about the $46 billion China-Pakistan Economic Corridor which is passing through Pakistan-occupied Kashmir, as she noted that it violates India's sovereignty. On the status of Doklam, since after the Modi-Jinping meet at Wuhan, Minister of State for External Affairs VK Singh told Rajya Sabha on 23 August 2018, that there have been no new developments at the site of the face-off with China in Doklam and its vicinity, and status quo prevails in the area. "Since the disengagement of Indian and Chinese border personnel in the Doklam area on August 28, 2017, there have been no new developments at the faceoff site and its vicinity. The status quo prevails in this area," Singh said in a written reply to a question on whether China has constructed new roads in the southern part of the Doklam Plateau.[16]

However, on 26 July 2018, during the US Congressional hearing of the House Foreign Affairs Sub-Committee for Asia and the Pacific, Congresswoman Ann Wagner made the claim and posed a question to a State Department official, Alice G Wells, on Beijing's actions in the Himalayan region and compared them with its manoeuvre in the disputed South China Sea. "Although both countries backed down, China has quietly resumed its activities in Doklam and neither Bhutan nor India has sought to dissuade it. China's activities in the Himalayas remind me of its south China Sea policies. How should our failure to respond to the militarisation of the South China Sea inform the international response to these Himalayan border disputes?" Wagner asked, but did not elaborate on her claim of China resuming its activities.

In her response, Wells, the Principal Deputy Assistant Secretary of State for South and Central Asia, did not directly refer to Doklam, but told Wagner and other lawmakers: "I would assess that India is vigorously defending its northern borders and this (the situation at the northern borders) is a subject of concern to India". In April 2018, Minister of State for Defence Subhash Bhamre stated in Rajya Sabha, "In the year 2017, the number of transgressions were 426 as against 273 in the year 2016".[17] China's old policy/strategy of crawling and clutching whatever, wherever, whenever continued, despite Doklam stand-off resolution and Wuhan summit.

Despite the growing the bonhomie, the Chinese still played the spoiler with news reports that the intrusions were well on their way, as reported by The Tribune newspaper, "The People's Liberation Army (PLA) has allegedly intruded into the Demchok sector in Ladakh along the Line of Actual Control (LAC) and installed tents. The alleged intrusion occurred in the Charding-Nilu Nala area in the Demchok sector in July 2018. The PLA installed five tents in the area but later removed three of them after the Indian Army and PLA held a Brigadier-level meeting a few days ago. According to sources, PLA men, in civvies, had intruded around 300-400 metres inside the Indian territory in the Demchok region and put up five tents.

They were posing as nomads and had also brought cattle with them. "Even after showing flags, which is the standard procedure on the LAC to express dissent, they continued to stay put in the region," a source told *The Tribune*. "After repeated requests, the PLA agreed to the Brigadier-level talks. Thereafter, three tents were removed, but two tents are still there. PLA men in civvies continue to occupy the area," the source added. Despite repeated calls, there was no response from the Army."[18] Unfortunately, this happened at a time when the Chinese defence minister was scheduled to visit India. All these gestures do point towards the fact that even if New Delhi would go the maximum possible way in conveying to the Chinese its genuine intentions, the Chinese would still prefer keeping the pot boiling to extract greater concession by raising the threshold.

The fifty years of border management mentioned, the stand-off at Doklam and many other earlier instances of transgressions and incursions by Chinese PLA across the LAC very often led to grappling/ wrestling by soldiers of both nations, but fortunately all ended by dialogue at field commander to diplomatic level.[19]

It must be noted that Wuhan happened almost immediately after India's maiden participation the Shanghai Cooperation Organisation's (SCO) 15th Defence Ministers Meeting held at Beijing on April 24, 2018. Speaking at this meet Defence Minister Nirmala Sitharaman highlighted India's keen interest in developing an expanded partnership with the broader Eurasian region. India sought to build on long-standing ties of deep mutual trust and confidence with Russia, vibrant historical and cultural linkages with countries of Central Asia and closer development partnership with China and to further enhance and deepen ties with all member countries for mutual benefit.[20]

Mrs. Sitharaman said India would work with SCO partners to energize and revitalize age-old ties of affinity with countries of the region. She sought a forward-looking partnership based on robust dialogue and concrete initiatives to enhance economic, trade and cultural cooperation and mutually beneficial interactions on defence and security matters.[21]

Greater communication among member countries within the region was essential for progressive trends towards stability and peace to reassert itself, she said, and to arrest the current drift in ties between major powers. She emphasised that many problems that confront the region, such as climate change, cyber security, narcotics trafficking, or violent transnational crime require solutions based on cooperative frameworks that involve all countries and stakeholders. This is particularly necessary to address the persistent threat of cross-border terrorism and extremism.[22]

International terrorism is today the most serious threat to peaceful societies, she said. Terrorism threatens to derail our developmental aspirations and create sustained instability both within our countries and across national borders and that the member countries should closely coordinate and adopt a policy of zero tolerance towards terrorism. India will continue to engage strongly against terrorism with the SCO-Regional Anti-Terrorism Structure based in Tashkent. Strongly condemning yet another vicious terrorist attack in Kabul, Mrs.

Sitharaman said SCO must adopt an uncompromising approach towards the persisting threat of terrorism in Afghanistan, as it is essential to advance peace and prosperity in the region. Since defence cooperation, especially enhanced linkages between armed forces is an important dimension of SCO, Mrs. Sitharaman said India is keen to explore the full potentialities of this engagement and will engage with a positive approach on all issues related to defence cooperation within the SCO framework.[23]

She then elaborated: "India has already commenced practical steps to take forward defence engagement under the framework, as reflected in our first ever presence at this ministerial meeting and participation of the Indian Army band at the Fanfare for Peace military tattoo being held in conjunction with our meeting today. As we move ahead, India will also explore the possibility of coordinating some SCO defence activities in the coming years.... As India enjoys excellent bilateral defence cooperation with a large number of SCO countries especially with Russia," she said, adding that cooperation in the SCO framework will help reinforce India's efforts to strengthen bilateral cooperation with the partners in the region in the field of defence."[24]

With that, Defence Minister Sitharaman confirmed India's participation in a multi-nation counter-terror military exercise in Russia in September 2018, under the framework of the SCO, which after many years, will pitch Indian and Pakistani armies together along with China's PLA and armies of several other countries. Indian and Pak armies have in the past, operated alongside or as part of the same international military field formation in United Nation's peacekeeping missions. However, in the highly charged Indo-Pak relations since the past years, this was the first time that the two adversary armies will operate together.

As an SCO member, India sees itself in a position to play a major role in addressing the threat of terrorism in the region. It is also keen on deepening its security-related cooperation with the SCO and its Regional Anti-Terrorism Structure (RATS) which specifically deals with issues relating to security and defence.[25]

For India and China two powerful and progressing nations, it simply does not make any sense to be involved in frequent dissent across their borders and enhancement of the arms race. It will be of great benefit to the large populations of both China and India, if the former sincerely shifts from its hegemonic tendency to focus on trade, technical cooperation and all other mentioned progressive pursuits.[26]

And very important for the entire South Asian region is to rid it of the spreading cancer of terrorism. Indian Army and its security forces have maximum experience in countering terrorism. Will China decide to cooperate with India to end terrorism, which mainly emanates from Pakistan and also affects China? If China does so, terrorism in South Asia can be obliterated.

The use of the Tibet card has been subdued for the past two years now. In return, there was nothing forthcoming from the Chinese side. India went to the latest border talks then with some expectations, but the stalemate continued.

The 21st Meeting of the Special Representatives of India and China was held on 24th November 2018 between National Security Advisor Ajit Doval and State Councillor and Minister of Foreign Affairs of China Wang Yi, who met in Chengdu. The official release stated that the talks were productive, of which some points are worth consideration. Some key points are highlighted below:

> 1. The representatives "underlined the importance of approaching the boundary question from the strategic perspective of India-China relations and agreed that an early settlement of the boundary question serves the fundamental interests of both countries. 2. The Special Representatives agreed that pending the final resolution of the boundary question, it is important to maintain peace and tranquility in the border areas and to ensure that the boundary question does not affect the overall development of the bilateral relationship. In this context, they noted the mature handling of issues relating to the India-China border areas since the Wuhan Summit. 3. Acknowledging the importance of predictability in border management, and in that context, underscoring the importance of maintaining strategic communication at all levels, the Special Representatives held discussions on various confidence building measures to promote exchanges and communication between their border personnel. They directed the bilateral Working Mechanism on

Consultation & Coordination for Border Affairs to work out further details in this regard."[27]

Seen from the perspective for the worsening ties in 2017, the meeting was definitely reflective of the willingness of both the sides to start a meaningful dialogue after it was realized that stand-offs like Doklam could be mutually destructive for both the sides. However, the text of the talks, despite the optimism, once again demonstrated that there was nothing novel in the press release. The talk of maintaining peace and tranquility, regular channels of communication and CBMs was only a reiteration of things agreed in the previous meetings. Even the *Global Times* accepted that "two countries are often trapped in a vicious circle" and that "if the neighbors could figure out a solution, it would fundamentally improve ties and play a significant role in developing bilateral ties."[28]

The above status-quoist view was also substantiated by Army Chief General Bipin Rawat's speech in January 2019, when he described the border situation stating "We have been able to maintain peace and tranquility along the Chinese border, particularly after the Wuhan summit. Common directions were issued, and they are being followed."[29] A report published in Outlook also reiterated that there has been no concrete progress on the core issues between both the countries. In fact, the article even reported how the hotline decision between the senior most army officers had been in limbo for some time. The Indian Army wants the hotline to be between the Director General of Military Operations (DGMO) in Delhi and the Central Military Commission (CMC) of China based in Beijing. The People's Liberation Army (PLA) wants the hotline between the DGMO in Delhi and the Western Theater Command (WTC) based in Chengdu of Sichuan province.[30]

Even "NSA Ajit Doval and Chinese State Counselor & Foreign Minister Wang Yi could not persuade the Army Generals to resolve the issue" in the 21st round of talks, the report further stated.[31] The 12th WMCC meeting was held last March where "both sides reviewed the situation along the India-China border areas and discussed ways to effectively manage borders".[32] The statement of the 13th WMCC meeting which took place in New Delhi on 31st January 2019, read:

[T]he two sides reviewed the progress on implementation of various confidence building measures (CBMs) to enhance mutual trust and understanding. The Indian side reiterated the importance of maintaining peace and tranquility in the border areas as a prerequisite to smooth development of overall bilateral relations.[33]

There was a substantial decline in the border transgressions from the PLA soldiers. Compared to 2017, 2018 was relatively more peaceful in this context. The relative peace on the border did not affect other aspects of the Sino-India ties as well. There was no concrete change in Chinese stance. Post Wuhan, India had expected some change over the NSG (Nuclear Suppliers Group) issue but in January 2019, Chinese foreign ministry once again clarified that its long-held stand over blocking India's NSG bid would continue.[34]

"We will uphold the NPT mechanism. We underscore its importance as the cornerstone of international non-proliferation system and also an important component of international security...we promise to enforce the NPT fully and comprehensively and gradually realise our goal of a nuclear weapon free world and do our best to solve the nuclear non-proliferation issues through political and diplomatic means for the peaceful use of nuclear energy and international cooperation," Chinese Foreign Ministry spokesperson Geng Shuang stated.[35]

However, China's objection to Modi's tour of Arunachal Pradesh in February 2019 only confirmed that China's compulsions and complexes about its relationship with India persist. It remained to be seen when and how, if ever, China will overcome these and opt for meaningful ties with India which can actually benefit both. Summing it up, the only positive development had been the good optics surrounding the bilateral ties.

Pulwama Attacks and Aftermath: The Chinese Backstabbing

On February 14, 2019, a dastardly attack by Pakistani proxy Jaish-e-Mohammad attacked a CRPF convoy at Pulwama claimed more than 40 personnel's lives. The entire international community stood behind India and condemned the attack, except the Chinese who did not even give a scant acknowledgement of the role of Pakistan sponsored terrorists. The attacks only brought back the old wounds of China's non-cooperation in the United Nations whenever India tried to push the case against Masood Azhar and his outfit.

China's two statements, merely paying lip service and condemning the terrorist attack by the Jaish-e-Mohammad (JeM) at Pulwama in Jammu & Kashmir and also opposing Prime Minister Narendra Modi's visit to Arunachal Pradesh, only prove that neither Doklam nor Wuhan seem to have made any difference to its attitude towards India. Condemning the Pulwama attack, in which 45 men from the Central Reserve Police Force were killed in a ghastly attack claimed by the JeM while vetoing the declaration of JeM chief Masood Azhar as an UN-designated global terrorist is meaningless.[36] Both these matters are typical of China's 'sweet and sour' diplomacy.

Condemning China for opposing Modi's visit to Arunachal Pradesh, India yet again reminded its recalcitrant neighbour that, "the State of Arunachal Pradesh is an integral and inalienable part of India. Indian leaders visit Arunachal Pradesh from time to time, as they visit other parts of India. This consistent position has been conveyed to the Chinese side on several occasions," read a statement issued by the Ministry of External Affairs after the Prime Minister's visit. The Indian rebuke was in response to the spokesman of the Chinese Ministry of Foreign Affairs' remarks which called for New Delhi to "respect the interests" of the Chinese side while objecting to Modi's visit to Arunachal Pradesh. "The Chinese government has never recognized the so-called "Arunachal Pradesh and is firmly opposed to the Indian leader's visit to the East Section of the China-India boundary," Chinese Foreign Ministry Spokesperson Hua Chunying said in a statement. Beijing "warned" India to "refrain from any action that may lead to escalation of disputes," adding, "China urges the Indian side to bear in mind the common interests of the two countries, respect the interests and concerns of the Chinese side, cherish the momentum of improvement in bilateral relations, and refrain from any action that may lead to the escalation of disputes or complicate the boundary question."[37]

The Line of Actual Control (LAC), that demarcates the Indian and

Chinese territory, traverses five Indian states, including Arunachal Pradesh. Since the military standoff at Bhutan's Doklam plateau ended in August 2017, the tension has remained, even as the troops of both India and China disengaged. Numerous instances of Chinese troops crossing the LAC in the Arunachal sector have been reported since then. Modi was on a whirlwind tour of the north-eastern states of Arunachal Pradesh, Assam, and Tripura last week, inaugurating projects with just a few months to go for the 2019 Lok Sabha elections.[38]

Following the official bilateral visit of China's State Councilor and Defence Minister Gen. Wei Fenghe to India from 21-24 August 2018, marked by extensive discussions between him and Defence Minister Nirmala Sitharaman as well as Defence Ministry and Army officials and considering the Chinese renewal of activity in at least North Doklam and intrusions in other sectors like Demchok, this writer had expressed doubts about any meaningful effects of that meeting.

The (supposedly) unprecedented Narendra Modi-Xi Jinping meeting at Wuhan made waves because it was approached and organized/implemented differently compared to any previous Sino-Indian summits. Wuhan should have resulted in improvement of some basic essentials that India considers most important, i.e. peace on the Line of Actual Control (LAC), without the almost daily border dispute issues, fair-trade ties, hassle-free politico-diplomatic relations and good/social, business, cultural and educational exchanges.[39]

"Dragon-elephant Tango" Reality?

The Chinese assurances as usual have turned out to be less than promising in pacifying India's concerns even after a serious incident like the Pulwama carnage. A few days after the Chinese scuttled the UNSC efforts with the technical hold, the Chinese Ambassador to India wrote an article titled "Dragon-elephant tango" for *Indian Express* on 3rd of April 2019. Beginning with a description of the nascent beginnings of the Sino Indian relationship after the Communists took power, the ambassador categorises the relationship in four phases, namely:[40]

1. "Honeymoon period" till the Panchsheel days and Nehru's 1955 Bandung visit.

2. "Frozen Period", that began after the 1962 war and lasted till the end of the 1980s, when Rajiv Gandhi finally broke the ice with his 1988 visit.
3. "Recovery Period", which lasted from the "1990s to the 17th National Congress of the Communist Party of China".
4. "Acceleration Period" from the Communist Party's 18th National Congress in 2012 onwards till April 2020.

However, on May 5 and 9, 2020, in about four areas on the LAC, PLA violated the spirit of the peace and tranquility agreements by using crude weapons like iron rods studded with nails, rods with barbed wire coiled on them and stones. While there were no deaths, there were over 100 Indian Army personnel injured. Then on June 15, 2020, at Galwan, PLA, using the same kind of weapons mentioned, killed a Colonel and 19 soldiers of 16 Bihar Regiment, thereby totally violating all aspects of all the peace and tranquility agreements. Indian Army personnel soon afterwards, avenged this attack killing almost thrice the number of PLA soldiers and instilling fear into them.

The article then had its six observations describing the positives and new milestones achieved in the bilateral relationship and called upon the Wuhan consensus to be translated into action for the betterment of this relationship. Ending on a positive note, it suggested a four-prong approach to cooperation, namely negotiating and signing "China-India Treaty of Good-Neighbourliness and Friendly Cooperation", exploring free trade agreements, initiating consultations on early harvests of the boundary question, and achieving synergy on the Belt and Road Initiative."[41]

While it can be argued that the article was to pacify a fuming New Delhi and it indeed emphasized on the gradual progress in the relationship, it still stopped short of providing any concrete answer to the bilateral irritants and the Sino-Pak nexus which has kept the Security Dilemma hyperactive in the region. The main conclusion of the article was clear, that issues like the technical hold in the UNSC should not prevent both the nations from undoing all those gains reaped in the bilateral relationship, which is still progressing at a decent pace, if not taking a negative trajectory. It seems that in the article, despite all the good intentions, the Ambassador seems to have overlooked India's sensitivities towards the Pakistan sponsored proxy warfare and also China's efforts to unilaterally change the status quo on the LAC. Nevertheless, the article did confirm that bilateral ties are not in the best of the terms, yet there is a huge scope of improvement and numerous benefits still remain to be reaped.

While India's ties with her neighborhood and especially China may continue to have ebbs and flows, it may not lose focus of its efforts to emerge as a leading global power, both in the hard and soft power. The Anti Satellite Missile test on 27 March 2019 is a major achievement on these lines and more importantly, a revolution in the way India shall look at warfare and formulating its global strategic outlook. China, and Pakistan should be the first nations to be affected by this test.

On March 27, India successfully tested its ASAT missile by targeting a satellite hovering some 300 kilometers above the earth. Titled "Mission Shakti", the achievement was a major milestone as well as a quantum leap in India's offensive capabilities. After US, Russia and China, India became the fourth nation to have successfully conduced such a test.

In comparison to this, China carried out its ASAT test in 2007 and therefore its trajectory can be said to be a decade ahead of the Indian progress. India conducted its test in the Low Earth Orbit, while on the other hand the Chinese have looking towards developing capabilities "targeting high altitude satellites at 36,000 km" above the earth.[42] In addition, an expert interview in The Hindu also points out to the Chinese development of "laser based weaponry and cyber weaponry", which in combination with ASAT capabilities will go a very long way in transforming the nature of warfare. Given the territorial and deeply geopolitical nature of Sino-Indian dispute, India needs to catch up and is speedily catching up with changing nature of war to avoid spilling over of the bilateral irritants to other realms where bilateral rivalry could tip the precarious strategic balance maintained on the border.

Another 'informal' summit was held at Mamallapuram, Tamil Nadu (50 kms from Chennai) in October 2019. To celebrate the 70th anniversary of diplomatic relations the two countries decided to organise 70 activities including a conference on a ship voyage that will trace the historical connection between the two civilisations. The aims were, a high-level economic and trade dialogue mechanism to be established with the objective of achieving enhanced trade and commercial relations; mutual investments in identified sectors will be encouraged through the development of a manufacturing partnership and sister-state relations to be established between Tamil Nadu and Fujian Province.

Mr G. Parthasarthy, writing an article titled Looking beyond the Mallapuram summit, in the Business Line of October 25, 2019, commented that the Narendra Modi-Xi Jinping summit in Mamallapuram was certainly an international publicity bonanza for the leaders of the two of the most populous countries in the world, with Mamallapuram—the site of the ancient Tamil Kingdom from which traders set sail for China several centuries ago—as the backdrop. "But one has to be careful in assessing the impact of the Modi-Xi meeting on China's approach to India...we should remember the serious misgivings about China using coercive action to enforce its maritime boundary claims over countries like Japan, South Korea, Vietnam, Malaysia and Indonesia. We also cannot ignore the Chinese machinations to back leaders and political parties all across South Asia that pose a risk to India".

There is clearly a Chinese attempt to create and foment differences with our South Asian neighbours, such as the Maldives, Sri Lanka, Nepal and Bangladesh. Worse still, China has no regrets about its policies on Jammu and Kashmir—despite the abject failure of its attempts to internationalise the issue in the UN's Security Council, Human Rights Commission and even the UN General Assembly. China's support for Pakistan was reiterated when Prime Minister Imran Khan visited Beijing on the very day that President Xi was heading to Mamallapuram. There should be no illusion that Beijing will continue to use Pakistan as an instrument for strategic containment of India by strengthening the former's nuclear, missile and conventional weapons capabilities.

Despite these policies, New Delhi would be well advised to continue its dialogue with Beijing to resolve differences on the border issue, based on the principles agreed upon in 2005 by the then Prime Minister Manmohan Singh and former Premier Wen Jiabao.

2019 became a very interesting phase in the Sino-Indian ties characterized with the continuing tensions as seen in the post-Pulwama Sino-Pak solidarity, China's nominal attempts to pacify Indian anger and India's attempts to change the regional status quo through Balakot airstrikes and filling the gap in its strategic capabilities with the ASAT test. While cognizant of the geostrategic challenges and other capability gaps, New Delhi indeed worked at a very fast pace to assert itself in the regional domain. Sino-Indian tensions, while definitely present, still do not appear to go out of control given the growth in crisis management mechanisms, but at the same time the key bilateral irritants too do not appear to be withering away, given China's quest to balance against India by deepening its ties with Pakistan through multifarious means, be it military cooperation, investments or the forex bailouts it has been infusing to prevent the Pakistani foreign exchange reserves from crashing. With these challenges, India had to pave its way out and constructively engage with China, without losing sense of the larger strategic challenges.

Some Interesting Findings About the Wuhan Virus

The Huanan Seafood Market, where-wild animals are sold, but no bats, became a source of an unknown pneumonia. Of the 41 cases, 14 were unrelated to seafood. Beijing suppressed information for first 6 weeks.

On December 30, 2019, Wuhan-based doctor Li Wenliang posted information about the virus on WeChat, China's most popular social media platform. Recognizing the potential ramifications of this infectious disease, he utilized the tools available to him in an attempt to raise public awareness—a commendable action in the eyes of any rational observer. Instead, he was seen as a threat, to both the careers of the local officials who called him into questioning and, by extension, to the legitimacy of the Chinese Communist Party and Xi himself. Li was swiftly punished by local public security officials for "spreading rumors" in early January. Tragically, he died in February after contracting the virus.

In a documentary presented by *The Epoch Times* and *NTD, Epoch Times* investigative reporter Joshua Philipp takes an in-depth look at the progression of the pandemic from January to April 2020 exposing some startling and sinister goings on.

From the Huanan Seafood Market in Hubei Province to the scandals at the Wuhan Institute of Virology, from long-running experiments on viruses to military takeovers, suspicious activities arise from every corner. Through vigorous investigations and the piecing together of hidden information, the documentary will unearth a more complete understanding of the situation surrounding the rise of this pandemic.

Suspicions uncovered from official reports and publicly available information also sprouted more questions, leading to surprising findings and inquiries.

The CCP virus, which originated from China, has rampaged through the world and caused more than 80,000 deaths, infecting at least 1.4 million.

The true number of deaths and infections is unknown due to the underreporting of cases from mainland China.

#CCPvirus #Wuhan #Coronavirus

Shi Zhengli, a Chinese virologist and writer, is a researcher at the Wuhan Institute of Virology (WIV), which is part of the Chinese Academy of Sciences (CAS). Shi and her colleague Cui Jie found that the SARS virus originated in bats. A member of the Virology Committee of the Chinese Society for Microbiology, she is an editor of the Board of *Virologica Sinica*, the *Chinese Journal of Virology*, and the *Journal of Fishery Sciences of China*.

She graduated from Wuhan University in 1987, received her master's degree from the Wuhan Institute of Virology, Chinese Academy of Sciences (CAS) in 1990 and her Ph.D. from Montpellier 2 University in France in 2000.

In 2005, a team led by Shi Zhengli and Cui Jie found that the SARS virus originated in bats. The results were published in *Science* in 2005 and *Journal of General Virology* in 2006.

In 2014, Shi Zhengli was involved in an investigation of bat coronaviruses, specifically gain of function experiments involving both the SARS and bat coronaviruses, a joint research of University of North Carolina and Wuhan Institute of Virology, with Ralph S. Baric as principal investigator. That same year funding for the project in the

US had been paused due to the moratorium on risky virology studies involving influenza, MERS & SARS viruses, that was announced by the US government that year. Similar work, however, continued in Wuhan, China.

During the 2019–20 coronavirus pandemic, Shi and twelve other Institute scientists formed an expert group on the research of Severe acute respiratory syndrome coronavirus 2 (SARS-CoV-2). In February 2020, researchers led by Shi Zhengli published an article in *Nature* titled "A pneumonia outbreak associated with a new coronavirus of probable bat origin" and in a post on bioRxiv, said that the SARS-CoV-2 is in the same family as SARS and closest to one found in bats. In February 2020, her team published a paper in *Cell Research* showing that remdesivir, an experimental drug owned by Gilead Sciences, had a positive effect in inhibiting the virus in vitro, and applied for a patent for the drug in China on behalf of the WIV. Shi co-authored a paper labelling the virus as the first Disease X.

In February 2020, the *South China Morning Post* reported that Shi's decade-long work to build up one of the world's largest databases of bat-related viruses gave the scientific community a "head start" in understanding the virus. The *SCMP* also reported that Shi was the focus of personal attacks in Chinese social media who claimed the WIV was the source of the virus, leading Shi to post: "I swear with my life, [the virus] has nothing to do with the lab", and when asked by the *SCMP* to comment on the attacks, Shi responded: "My time must be spent on more important matters". *Caixin* reported Shi made further public statements against "perceived tinfoil-hat theories about the new virus's source", quoting her as saying: "The novel 2019 coronavirus is nature punishing the human race for keeping uncivilized living habits. I, Shi Zhengli, swear on my life that it has nothing to do with our laboratory".

Shi Zhengli has also reportedly been referred to as 'batwoman'.

The Corona virus/Covid 19 emanating from a laboratory in Wuhan, only made it obvious that despite China officially being a signatory to conventions related to no use of chemical and biological weapons, it never actually stopped experimenting on them. Given the Communist Party of China's (CPC) and the People's Liberation Army's (PLA) compulsions of never-ending efforts of global domination, ensuring a force-multiplier/alternative to overcome reverses with loss of troops in case of a war against India and with the presence of PLA in a number of China's laboratories, particularly the laboratory in Wuhan, are factors which leave little doubt of China's 'research' in the field of biological and possibly even chemical weapons. And of course, China is not at all obliged to be transparent. The CPC completely controls media. So, it remains to be seen what all of China's statements following the Covid-19 outbreak are true.

China's expulsion of American journalists from the *Washington Post*, *New York Times* and the *Wall Street Journal* in the third week of March 2020 was in retaliation against the US' decision to limit the number of reporters from Chinese government-controlled media outlets who may work in the US. While the US is a democracy, where freedom of its media reporting on other countries is often selective, or in line with the government's or the opposition's policies, in China the media is under total control of its Communist government. An official document outlining the political goals of the People's Liberation Army, was revised in 2003 to strengthen the aspect of "media warfare" being an explicit part of Beijing's military strategy aimed at influencing public opinion overseas in order to steer foreign governments into making policies favourable towards China's Communist party. Former CIA analyst Peter Mattis, now a fellow in the China programme at the Jamestown Foundation, a security-focused Washington think tank opined, "Their view of national security involves pre-emption in the world of ideas.... The whole point of pushing that kind of propaganda out is to preclude or preempt decisions that would go against the People's Republic of China."

Newsweek magazine reported on 30 March 2020 that a large number of urns at a funeral home in Wuhan, the city's official cremation rates and reports of an overstressed health care system have led to speculation that Wuhan's real COVID-19 death toll could be in tens of thousands. So far, Beijing has confirmed roughly 81,000 cases and 3,300 deaths, mostly in Wuhan, the epicentre of the virus' outbreak. Many people, including U.S. politicians have reportedly accused China of underplaying their real coronavirus death figure. There has been scepticism over Chinese officials' attempts to cover up the severity of the outbreak in the early stages—before the disease became widespread overseas—and the numerous revisions made to how domestic cases are counted. Wuhan's medical system came under great stress during the height of the outbreak in China, which further raises questions about the officially reported 2,535 deaths.

According to Federation of American Scientists, Weapons of Mass Destruction publication online, China is widely reported to have active programs related to the development of chemical and biological weapons, although no details of these programs have appeared in the open literature. China is believed to have an advanced chemical warfare program that includes research and development, production and weaponisation capabilities. Its current inventory is believed to include the full range of traditional chemical agents. It also has a wide variety of delivery systems for chemical agents to include artillery rockets, aerial bombs, sprayers, and short-range ballistic missiles. Chinese forces have conducted defensive CW training and are prepared to operate in a contaminated environment. As China's program is further integrated into overall military operations, its doctrine, which is believed to be based in part on Soviet-era thinking, may reflect the incorporation of more advanced munitions for CW agent delivery. China has signed and ratified the CWC. On 30 December 1996 the Standing Committee of the National People's Congress China ratified the Chemical Weapons Convention [CWC]. Previous, dual-use chemical-related transfers to Iran's chemical weapons program indicate that, at a minimum, China's chemical export controls are not operating effectively enough to ensure compliance with China's CWC obligation not to assist anyone in any way to acquire chemical weapons. In March 1997 Israeli authorities arrested an Israeli businessman, Nahum Manbar, for allegedly selling Chinese chemical weapon components to Iran.

On May 21, 1997, pursuant to the Chemical and Biological Weapons Control and Warfare Elimination Act of 1991, the US Government imposed trade sanctions on five Chinese individuals, two Chinese companies, and one Hong Kong company for knowingly and materially contributing to Iran's chemical weapons program. These individuals and companies were involved in the export of dual-use chemical precursors and/or chemical production equipment and technology. The Chinese companies were the Nanjing Chemical Industries Group (NCI) and the Jiangsu Yongli Chemical Engineering and Technology Import/Export Corp.

In 1939 the Japanese army established the Unit 731 germ-warfare research center in Harbin, where Japanese medical experts experimented on Chinese, Soviet, Korean, British and other prisoners.

China possesses an advanced biotechnology infrastructure as well as the requisite munitions production capabilities necessary to develop, produce and weaponize biological agents. Although China has consistently claimed that it has never researched or produced biological weapons, it is nonetheless believed likely that it retains a biological warfare capability begun before acceding to the BWC. China is commonly considered to have an active biological warfare program, including dedicated research and development activities funded and supported by the Government for this purpose. There is essentially no open source data on the subject of Chinese BW activities, and many legitimate research programs use similar, if not identical equipment and facilities.

Lt. Col. Dany Shoham, who studied Chinese biological warfare and was a senior analyst with Israeli military intelligence for biological and chemical warfare in the Middle East and worldwide, is reported to have made a startling revelation that China's most advanced virus research laboratory, the Wuhan Institute of Virology, is linked to Beijing's covert bio-weapons program. If true, this could have huge consequences on the world of biowarfare. An Israeli biological warfare analyst has said that the deadly animal-borne coronavirus spreading globally may have originated in a laboratory in Wuhan linked to China's covert biological weapons program.

"Certain laboratories in the institute have probably been engaged, in terms of research and development, in Chinese [biological weapons], at least collaterally, yet not as a principal facility of the Chinese BW alignment," Shoham and also informed that work on biological weapons is covertly conducted as part of dual civilian-military research. Though China has denied having any link to biological weapons, a US State Department report last year has suspected covert biological warfare work in China. The report had cited Gao Fu, director of the

Chinese Center for Disease Control and Prevention, as telling Chinese state-controlled media that initial signs indicated the virus originated from wild animals sold at a seafood market in Wuhan.

GreatGameIndia, dated January 24, 2020, stated that China's Biological Warfare Program is believed to be in an advanced stage that includes research and development, production and weaponization capabilities. Its current inventory is believed to include the full range of traditional chemical and biological agents with a wide variety of delivery systems including artillery rockets, aerial bombs, sprayers, and short-range ballistic missiles.

The Wuhan facility was reported to have studied Corona viruses in the past, including the strain that causes Severe Acute Respiratory Syndrome, or SARS, the H5N1 influenza virus, Japanese encephalitis, and dengue. The SARS virus had escaped from high-level containment facilities in Beijing multiple times, reported newsmax.com Jan 25, citing Richard Ebright, a molecular biologist at Rutgers University in Piscataway, NJ, and the Nature magazine.

In 1993, US intelligence officials stated that it was highly probable that China had an active and expanding offensive BWs program, following assessment that two civilian-run biological research centers were actually controlled by the Chinese military. The research centres were known to have engaged previously in production and storage of BW. The American suspicions intensified in 1991 when one of the suspected biological centres was enlarged. Suspicions heightened further after Beijing made, according to a US official, a 'patently false' declaration to the United Nations (UN) that it had never made any germ weapons or conducted any work to bolster defences against a biological attack.

The Chinese Foreign Ministry subsequently described all this as groundless, denying that China had a germ weapons programme. In 1995, President Clinton transmitted to the US Congress his statutory annual report, Adherence to and Compliance with Arms Control Agreements. On China, it said:

> '[T]here are strong indications that China probably maintains its offensive BW program.' In its Chemical and Biological Defense Program Annual Report and the Chemical and Biological Defense

Program Performance Plan for 2001, the US Department of Defense was even more specific, contending: 'China possesses the munitions production capabilities necessary to develop, produce and weaponize biological agents'.

Convening a hearing on China's proliferation practices in 2003, the US–China Economic and Security Review Commission was informed as follows:

> The US believes that despite being a member of the Biological Weapons Convention, China maintains a BW program in violation of its BWC obligations. The United States believes that China's consistent claims that it has never researched, produced or possessed BW are simply not true, and that China still retains its BW program.

Although China has submitted its voluntary annual BWC confidence-building measure (CBM) data declarations every year, the US Department of State assessed in 2005 that the information submitted therein continued to be 'inaccurate and misleading'. Further, 'BWC CBMs since 1991 have called on the States Parties to declare, among other things, their past offensive activities, which China has not done. On the contrary, China insists it never had such a program at all.'

Likewise, in 2007, Defense Intelligence Agency (DIA) testimony for the US Senate, the Select Committee on Intelligence, entitled *'Current and Projected National Security Threats'* (in both open and closed sessions), contended that the DIA believes China 'continues to maintain some elements of an offensive biological weapons program.'

The Central Intelligence Agency (CIA), the DIA and intelligence agencies in other countries most probably continue to carefully follow and monitor China's Biological Warfare Program. Irrespective of publicly bringing out their findings—if partially—or totally keeping them, Beijing's BWP entirely persists in all likelihood. It is assumed that it includes an extremely secretive operational, sizable BW arsenal, extremely hidden, which is steadily being upgraded.

China's Biological Warfare Programme: An Integrative Study with Special Reference to Biological Weapons Capabilities by Dany Shoham published in *Journal of Defence Studies*.

According to *The Print*, dated July 11, 2020, in an interview to US-based *Fox News* published July 10, 2020, Dr Li-Meng Yan, who has specialised in virology and immunology at Hong Kong School of Public Health, claimed Chinese authorities knew about the deadly virus in December last year, but hushed it up. She even claimed that her own institute, which is affiliated with the World Health Organization (WHO), had asked her to stay silent about it. She also mentioned in the interview, that had China been transparent about the full dangers of the virus early on, then it would have helped the international community to understand and cope with the virus in a much better way. Yan, who fled to the US in April, 2020 alleged if she had spoken up about the virus in China, she would have been killed and, hence, fled to the US, "to tell the truth of the origins of Covid-19 to the world". She said she had to rely on her friends from the medical community for information as no expert from outside the mainland was allowed to visit the area. She said one of her friends from the Centre for Disease Control and Prevention in China told her that the virus started spreading from human to human on 31 December, which was only confirmed by the WHO in January. Even after reporting her findings to her supervisor, Dr Poon, who is an expert in the field, he allegedly did not raise alarm and asked her to continue her investigation. Yan alleged he told her "to keep silent, and be careful" or all of them will be in trouble.

As on May 29, 2020, Worldometer recorded that 213 countries and territories around the world were reported to have a total of 5,932,184 confirmed cases of the exceptionally dirty and dangerous Coronavirus Covid-19 that originated from Wuhan, China, and a toll of **362,614 deaths**. Actual numbers of deaths and infections in China are unknown due to underreporting of cases by Chinese media, which is controlled by the Chinese Communist Party (CCP).

Some important questions come up. How is it that while this virus has travelled thousands of kms through human contact, its effect in Beijing, 1152 kms and Shanghai, 839 kms from Wuhan has been absolutely minimal? No Chinese political or military leaders have tested positive. All business areas in China are safe. Wuhan is reported to have been opened on April 08, 2020. Did China have an antidote/

vaccine for Covid-19, which may have been administered selectively well in advance in areas of Beijng and Shanghai? Reportedly, over 21 million mobile phones and 2,00,000 land lines in China had gone silent or had stopped functioning.

Share markets worldwide dropped down to half. Lockdowns to prevent or reduce the spread of the virus ruined many businesses and rendered millions of people jobless.

On December 30, 2019, Dr. Li Wenliang, 34, an ophthalmologist at Wuhan Central Hospital, posted information about the virus on WeChat, China's most popular social media platform. In early January 2020, Li was punished by local public security officials for "spreading rumours". He died in February after contracting the virus. Many other Chinese scientists and others who divulged any aspect of Wuhan being the source of the virus have reportedly been silenced. It was also reported that many persons working at WIV were missing and that under pressure, eating and hunting of wild animals got banned in Wuhan.

China Setting up Wuhan Kind Lab in Pakistan

Regarding biowarfare, China and Pakistan have entered a "secret three-year deal to expand potential bio-warfare capabilities", which includes running various research projects related to "deadly agent anthrax" this is a serious concern that exposes the nexus between China and Pakistan.[43] One report states that Wuhan lab was providing "extensive training on manipulation of pathogens and bio-informatics to Pakistani scientists to help Pakistan develop its own virus collection database" which may enhance the capability of Pakistan in genetic identification of viruses, access to dangerous microorganisms and use of genomic tools for research and infectious diseases. It further states that "China wants Pakistan to engage India and it wants to conduct potentially dangerous experiments on foreign soil, without subjecting its own people to risk."

The Economic Times of July 26, 2020, published a PTI report stating "Pakistan and China have concluded a secret deal to expand potential bio-warfare capabilities, including running research projects related to the deadly anthrax, an Australian media report has alleged, prompting

Pakistan to dismiss it as a "politically motivated and fake story." In an article published on July 23, Australia's investigative newspaper The Klaxon said China's Wuhan Institute of Virology has signed a covert three-year deal with Pakistan military's Defense Science and Technology Organization (DESTO) to collaborate research in "emerging infectious diseases".

Australian Journalist Anthony Klan, has also made a sensational revelation which was reported in Economic Times, July 25, 2020, that the Wuhan Institute of Virology of China and the Pakistan's military establishment have entered into a joint collaboration to produce "emerging infectious diseases" and "anthrax". Klan's view needs to be taken seriously in view of the nexus between China and Pakistan over the years.

Wuhan lab scientists have been conducting extensive research operations on deadly "animal-to-human" pathogens in Pakistan for several years. Studies involve over 7,000 Pakistani farmers, herders and others, and over 2,800 camels and other animals. The studies have been funded by China and appear to be a precursor to the secret new China-Pakistan military bio-program exposed by The Klaxon last month. Anthony Klan reports. ANTHONY KLAN EXCLUSIVE

A team of key Coronavirus scientists from China's Wuhan Institute of Virology have been conducting experiments of dangerous pathogens in "collaboration" with Pakistan for up to five years under the auspices of China's opaque Belt and Road infrastructure scheme. Following revelations last month that China and Pakistan's military have allegedly entered a secretive three-year deal to expand potential bio-warfare capabilities, it has emerged Wuhan scientists have been conducting research into deadly pathogens in Pakistan since 2015. The results of five studies conducted by Wuhan and Pakistani scientists have been published in scientific papers, each involving the "detection and characterisation" of "zoonotic pathogens". Zoonotic pathogens are infectious diseases that can pass from animals to humans. The studies involve experiments and genome sequencing of the West Nile Virus; MERS-Coronavirus; Crimean-Congo Hemorrhagic Fever Virus; the Thrombocytopenia Syndrome Virus; and the Chikungunya Virus. There is no vaccine or cure for any of those pathogens, which are among some of the world's deadliest and most contagious. One of the studies thanks Wuhan's National Virus Resource Centre for "providing the virus-infected Vero cells". Each of the five studies states it was "supported" by the "International Cooperation on Key Technologies of Biosafety along the China-Pakistan Economic Corridor".[44]

NOTES

1. https://economictimes.indiatimes.com/news/defence/indias-geopolitical-status-goes-up-after-doklam-standoff-ends/articleshow/60282585.cms
2. Ibid.
3. https://salute.co.in/will-wuhan-lead-to-lasting-peace-on-the-lac/
4. https://www.mea.gov.in/press-releases.htm?dtl/29853/IndiaChina_ Informal_ Summit_at_Wuhan
5. Ibid
6. Ibid
7. https://salute.co.in/will-wuhan-lead-to-lasting-peace-on-the-lac/
8. Ibid.
9. Ibid.
10. Ibid.
11. https://www.livemint.com/Politics/h6MqdRPeoiNWMcCMnJugAK/India-China-defence-ministers-meet-after-Doklam-standoff.html
12. https://www.livemint.com/Politics/h6MqdRPeoiNWMcCMnJugAK/India-China-defence-ministers-meet-after-Doklam-standoff.html
13. https://www.scmp.com/news/china/diplomacy-defence/article/2161221/india-and-china-increase-military-cooperation-after
14. https://nationaldefence.in/breaking-news/india-and-china-agrees-to-work-towards-full-implementation-of-ongoing-confidence-building-measures/
15. https://nationaldefence.in/breaking-news/india-and-china-agrees-to-work-towards-full-implementation-of-ongoing-confidence-building-measures/
16. https://economictimes.indiatimes.com/news/defence/no-new-developments-in-doklam-status-quo-prevails-government/articleshow/65151550.cms
17. https://www.outlookindia.com/website/story/govt-data-reveals-chinese-incursions-into-india-rose-to-426-in-2017-from-273-in-/307883
18. https://www.tribuneindia.com/news/jammu-kashmir/chinese-intrusion—in-demchok-sector/636379.html
19. https://salute.co.in/will-wuhan-lead-to-lasting-peace-on-the-lac/
20. https://nationaldefence.in/breaking-news/raksha-mantris-address-at-the-15th-sco-defence-ministers-meeting-in-china/
21. Ibid.
22. Ibid.
23. Ibid.
24. http://pib.nic.in/newsite/PrintRelease.aspx?relid=178875
25. http://24x7newscast.com/after-chinait-is-now-pakistan-to-carryout-friendly-military-regime-with-india/
26. https://salute.co.in/will-wuhan-lead-to-lasting-peace-on-the-lac/

27. https://economictimes.indiatimes.com/news/defence/india-china-underline-to-approach-boundary-question-from-strategic-perspective/articleshow/66786055.cms?from=mdr
28. http://www.globaltimes.cn/content/1129040.shtml
29. https://www.businesstoday.in/pti-feed/situation-along-border-with-china-improved-after-wuhan-summit-gen.-rawat/story/308870.html
30. https://www.outlookindia.com/website/story/india-news-opinion-no-progress-on-india-china-relations-govt-creates-optical-illusion-ahead-of-elections/323606
31. https://www.outlookindia.com/website/story/india-news-opinion-no-progress-on-india-china-relations-govt-creates-optical-illusion-ahead-of-elections/323606
32. https://www.mea.gov.in/press-releases.htm?dtl/30440/Press_release_ on_the_12th_Meeting_of_IndiaChina_WMCC
33. https://www.mea.gov.in/press-releases.htm?dtl/30961/13th+Meeting+ of+the+Working+Mechanism+for+Consultation+amp+Coordination+on+IndiaChina+Border+Affairs
34. https://timesofindia.indiatimes.com/india/china-signals-it-will-continue-to-block-india-from-nsg/articleshow/67766022.cms
35. https://www.livemint.com/politics/policy/india-must-sign-npt-to-gain-entry-into-nsg-china-1548936478869.html
36. https://southasiamonitor.org/list.php?type=sl
37. https://www.singaporestar.com/news/259460739/india-rebukes-china-for-objecting-to-pm-modi-arunachal-visit
38. Ibid.
39. https://salute.co.in/will-wuhan-lead-to-lasting-peace-on-the-lac/
40. https://indianexpress.com/article/opinion/columns/dragon-elephant-tango-india-china-relations-narendra-modi-xi-jinping-5657281/
41. Ibid.
42. https://www.thehindu.com/opinion/op-ed/is-indias-anti-satellite-test-a-game-changer/article26810081.ece
43. https://www.news18.com/news/india/news-of-chinese-lab-creating-anthrax-like-pathogens-in-pakistan-fake-says-its-foreign-office-2736129.html
44. https://www.theklaxon.com.au › home › wuhan-lab-co...25-Aug-2020—Wuhan lab scientists have been conducting extensive research operations on deadly "animal-to-human" pathogens in Pakistan for several years.

7

GALWAN AND KAILASH RANGE

In 1967 at Nathu La, Sikkim, when PLA upped the ante by using artillery, the Nathu La brigade commander who wanted to respond with artillery could only do so after approval by the government. When his request reached through proper channel to then Prime Minister Indira Gandhi, holding the defence portfolio also, she gave her approval. The end-result was about 400 PLA troops being killed and a convoy of Chinese vehicles and many bunkers being destroyed. Thereafter PLA pressed for resolution of perceived intrusions by Indian troops without use of force or firearms but instead, by discussion between the commanders on ground. If at all there was any physical confrontation following very frequent transgressions/incursions, almost always by PLA troops they were dealt with for 53 years, including the 73 days Doklam stand-off in 2017, by pushing/grappling or fisticuffs and eventually - every time - resolved by dialogue/ discussion between officers of both armies deployed on ground/ higher field commanders/diplomatic levels, as required. However, since early May 2020 onwards, PLA beat all earlier records of this mild form of unarmed combat.

On May 5, around 250 PLA soldiers attacked Indian Army personnel with iron rods, sticks, and even resorted to stone-pelting in the Pangong Tso (lake) area in which soldiers on both sides sustained injuries. On May 9, nearly 150 PLA troops attacked Indian Army counterparts in a similar way resulting in a face-off near Naku La Pass in the Sikkim sector. Varying reports of the injured on both sides ranged up to 100. Some more incidents initiated by PLA, including at Demchok and Daulat Beg Oldi (DBO), increased aggressive patrolling and fresh deployments in other sectors, were definite indicators of a considered ratcheting up by China. Indian Army reportedly matched and mirrored all Chinese moves. India's long overdue strategic infrastructural development including the construction of the 255 kms long Darbuk–Shyok-DBO road, including a bridge over the Galwan river, well inside Indian territory, miffed the Chinese, who came and pitched about 100 tents in that area.

While China falsely accused India of aggressively trespassing its territory and blocking PLA patrols, Chinese President Xi Jinping exhorted PLA to be prepared to defend the nation.

Interacting with this author, Lt Gen SL Narasimhan (Retd), Director General, Centre for Contemporary China Studies and Member, National Security Advisory Board, commented: "The increase in comprehensive national power of China seems to be driving this behaviour. Wolf warrior diplomacy, a euphemism for aggressive behaviour by China's diplomats has been on for a few months now.... It appears that PLA simply wants to assert its perception of the LAC. Therefore, India's armed forces must be prepared for a long haul and ensure sanctity of India's perception of the LAC. Also, efforts must continue to get the LAC clarified so that such incidents can be avoided".

On June 15, 2020, at Ladakh's extremely cold Galwan valley in high altitude, Colonel B Santosh Babu, Commanding Officer, 16 Bihar and 19 other ranks of this battalion and some other units were killed in the most violent and barbaric close-quarter confrontations over the past 53 years. PLA personnel attacked them with iron rods studded with nails, rods with barbed wire wound around one end and boulders/stones.

The confrontation reportedly erupted as the 16 Bihar detachment, which was overseeing PLA's disengagement process, tried to remove a Chinese tent at Galwan Valley. A physical fight started after the detachment objected to PLA, which did not follow the disengagement process agreed upon in earlier meetings between commanders of both armies. The Chinese soldiers targeted Colonel Babu and killed him with the deadly weapons. The fact that PLA troops were armed with such weapons makes it obvious that such an attack was well planned by the Chinese.

In fact, since early May 2020 onwards, PLA beating all earlier records of mild form of unarmed combat by using crude barbaric weapons, violated all agreements made for "peace and tranquility", including those in both the 2018 Wuhan and 2019 Mamallapuram summits.

Following the June 15, 2020 evening attack by PLA and the Indian Army's quick response, while China did not disclose PLA's fatal casualty figure, believed/widely reported then as 43, much later was officially disclosed as four. However, later there were reports of PLA losing over 100 personnel. Indian troops who reorganised themselves and returned later to avenge the killing of their 20 comrades, ironically but very significantly did not carry firearms. While few of them-the Sikh troops-carried kirpans (daggers), most of the others disarmed the Chinese soldiers of their crude weapons and used the same very effectively against them. Some of the Indian soldiers fought with bare hands and altogether they killed many times more Chinese than the 20 Indian brave-hearts killed.

While PLA's strategic infrastructural development in many parts of the Chinese side of the LAC has been going on since decades, the same much required, long overdue and vitally important task on India's side began in recent years. One such major project completed at a faster pace is the construction of the 255 kms long Darbuk–Shyok–DBO road, also called the Sub-Sector North road, including a bridge over the Galwan river, well inside Indian territory, which miffed the Chinese. They did not react much to the construction of road mentioned per se, but it is a lateral to this road with bridge over the Galwan river leading towards the LAC, which became a strong reason for the May 2020 standoff and that too after PLA inducted 5000 additional troops with artillery guns and infantry combat vehicles at locations close to the LAC and pitched 100 tents.

Driven by its hegemonic mindset along with constant greed for power and grabbing foreign territories, the Chinese Communist Party (CCP)-PLA combo has always been paranoid about its adversaries or neighbours or target nations improving strategically or acquiring more or better weaponry. Some earlier developments, which also irked the Chinese were two exercises conducted by Indian Army in September and October 2019 in India's forward areas of Ladakh and Arunachal Pradesh, respectively.

The one in September 2019 was an integrated military exercise involving tanks, mechanised infantry, paratroopers and various other arms of service in eastern Ladakh and that too, just days after a faceoff between the Indian and Chinese troops in the region. The second one in Arunachal Pradesh was an exercise to test the capabilities of the newly conceived integrated battle groups, which was carried out in phases in the upper reaches of Arunachal Pradesh near Tawang and faced some resistance from China but the matter was resolved through diplomatic channels. Also, a greater irritant for China in the larger context is India's abrogation of Articles 370 and 35A, since August 05, 2019 along with Jammu & Kashmir and Ladakh being designated as separate union territories.

Having made the aggressive May 2020 military moves, that too during the peak period of the Covid 19, also referred to as the Chinese/CCP virus' worldwide outbreak and then accusing India of aggressively trespassing its territory and blocking PLA patrols and President Xi Jinping exhorting PLA to "be prepared to defend the nation" was a clear indication of China drawing a red herring / attempting to distract attention of China being the emanator of the deadly virus and 125 nations raising issues against it.

After about twelve meetings since the first week of May on the LAC, on June 06, 2020, the Indian and Chinese corps commanders were to meet to discuss and resolve the stand-off in Eastern Ladakh at Moldo on the Chinese side of the LAC. However, the Chinese commander who met Lt Gen Harinder Singh, GOC, 14 Corps, was Maj Gen Liu Lin, commander of South Xinjiang Military Region. The Chinese appointing an officer one rank junior to meet/confer with Lt Gen Singh was a clear move aimed as an insult-unbecoming but not surprising. They addressed the ongoing tussle in Eastern Ladakh over the heavy military build-up by the PLA along the LAC there. This was soon followed by another Maj Gen level meeting.

On June 09, 2020, it was reported that PLA's process of moving back had begun but only in the areas around patrolling points 14 and 15 in Galwan Valley and another in the Hot Spring area, but not in Pangong Tso.

On June 15, 2020, it was this process that Col Babu and a detachment of 16 Bihar were overseeing, when the PLA troops attacked with the deadly crude weapons mentioned earlier. In doing so the PLA adhered to its post-1967 Sikkim skirmishes method of not using firearms against Indian Army, but resorting to medieval methods and yet again violating/neutralising every agreement for peace and tranquillity on the LAC since the past many decades, including Wuhan and Mamallapuram, or for that matter, any discussions by India's 14 Corps Commander on June 06, 2020 or thereafter by Maj Gens.

The fact that such moves were made against India during the peak period of Covid19's worldwide contamination only confirmed that China is aiming at total world dominance-both economic and military. While militarily, India has been a thorn in China's side, with the countrywide anti-China sentiment building up on the streets in India as the 20 brave soldiers last rites were being seen on tv screens, China felt the economic sting too.

The May 2020 and much more so in June 2020 Chinese attacks amply indicated that China intended to continue its hegemony with more force and try to change the status quo of the LAC by driving out Indian troops from some of their locations well within Indian territory.

The CCP-PLA had obviously planned this major attempt to change the status quo on the LAC by also involving Pakistan and Nepal, which gave New Delhi an unpleasant surprise of cartographic changes including Lipulekh etc. That too is an old Chinese ploy of beginning hegemony. Pakistan in any case is China's long-term lackey and may already have been part of its grand plan. It has kept India's security forces quite busy in Union Territory Jammu & Kashmir.

The gloves were indeed off. It was also a reminder that New Delhi must ensure that Indian Army's mountain corps be made fully ready for foiling further Chinese military moves. While PLA may be feeling gung-ho about launching land-grabbing moves, Indian Army must be allowed to respond to PLA in the "language that it best understands"- like at Nathu La (1967) with use of firearms or at Sumdorong Chu (1986-87) without use of firearms. CCP-PLA must also keep in mind that PLA has for many decades been an optically grand but un-blooded army.

PLA finally got blooded-literally-after 53 years on the night of June 15-16, 2020, when their soldiers killed 20 Indian troops and then lost many more when group of Indian Army's soldiers of 16 Bihar along with Punjab, Mahar and Artillery regiments counter attacked them at Galwan. This will not be forgotten by PLA in a hurry.

"A part of the "China dream" is the establishment of a "unified global system", or empire, termed tianxia ("all under heaven" in Mandarin). Translating its enormous economic gains into coercive military power, China expects neighbouring nations to submit to its hegemony," stated former Naval Chief Admiral Arun Prakash in an article titled 'India will Need to bring order, alacrity to crisis management', widely published on June 25, 2020.

There seems no doubt that what transpired from early May, 2020, on the India-China Line of Actual Control (LAC) was part of the Chinese Communist Party (CCP)-Peoples' Liberation Army (PLA) combo's plan to be implemented taking advantage of the effects of the dirty and dangerous virus released from China's Wuhan Institute of Virology, which reached 214 countries and territories and shattered economies all over.

Following Indian Army's deadly response to Chinese People's Liberation Army (PLA) upping the ante at Nathu La and Cho La in Sikkim, in 1967, resulting in short of four hundred of its soldiers killed and a convoy of vehicles and many bunkers destroyed, the Chinese decided to settle all breaches of the perception-based and disputed Sino-Indian border termed as the Line of Actual Control (LAC), by discussion and not resorting to the use of force/firearms. In fact, the Chinese very smartly got this clause of not using firearms included in the second agreement in1996 on "peace and tranquillity" along the LAC. The first agreement was 1993, the 3rd, 4th and 5th ones were in 2005, 2012 and 2014 respectively. Except for ambushing and killing four riflemen of India's first and oldest paramilitary force, Assam Rifles at Tulung La in 1975 - not by bullets but by torture - PLA steadfastly continued its intrusions/incursions/transgressions/"straying" across the LAC, for almost 53 years till May-June 2020, including large scale ones at Sumdurong Chu in 1986-87 and Doklam in 2017, all of which were resolved by discussion and no use of firearms.

According to a US News report of July 13, 2020, the Chinese Ministry of Civil Affairs told families of those who died in the June 15-16, 2021 Galwan Valley clash that they must forgo traditional burial ceremonies and cremate the soldiers' remains and that any funeral services should be conducted remotely and not in person. Though the government has used the threat posed by the spread of the coronavirus as a pretext, the assessment concludes that the new rules are a part of a deliberate effort by Beijing to undermine public awareness and erase any enduring reminders of the violent clash.

The June 15 barbaric attack was because of Indian Army overseeing/verifying PLA's disengagement, which was not being adhered to as agreed upon in the first Corps Commander level meeting at Moldo on June 06, 2020. What also emerged was PLA's massive staging forward in many locations along the LAC. This was countered by Indian Army's mirror deployment.

After many meetings, with the corps commander level ones lasting as long as 15 hours - thanks to the Chinese - and discussions between lesser level military commanders and diplomats, a process of PLA disengaging reportedly began but still remains incomplete as PLA is not agreeing to back off at Pangong Tso.

With over five decades of trust having become a serious casualty and knowing the history of the CCP-PLA combo's hegemonic compulsions/perception of the Chinese being destined to dominate the world, even if a full-fledged withdrawal is effected by PLA, there is no guarantee that the same forward deployment will not be tried again. If so, with all the strategic infrastructure developed on the Chinese side and the terrain, the time required for PLA to stage forward will be much less than that for Indian Army.

While PLA's plans/intentions were implemented with bloody fatal effect in Galwan on June 15, when it initiated non-fatal violence at Daulat Beg Oldie and Pangong Tso (all in Eastern Ladakh) and at Naku La in Sikkim between May 05 and 09, 2020. Chinese troops were seen carrying iron rods in their haversacks even up to ten days later in East Kameng district, Arunachal Pradesh, although no violence was reported there. All these reports only pointed towards protocol about no use of force being violated by PLA as part of a premeditated plan. Technically, firearms were not used, but "peace and tranquillity" was shattered by PLA.

India's stand was very clear – status quo ante as in April 2010. While both Prime Minister Narendra Modi's July 03 visit followed up by Defence Minister Rajnath Singh's visit coinciding with Indian Army's exercise including a parachute drop and movement of tanks, were also meant to send a message to the Chinese, New Delhi must always be mindful of Beijing's ambitious plans, deviousness and doggedness and expedite all measures to make good long-standing deficiencies/urgent operational requirements. Lessons from the past must be learnt and factored into India's diplomacy and defence planning meaningfully/effectively.

Even if PLA does get back to April 2020 status of deployment, it will have to be watched hawk-like, because its aim is to occupy all commanding heights and tri-junctions. The Army's task of monitoring will be much more effective if Central strategic intelligence, is consistently shared with it. Incidents like losing twenty Indian Army braves on June 15 can possibly be avoided. And another important reason to keep the Army updated on PLA's movements and locations is that it even if it disengages and de-escalates by reverting to its April 2020 deployment, the possibility of it repeating such a staging forward again cannot at all be ruled out.

It must be recalled as brought out by Lt Gen P.G. Kamath in his article, *China Lies and India Believes: The Road Ahead*. "Look at Doklam Plateau; though we have not allowed them to build a road from Batang La to Gyemochen, Chinese have occupied the whole of the Bhutanese plateau of 89 sq km and have built an alternative road further east of the road that we had stopped. India can keep thumping its chest but the Chinese have stolen a march and are closer to the plains of India."

(https://www.linkedin.com/pulse/china-lies-india-believes-road-ahead-lt-gen-p-g-kamath/)

In late 2019, the Indo Tibetan Border Police (ITBP), under Ministry of Home Affairs, was enhanced by forming two commands at Chandigarh and Guwahati under additional director generals for better operational functioning of about 35-38 battalions deployed along the LAC, from Ladakh to Arunachal Pradesh. Interacting with this writer, Lt Gen J.S. Bajwa (Retd), author of *Modernisation of the PLA* (Lancer) and some other officers who have served on the LAC advised that all ITBP battalions deployed in the active sectors of the LAC must be fully under operational control of the Army. It may be relevant to quote an excerpt of a letter in July 2020 to the President, PM, Defence Minister and Services Chiefs by 144 veterans: "Over the decades, a substantial portion of the Army has been continuously deployed in its secondary role on internal security and counter-insurgency duties, at the cost of availability of troops for the Army's primary role of defence of territorial sovereignty. At the same time, large strength of the Central Armed Police Forces (CAPFs) are deployed in border areas in an essentially military role. This anomalous reversal of roles and duties now demands rationalization for efficiency and effectiveness in both internal and external national security".

In view of the CCP-PLA combo's plans and aims mentioned, New Delhi must take serious note of its over seven decades of history replete with thousands of hegemonic attempts and lies and the weak/conciliatory stance of Nehru and the Congress party, and the meaningless agreements since Panchsheel till date. The only exceptions were Lal Bahadur Shastri's assertiveness during the 1965 war against Pakistan and Indira Gandhi's assertiveness in 1967 against China and in 1971 against Pakistan. New Delhi must now evolve an assertive policy to be followed consistently, repeat, assertively and consistently, both on terrain and table.

Having gobbled territory of many of its former neighbours in the past and now having contaminated the world, it now poses a great threat to India's integrity. China's hegemonic greed is not only for India's land but also for the sweet water rivers that flow on it, for making microprocessors. Iqbal Chand Malhotra in his article *Smoking*

Mirrors: The illusion of the LAC, published in timesnownews.com, June 09, 2020, states, "For China, this water can only be harnessed from the Himalayas and the Karakorum's rivers. It has invested around US$ 25 billion to build five dams on the Indus River in PoK (Pakistan Occupied Kashmir) with water storage reservoirs of over 225 km in length."

It is high time the Chinese political and military leadership are made to realise that chronic hegemonism and doggedness in constantly trying to crawl and clutch Indian territories is not going to work anymore and that the LAC must be clarified.

While New Delhi made a beginning in striking economically against China by banning over a hundred apps and cancelling contracts, public sentiment against Chinese goods has shot up. Apart from burning Xi Jinping's posters, Indian shopkeepers refused to sell Chinese made Rakhis (decorative wrist bands) during the festival of Raksha Bandhan in August 2020. The economic stakes must be raised as high as possible. Sonam Wangchuk's overview of China is indeed worth knowing widely. His audio-visual presentation in very good Hindi is an incisive analysis of China in the post Covid stage, recommended that India beat bullet power with wallet power and boycott all Chinese goods-software within one week and hardware within one year.

India must also become politically and diplomatically far more aggressive. It must take on China for grabbing Tibet, its illegal occupation of Indian territories so far, its suppression and torture of Uighurs and most of all, its irresponsible 'experimentation' and use of biological warfare.

On the LAC, New Delhi must shed any hangover of Nehruvian tendencies and be prepared to be not always reactive but effectively proactive also. The mountain corps must be fully equipped. If more light tanks and aircraft or any other weaponry are required, some readymade ones should be speed-purchased.

For India's very survival and progress, it is time to change its narrative and power on land, air and sea. While Indian soldiers taught their Chinese counterparts a deadly lesson without firearms on the night of July 15-16, 2020, PLA will be well advised to desist from any more misadventures - without or with firearms.

After exactly 53 years since September 1967, of being reactive on the ground to thousands of moves/attempts by China's People's Liberation Army (PLA) trying its monkey tricks to grab India's land, Indian Army finally responded with some unprecedented "redeployment of troops" on the Line of Actual Control (LAC) to evict the PLA from some key heights and tactically advantageous positions and occupy them. To say the least, the Chinese were shocked as they saw a reversal of roles.

For over six decades the Chinese always bullied on the table and bulldozed on terrain, always grabbing or nibbling to grab further chunks of Indian territory. Many parts of current China were independent sovereign nations, the largest being Tibet. In fact, all of the India-China boundary is what China captured and refers to as Tibet Autonomous Region.

An official press release stated that on the night of 29/30 August 2020, PLA troops violated the previous consensus arrived at during military and diplomatic engagements during the ongoing standoff in Eastern Ladakh and carried out provocative military movements to change the status quo. Indian troops pre-empted this PLA activity on the Southern Bank of Pangong Tso Lake, undertook measures to strengthen our positions and thwart Chinese intentions to unilaterally change facts on ground. The Indian Army is committed to maintaining peace and tranquillity through dialogue, but is also equally determined to protect its territorial integrity. Till September 03, 2020, four Brigade Commander level Flag Meetings failed to resolve the issues.

It has been seen over seven decades that talks are an old trick of the Chinese Communist Party (CCP) and PLA combo, with the aim of buying time and not very often following any agreement. Nonetheless, the Indian government and Indian Army have always been amenable to talks for the sake of peace and tranquillity, even so after PLA shattered every peace agreement from May 05 to June 15, 2020. Lies, deception and total disregard of signed agreements have been part of the CCP-PLA combo's standard operating procedure or rather, its very philosophy.

Ever since the PLA freaked out-in May 2020-Indian Army was rather reticent in sharing some realities, that too at a time when some much overdue and never before like decisions and actions were taken, shocking the Chinese like never before and breaking the jinx of Indian Army only reacting and that too with one hand tied behind the back.

Col Danvir Singh (Retd), Associate Editor, *Indian Defence Review*, who served as a Company Commander in the Chushul Garrison in 2004-2005, needs to be thanked for an elaborated version of what transpired after before and after August 29, 2020, which shocked PLA like never before and surprised the world.

In early August 2020, the newly inducted Mountain Division including Tibetan troops of the Special Frontier Force (SFF), was fully acclimatized. They had begun reconnaissance and validated their offensive plans which were so secret that even the holding formation troops were unaware of what was going on. Options were carefully drawn and diligently vetted.

By 24 August 2020 one plan was finally given the go ahead. The plan involved the retaking of certain commanding heights by evicting the Chinese forces.

Simultaneously, Chief of Defence Staff, General Bipin Rawat cautioned the nation to stay prepared for any eventuality, even if that meant war.

The final phase of the retaking the objectives was planned to be completed in 120 minutes flat. Tanks, artillery guns/missiles and air defence were all well poised to counter and destroy any PLA attempt to thrust into the Chushul valley. Air defence troops were also deployed with shoulder fired anti-aircraft Igla missiles, networked and coordinated to shoot down any Chinese aircraft interfering with our advancing troops.

The Chinese on their side had their mechanized combat team located in Spangur near Moldo. They had 33-ton T15 light tanks designed to fight a battle in this high-altitude region. The Indian troops, fully geared for action, with all ends tied, contingencies catered for and rehearsed were ready to strike. Their objective was Spangur Bowl, an area south of Pangong and east of Chushul.

The features dominating the Spangur gap provided great tactical dominance and huge strategic advantages were Black Top, Helmet, Magar and Gurung Hills stretching right up to Rezang La. Under cover of darkness, Indian infiltrating troops moved up to the LAC, established their release points and waited for the green signal. Some troops mounted on high mobility vehicles drove straight up to the objective—the 3 km ridgeline on the hill alongside Requin.

At the word go, these troops crossed over into the enemy claimed territory with lightning speed and occupied the hill features, beating their own planned timings well under 120 minutes. Before dawn, one complete infantry brigade with over 2,000 troops was holding the heights overlooking the Spangur Bowl. Armed with French Milan anti-tank missiles and Carl Gustav rocket launchers, Indian troops had literally rendered the Chinese armoured tanks at Moldo redundant and out manoeuvred. On 31 August, the Chinese garrison at Moldo was virtually under siege.

When the greatly shocked Chinese mustered their club wielding troops and advanced towards the positions now held by Indians Army, more shocks awaited them. The Indian troops warned the advancing PLA men, who continued with their advance. The Indian troops fired a few warning shots in the air and the Chinese, seeing the aggressive posture, fled, only to return a little later.

This time they came with their armoured personnel carriers, driving on their cemented road from Moldo to Rezang La. But this advance also came to a halt and was followed by a hasty retreat because the Indian troops were at a stone's throw from the Moldo garrison, dominating each and every move of the PLA. The sight of anti-tank missiles and rocket launchers deterred the move of the Chinese armoured personnel carrier and halted them in their tracks.

The Chinese had realised that not only were they outnumbered but totally out-flanked, making their position untenable. Any armed clash hereafter would prove suicidal. The annihilation of Moldo garrison was assured for the Chinese had clashes erupted. The Indians by now were firmly dug in.

Subedar Nyima Tenzin of the SFF died on August 30 when he

stepped on a mine near the south bank of **Pangong Tso** during the action of occupying the strategic heights. Sending a strong message to China, BJP general secretary Ram Madhav attended Subedar Tenzin's funeral conducted with full military honours.

Army Chief Gen MM Naravane, who toured Ladakh from 02 to 04 September, said the situation along the Line of Actual Control (LAC) is "tense" but added that the nation can count on the Chief of the Air Staff, Air Chief Marshal RKS Bhadauria, visited frontline air bases in Eastern Air Command on 02 September 2020. Respective Air Officers Commanding apprised him of the readiness state and operational preparedness of the combat units under their command. The Air Chief also met and interacted with air warriors serving in these units and lauded the focussed efforts by the station personnel towards maintaining proficiency in all roles envisaged and urged them to continue performing their duty with due diligence.

Following PLA's gross violation of all India-China peace agreements on 15 June 2020 by brutally killing 20 Indian Army personnel and Indian Army's quick fierce revenge attack without firearms, killing 3 or 4 times more PLA soldiers, PLA air force fighter aircraft and helicopter activities heightened along the LAC. Its fighters and strategic bombers staged forward and were detected flying near the Indian territory maintaining the 10 km plus distance from the boundary. Chinese helicopters had been flying their very close to the LAC in all the troubled sectors including the Sub Sector North (Daulat Beg Oldie sector), Galwan valley near Patrolling Point 14, Patrolling Point 15, Patrolling Point 17 and 17A (Hot Springs area), Pangong Tso and Fingers area.

This was countered by deployment of India's quick reaction air defence missile including the Akash missile, which can take down very fast-moving combat aircraft and drones in few seconds. Many modifications and upgrades have already been done in it to make it suitable for deployment in the high mountainous terrain. IAF's fighter aircrafts have also been very active in the Eastern Ladakh area. The surveillance gaps have also been plugged and no enemy aircraft would be able to go undetected India's forces. Soon after the Chinese transgression into Indian territory in early May 2020 and their aircraft began entering very close to Indian air space and frequently up to their claim lines in the Ladakh sector including a construction site close to the Galwan valley, IAF sent its Su-30MKIs to Eastern Ladakh, where formidable air defence systems of both Indian Army and IAF have been to prevent any misadventure by PLA or/and its air force. It was also reported that India would very shortly after acquiring a highly capable air defence system from a friendly country which can be deployed and the entire area can be taken care off to prevent any enemy flying there.

When General Wei Fenghe, State Councillor and Defence Minister of China, made urgent requests, or as the media put it "begged India for talks", Defence Minister Rajnath Singh met him on September 04, 2020, in Moscow on the side-lines of the Shanghai Cooperation Organisation (SCO) meeting.

In the two and a half hours meeting Mr. Singh categorically conveyed India's position on the developments along the LAC including at Galwan valley in the last few months and emphasised that the actions of PLA, including amassing of large number of troops, their aggressive behaviour and attempts to unilaterally alter the status quo violated the bilateral agreements and was not in keeping with the understandings reached between the Special Representatives of two sides. The Indian Defence Minister stated clearly that while the Indian troops had always taken a very responsible approach towards border management, there should be no doubt about our determination to protect India's sovereignty and territorial integrity. Given the CCP-PLA combo's record of reneging on all past peace and tranquillity agreements, lies, deceit, sustained attempts at bullying India till some years ago and this meeting full of platitudes by Gen Fenghe, the immediate future of the stand-off or talks appears to be bleak. While China has specialised in projection/propaganda of its military being powerful in numbers weapons and equipment, it should not be opting for an armed confrontation/war. Indian Armed Forces are preparing for the worst and if push comes to shove, it may not be wrong at all to predict that losses on China will be heavy. Meanwhile the least India can expect is an extended eyeball to eyeball stand-off, but, for a change, with Indian Army being on some commanding heights.

Rattled like never before, on September 06, 2020, Chinese troops attempted to approach Indian troops, but could not do anything except firing shots in the air, while Chinese government and the media it controls made a great issue and again, lying.

In ten months since China launched a dirty and dangerous biological weapon aimed at contaminating the world, surveillance systems have detected some of its military moves.

Satellite images showed how Kailash Manasarovar, a venerated place of religious pilgrimage for Hindus now resembled a battle zone with heavy military presence. This was reported in Defence News on August 23, 2020 and it was added that China's enhancement of military facilities near Mount Kailash included deployment of surface-to-air missiles (SAM) with fresh constructions that started in April 2020 being completed by September 2020. Mount Kailash and many areas along Manasarovar, including Rakshastal and Gauri Kund, are revered by Hindus and Buddhists. Satellite images from August 16, 2020 indicated possibly, HQ-9 SAM system under tarpaulin covers. This also amounts to desecration and defacing or destruction also of the holy site.

A TV news network showed visuals of young Chinese soldiers sitting in a bus crying, reportedly on their way to the Sino-Indian Line of Actual Control (LAC), juxtaposed by Indian soldiers playing kabaddi in 3 feet of snow, somewhere near the LAC. The Chinese soldiers, mostly single children of their parents owing to Chinese Communist Party's dictat, were most likely ccrying as they had heard of the fate of their senior comrades in Galwan valley on June 15-16, 2020. This video was reportedly released by Taiwan and was stoutly denied by China's state – controlled mouth piece, *Global Times*.

That was the day when Chinese troops broke all agreements for peace and tranquillity and also broke all records of military confrontation by killing 20 Indian soldiers including their battalion commander on June 15 2020, by using, not firearms, but medieval barbaric weapons. The intense revenge counter-attack by Indian soldiers shortly thereafter resulted in 3 or 4 times more Chinese soldiers being killed without use of firearms and 14 Chinese soldiers being barehandedly thrown into the freezing waters of the Galwan river by a single young Indian Army brave-heart Gurtej Singh, who also died. Some Chinese personnel were captured too. Earlier on June 05 and 09,

2020, Chinese troops resorted to stoning and attacking with medieval weapons at East Ladakh and Naku La (pass), Sikkim respectively, injuring over 100 Indian soldiers, but with none killed. But even then, PLA violated the spirit of all past agreements.

The other unexpected and unprecedented rude shock to PLA was when some commanding new heights were occupied by Indian Army - including its Tibetan troops of Special Frontier Force for the first time since its raising in 1962 - between August 29 and the second week of September include Magar Hill, Gurung Hill, Recehen La, Rezang La, Mokhpari and the dominating height over Chinese positions near Finger 4. After being shocked again, PLA, is frustrated like never before and reportedly been forced to plan for its troops to spend the coming snow-filled winter facing the Indian Army troops.

Before and after these incidents there were many rounds of talks between military commanders. The corps commander level meet on September 21 which reportedly went on for fourteen hours was also unconclusive. Talks between Prime Minister Narendra Modi and President Xi Jinping, which, viewed retrospectively, amount to China making a mockery of them. When PM Modi was hosting Xi and his wife at the Sabarmati riverfront, Chinese troops had intruded into Chumar. And the greatest irony is Xi inviting PM Modi to Wuhan, from where, China launched its biological attack on the world. During the foreign and defence ministers meetings in September 2020, the Indian Ministers stated whatever the Chinese had done/should not have done, but both meetings were inconclusive.

The brigadier-level talks between Indian and Chinese armies on September 07, 2020, led to much heat from both sides and resulted in their deciding against holding in-person talks. Both the military commanders then exchanged heated arguments over the hotline. This was on September 8, 2020, a day after Chinese soldiers attempted to dislodge Indian forces which occupied strategic heights in Mukhpari peak and Rezang La areas in Ladakh on the night of August 29-30, 2020. PLA's attempts to dislodge Indian soldiers on the newly occupied heights by its group of soldiers armed with staves and firearms were thwarted. The heated exchange on the hotline was over Chinese troops' attempt to approach Mukhpari Peak, dominated by Indian forces as well as the PLA's use of medieval weaponry.

What emerged from a look back at the talks mentioned and those from 1993 till 2020, both politico-diplomatic and military, including maybe thousands of talks held by commanders on ground from 1967 till 2020 is the characteristic lies, deceit, utter lack of sincerity, bullying attitude and an unending greed for land, particularly that with valuable natural resources, which makes them to continuously keep creeping across the LAC, about which they refuse to declare their claim lines. Not declaring their claim lies, suits PLA so that it can try to claim any area based on Chinese perception. Some Indian Army veterans who faced the monkey tricks of PLA during their service believe, this unresolved border should be referred to as the Line of Existing Control, not 'Actual' control.

The 1981 parallel track policy of working to build harmonious ties even as the two countries sort out the boundary issue has not paid any dividends to India. Instead, India has lost territory since then, letting 65 patrolling points defined by the China Study Group in 1976 turn into the de facto LAC in Ladakh. The patrolling points are well within the Indian perception of the LAC but the movement of the Indian forces to these points has been curtailed by the presence of Chinese troops, face-offs with PLA patrolling parties and on occasions, the harsh weather and mountainous terrain.

It is under the guise of a summer exercise that PLA marshalled a large force with all supporting units of tanks, guns, missiles etc and used it Galwan, and Pangong Tso, in June 2020 after Depsang and Daulat Beg Oldie in May 2020.

PLA showed no intentions of disengaging or de-escalating. In fact, it frustrated and feverishly proceeded with efforts to grab parts of Bhutan.

With the after effect on PLA's morale by Indian Army's revenge counter attack on June 15-16, 2020, at Galwan and the unprecedented occupation of commanding heights since August 29, 2020, raising India's bargaining leverage substantially, India must press forward till mid-October 2020/till the snows set in, to occupy even more such positions. And simultaneously India must assertively begin using all cards against China, from Aksai Chin onwards at least. India should refuse to hold any further talks with China till it does not relent. This is the time after seven decades when India must begin to keep rubbing China with all that it has done by way of bullying India during the decades of India's Congress government rule - except for Prime Ministers Lal Bahadur Shastri (1965) and Indira Gandhi (1967 at Nathu La/Cho La and 1971) - till mid-2014 being too soft and ever-bending. While the BJP government has been assertive relatively, it needs to go quite a bit further to ensure that the post August 29, 2020 gains are maintained and not frittered away by falling back as a result of any further/future talks. It is critically important to break the Nehruvian jinx of not using force when required and when it would have been effective, or not using enough of it and now determinedly take on all issues to change the narrative with China. Given China's military intentions and aim, taking advantage of the pandemic, which it engineered, it is vital for India to take proactive and powerful measures to ensure its security and integrity.

Indian Army's post-August 29, moves were going to force PLA into camping the 2020-21 winter with extra clothing and equipment. If the Chinese leadership was pig headed enough to think it could pitch PLA into a winter war, which today is technologically possible, it would only mean a heavy price to pay by way of body-bags and its economy. While Indian Army troops are quite used to extreme cold climate and are quite adept at maintaining tanks in such temperature conditions, PLA soldiers may find the going a bit tough to put it mildly.

It got quite amply proved in 1967 in Sikkim and again in 2020 in Eastern Ladakh that PLA is not made of super-soldiers. On June 15-16, when Indian soldiers counter attacked them, many of them were reportedly howling in pain and fear, shocked at the fierceness and physical strength of their attackers. But what was achieved on August 29-30, 2021 and which shocked CPC-PLA was historically unprecedented. It also was the result of a huge logistic process involving massive movement of men and materials by air and land.

At a time when Defence Ministry and Indian Army were quite reticent in sharing details about the Army's operational movements, one of the precautions to maintain complete secrecy for achieving total surprise against the enemy, on September 27, 2020, ANI aired a briefing by Maj Gen Arvind Kapoor, Chief of Staff of the Corps in Eastern

Ladakh. All areas of the Ladakh range fall in the highest mountainous regions. The region receives heavy snowfall during the month of November. Apart from this, the minimum temperature here reaches around –30 to –40 degrees. In these cold conditions, many times the roads connecting Ladakh are also closed. Kapoor informed how well the Army was ready for deployment in winters, with stocks essential supplies, greatly improved living conditions and that all our troops and equipment are well prepared, no matter how difficult the weather is. Briefly referring to deployment of tanks at such high altitude and their effectiveness, he added that with this deployment, India had given a clear message to China that in the event of war it will not refrain from entering its occupied territory.

By end of January 2021, it became obvious that CPC-PLA were feverishly trying for a disengagement with a major aim of making Indian Army vacate Kailash Range.

On February 11, 2021, Defence Minister Rajnath Singh reportedly informed the Rajya Sabha that the disengagement agreed to in the North and South Bank of the Pangong lake includes: both sides to cease their forward deployments in a phased, coordinated and verified manner; Chinese troop presence in the North Bank to continue east of Finger 8; Indian troops to be at Dhan Singh Thapa Post near Finger 3; similar action to be taken in the South Bank by both sides; structures built by both sides since April 2020 on both banks to be removed and landforms restored; temporary moratorium on military activities by both sides in the North Bank including patrolling; patrolling to be resumed only when both sides reach a subsequent agreement, and; implementation of the agreement will substantially restore the situation to that existing prior to commencement of the standoff last year. He also made it clear that there are outstanding problems to be addressed, including at Hot Springs, Gogra and Depsang, which would be taken up within 48 hrs of the completion of the Pangong Tso disengagement.

Defence Ministry issued a statement conveying that some misinformed and misleading comments were being amplified in the media and on social media about the disengagement at Pangong Tso. Any allusion that Indian territory is up to Finger 4 is categorically false. India's territory is as depicted by the map of India and includes more than 43,000 sq km currently under illegal occupation of China since 1962. Even the Line of Actual Control (LAC), as per the Indian perception, is at Finger 8, not at Finger 4. That is why India has persistently maintained the right to patrol up to Finger 8, including in the current understanding with China. Permanent posts of both sides at the north bank of Pangong Tso are longstanding and well-established. On the Indian side, it is Dhan Singh Thapa Post near Finger 3 and on the Chinese side, east of Finger 8. The current agreement provides for cessation of forward deployment by both sides and continued deployment at these permanent posts. The statement ended by asserting that India has not conceded any territory as a result of this agreement. Contrarily, it has scrupulously respected the LAC and prevented any unilateral change in the status quo.

In an article titled "Blurring The All-Important Line: The Faux Pas of Ladakh Disengagement", in news18 opinion, dated February 13, 2021, Lt Gen Prakash Katoch (retd) stated that it is quite evident that China has effectively shifted the LAC westwards and any so-called buffer zones will also be in Indian territory to the advantage of the PLA. He further stated that if disengagement was to be discussed in a phased manner, we should have ensured that Depsang got the top priority given its strategic importance and the fact that the PLA is lodged 20 km deep at the Y-Junction where it had also intruded in 2013 and the issue was discussed then in Parliament.

Katoch further stated: "Agreeing to vacate Kailash Range, hilltops covering the Spanggur Gap and heights around Chushul that are dominating PLA's Moldo Garrison is a strategic blunder for which India may pay dearly in future. We don't seem to have learned any lessons from the return of the Haji Pir Pass to Pakistan (1966). For China it is a masterstroke, especially without any discussion on disengagement in Depsang and other friction points. These were what gave India an edge, as mentioned by Rajnath Singh. So why give up this edge before discussing overall disengagement? The proposed moratorium to recommence patrolling may take a few months as it will only be discussed after complete disengagement has been effected. Till then, our troops will not be able to patrol east of Finger 3 in the North Bank of Pangong lake. With the PLA at the Y-Junction in Depsang, the ITBP stopped patrolling to Patrol Point (PP) 10, 11, 11A, 12 and 13 – all of which are short of the LAC. Other friction points include PP14 in Galwan Valley, PP15 in Hot Springs and PP17A in Gogra Post area".

Even after the disengagement began, Army Chief Gen MM Naravane reportedly stated that China's rising footprint in India's neighbourhood and its attempts to unilaterally alter the status quo along disputed borders, led to confrontation and mutual distrust. He also expressed his apprehensions about the then recent shift by the US, which allowed China to "leverage" against India and that China was also expected to involve Pakistan further against India.

On February 19, 2021, it was reported that disengagement North and South banks of the Pangong Lake had been completed, From the South bank, the Chinese withdrew 130-140 tanks, 30 artillery guns and about 2,000 troops. From the North Bank, where there were no tanks, they withdrew 4000-5000 troops and 30 artillery guns. While the alacrity and completeness of this phase of disengagement by the Chinese is indeed a surprise, it remained to be seen what would ensue after the next commanders' meeting and there remained no doubt that the Chinese would have to be watched sharply 24x7.

On July 31, 2021, the 12th round of corps-commander-level talks between India and China, which were held at the Chushul-Moldo meeting point on the Chinese side of the LAC. By August 05, 2021, Indian Army and PLA completed troop disengagement from the Gogra area of eastern Ladakh, after 15 months of a "sensitive face-off". As reported by The Print, the disengagement process included removal of all temporary structures and other allied infrastructure by both sides, and restoration of landform to pre-stand-off period. Defence Ministry/ Army sources were cited stating that while this disengagement process, which was first initiated in the area in 2020 but not completed by China, a buffer zone has been created in which no patrolling will take place in the area "in the foreseeable future".

Lt Gen Prakash Katoch, wrote in Strategic Affairs India that according to news reports of August 25, 2021, India and China are to soon have the 13th round of Corps Commander-level talks to address the friction point (pseudonym for PLA intrusion) at Hot Springs. The report, however, said that an invite was being sent to the Chinese for the fresh round of talks to address the dispute in the Hot Springs area, which meant that its approval depended on whims and fancies of China. The news report further said that this would be the "last" of the new friction points to be resolved that emerged post-May 2020.

There seemed no mention of Depsang and Demchok. Depsang is the deepest PLA intrusion across the Line of Actual Control (LAC) where the PLA is not permitting Indian patrols to go to the locations of their protective patrols (PP) which themselves are short of the LAC.

Tsewang Dorji, research fellow at the Tibet Policy Institute in Dharamsala. maintains that in future whatever happens inside Tibet may matter for the Indian security environment and also that of Asia as well. In his article, courtesy BDL, June 21, 2021, he stated: that for past few years the People's Liberation Army of China has enhanced its technological capabilities and has conducted various live-fire military exercises along the Himalayan border.[1] Since 2015 the military exercises near border increased and as Xi came to power a major reorganisation of PLA was done in 2015 and seven military regions were reorganised into five theatre commands.[2]

From that time there were intensive military exercises including different theatre commands. Satellites images also proved that "PLA Has been actively upgrading its military infrastructure" and increased transport network and military infrastructure across Tibet bordering India, while pressurising India to halt its road construction in Galwan valley and Pangong Tso.[3]

Six decades ago George Ginsburgs and Michael Mathos stated that Tibet is the most important part strategically and "he who holds Tibet dominates the Himalayas piedmont; he who dominates the Himalaya piedmont threatens the Indian subcontinent; and he who threatens the Indian subcontinent may well have all of South Asia within his reach and, with it, all of Asia."[4]

For the past few years, the People's Liberation Army (PLA) has upgraded its high-tech weapons and conducted a series of live-fire military exercises along the Himalayan borders and in Tibet. For Instance, *Global Times* reported on 5 January, 2020 that "China's latest weapons including the Type 15 tank and the new 155-millimeter vehicle-mounted Howitzer were deployed in Southwest China's Tibet Autonomous Region as the People's Liberation Army (PLA) began a first round of exercises in 2020...".

After Xi Jinping came to power, a major reorganisation of the PLA was carried out in 2015 and later in February 2016, the seven military regions were reorganised into five theatre commands. During the official flag-conferring ceremony held in Beijing on 1 February, 2016, Xi, also chairman of the Central Military Commission (CMC), "urged the theatre commands to improve their ability to command and strengthen joint command and action to complete the tasks of routine combat readiness and military actions".

Since then, there have been different intensive military exercises which also involved joint military exercises between different theatre commands, including the Western Theatre Command, which overlooks the security of East Turkestan (Xinjiang) and Tibet. All this centralisation of the command system indicates that China is planning to create a new front in the Indo-Tibet border. n other words, China's growing number of military exercises in Tibet increases the threat that India faces.

During the military and diplomatic stand-off along the LAC on the Galwan Valley in June last year, despite pursuing a negotiation with India, satellite images proved that the PLA has been actively upgrading its military infrastructure. While pressuring India to stop the construction of roads in the Galwan Valley and Pangong Tso, China continues to develop an enhanced transport network and military infrastructure across Tibet bordering India.

This was further proved by the satellite images released by the space technology company Maxar. The structures consisting of bunkers, tents and storage units for military hardware built by the PLA overlooking the Galwan River were not visible in aerial photographs earlier in June. Hence, in dealing with India, there is a dualistic approach from Communist China.

It was reported in *Hindustan Times* on 20 November, 2020 that "Military commanders and national security planners who spoke on condition of anonymity said that over the past month they noticed the

PLA engage in road construction at Churup village right across Kaurik pass in the central sector and that it has placed new container housing modules around Tunjum La, north of the contested Barahoti plains in Uttarakhand, just 4 km from the 565 km LAC in Himachal Pradesh and Uttarakhand".

However, the construction of a road right across Kaurik pass threatens the security of India. Not only this, the existence of the East Turkestan-Tibet highway, which is closer to Kaurik pass, is one of the important strategic roads for the deployments of PLA's soldiers and military hardware during the time of 1962 border war with India.

On May 29, 2021, Chief Minister of Himachal Pradesh Jai Ram Thakur along with Director-General of Police Sanjay Kundu visited the forward areas of Lepcha in Kinnaur and Lahaul-Spiti districts. companied by cabinet minister Dr Ram Lal Markanda, after the inspection, the chief minister was quoted in *Outlook* as saying, "It's true that China is building roads and ramping up other infrastructural projects along the state's borders in the Tibet region. It appears China is planning to set up its surveillance network at some vantage point which is located at a higher elevation so as to keep an eye on our side of the borders".

These continuous Chinese infrastructure developments on the Tibetan Plateau further confirm the importance of Tibet.

From a strategic point of view, Himachal Pradesh is important because it shares a 260-kilometre-long porous border with Tibet in Kinnaur, Lahaul and Spiti districts. Of the total border length, 140 kilometres lie in the Kinnaur district, while 80 kilometres come under Lahaul and Spiti districts. In addition to this, the outfitting of 5G at the radar station in Tibet will further enhance the military communications and support a sprawling network for the rapid deployment of army and weapons along the India-Tibet border.

For the past decade, in the name of poverty-alleviation programmes, nearly 266,000 Tibetan nomads and farmers have been transferred into 960 new relocations near Tibet's border with India. The long-term plan of these mass relocation programes is to occupy and safeguard the Tibet border. Moreover, in Tibet, the party-state has systematically connected the major isolated border villages to highways and most of the border villages are now brought under the centralised surveillance system network.

In 2017, Communist China released its plan for the 'Construction of Villages of Moderate Prosperity in Border Areas (2017-2020)'. The objective of this plan is guided by Xi's governing strategy for Tibet: "[To] govern the country well we must first govern the frontiers well, and to govern the frontiers well we must first ensure the stability of Tibet".

Despite the 11 rounds of talks between Corps Commander-level between India and China over the Indo-Tibet border, China hasn't given up its expansionist policy towards the Himalayas.

From the military preparedness and strategic calculation, it seems China's "early harvest strategic move" is likely to shift towards the Tibet-Himachal borderland.

Around six decades prior, George Ginsburgs and Michael Mathos aptly summed up the importance of Tibet in the following words: "He who holds Tibet dominates the Himalaya piedmont; he who dominates the Himalaya piedmont threatens the Indian subcontinent; and he who threatens the Indian subcontinent may well have all of South Asia within his reach and, with it, all of Asia".

In short, in future whatever happens inside Tibet may matter for the Indian security environment and also that of Asia as well.[5]

PLA's brutal killing of 20 Indian Army personnel on June 15, 2020 was not only the third incident along with a massive military build-up on the LAC signifying a Second Chinese Aggression, so to speak, but also a bloody mockery of all agreements on peace and tranquillity and confidence building measures undertaken by India and China. And yet after that there were 13 rounds of military commanders' talks, all of which were quite typically not only painfully stretched out by PLA commanders, but also in which they were most unreasonable and persisted in their bullying tactics. What again became quite obvious was that they do not want any resolution of a border which is not theirs anyway. Not satisfied by forcefully occupying two million five hundred thousand square kms of the very rich landmass of Tibet in the 1950s, they have been continuously trying to nibble or grab whatever, wherever possible.

The Indian Army statement issued after the 13th military meeting read: "The 13th round of India-China Corps Commander Level Meeting was held at Chushul-Moldo border meeting point on October 10, 2021. During the meeting the discussion between the two sides focused on resolution of the remaining issues along the LAC in Eastern Ladakh. The Indian side pointed out that the situation along the LAC had been caused by the unilateral attempts of Chinese side to alter the status quo and in violation of the bilateral agreements. It was therefore necessary that the Chinese side take appropriate steps in the remaining areas so as to restore peace and tranquillity along the LAC in the Western Sector. This would be in accord with the guidance provided by the two Foreign Ministers in their recent meeting in Dushanbe where they had agreed that the two sides should resolve the remaining issues at the earliest. The Indian side emphasised such resolution of the remaining areas would facilitate progress in the bilateral relations. During the meeting, the Indian side therefore made constructive suggestions for resolving the remaining areas but the Chinese side was not agreeable and also could not provide any forward-looking proposals. The meeting thus did not result in resolution of the remaining areas.

The two sides have agreed to maintain communications and also to maintain stability on the ground. It is our expectation that the Chinese side will take into account the overall perspective of bilateral relations and will work towards early resolution of the remaining issues while fully abiding by bilateral agreements and protocols."

China Military Online of October 11, 2021, Colonel Long Shaohua, spokesperson for PLA's Western Theatre Command stated on October 11: "Instead of misjudging the situation, the Indian side should cherish the hard-won situation in China-India border areas." During the meeting Shaohua is reported to have said, that the Chinese side made great efforts to promote the easing and cooling of the border situation and fully demonstrated China's sincerity of maintaining overall interests of bilateral military relations. However, he added, the Indian side still persisted in its unreasonable and unrealistic demands, which added difficulties to the negotiations. He further said that China is firm in its resolve to safeguard national sovereignty. This is most likely an indication that PLA has no intention of not only not disengaging from Indian territory illegally occupied but also stick to what all it claims. It has insisted on a 10-km long no patrol zone along the north bank of Pangong Tso, a 5-km long no patrol zone in Gogra, eye-to-eye deployment in Hot Springs area, PLA structures at Y-Junction 20-km inside Indian territory denying Indian Army patrols access to multiple patrolling points which anyway are short of the LAC, and PLA.

According to an extensive article by Amrita Nayak and Ankur Sharma in News18.com of October 14, 2021, "Thousands of Indian troops deployed at the icy heights along the Line of Actual Control (LAC) are bracing for a second consecutive winter in the harsh terrain amid tense ties with neighbouring China. Ahead of the long, cold haul, the troops have been equipped with the latest Finnish Sako sniper rifles, Israeli Negev Light Machine Guns, the American Sig Sauer assault rifles, as well as a variety of contemporary drones along with the indigenous K9 Vajra T guns and the M777 Ultra-Light Howitzers (ULH). Senior defence officials told News18.com that a massive logistical exercise is underway to provide the troops deployed at the LAC with tonnes of special rations and kilolitres of kerosene oil and special fuel oil, along with fresh habitat and additional sets of clothing suited to the extreme altitude and dipping temperatures over the next few months. India has also significantly ramped up infrastructure at the LAC, particularly in eastern Ladakh, with the construction of temporary shelters, roads and bridges for faster mobility of troops when needed. The Indo-Tibetan Border Police (ITBP) has increased the number of warehouses in the Ladakh region to store larger quantities of ration...with talks deadlocked, Indian troops will continue holding the newly-created posts at extreme altitudes along the LAC that were unoccupied prior to the Galwan Valley clashes in June 2020. The stalemate came a week after a face-off between Indian and Chinese troops in the Tawang sector in Arunachal Pradesh. As reported by News18.com first, a strong Chinese patrol had transgressed the LAC and attempted to damage some Indian unoccupied bunkers. A similar activity at Uttarakhand's Barahoti a month ago reflects China's intent to expand the scope of transgressions along the 3,488-km LAC. India is also procuring a large number of counter drone systems, many of which would be deployed at the LAC. Additionally, the IAF has operationalised its second Rafale squadron at Hasimara (Alipurduar district of West Bengal, near India's border with Bhutan) in July 2021.... The build-up of Chinese tanks and guns has also been matched by India with multiple armoured and mechanised units deployed in the area, defence sources said...the ITBP has also planned to recruit 10,000 additional *jawans*, in anticipation of the long haul that India is preparing for at the LAC. While the proposal has been given a green signal from the government, further processes are yet to be initiated.... In October 2021, the Defence Ministry announced the launch of five major road projects in Ladakh to be carried out by the Border Roads Organisation (BRO), including the Hanuthang-Handanbroke-Zungpal-Turtuk road to provide inter-valley connectivity between the Indus Valley and the Shyok Valley. The road will reduce travel time to 3.5 hours from the current nine hours. Aside from Ladakh, the BRO is also constructing multiple roads and bridges in Sikkim and Arunachal Pradesh close to the LAC. In June this year, Defence Minister Rajnath Singh had inaugurated a 20-km-long double lane Kimin-Potin road, along with nine other roads, in Arunachal Pradesh, and one each in the Union Territories of Ladakh and Jammu & Kashmir. In June 2021, Rajnath Singh had also inaugurated the Kyungam bridge on the Indus river on the Leh-Loma axis for improved connectivity and faster deployment of troops along the LAC. As many as 11 bridges were inaugurated in Ladakh at the time.... Sources in the government said one of the critical reasons why the latest military talks have not made headway is India's push for full disengagement at the remaining unresolved friction points, including the Hot Springs area and Depsang Plains, and not a piecemeal approach to the overall situation.... Army veterans who have served in different sectors along the LAC said the biggest problem at present is the trust deficit between the two countries. Lt. Gen. PJS Pannu (Retd), a former commander of the Leh-based 14 Corps which looks after the entire Ladakh and Kargil regions, told News18.com that whichever side executes the planned disengagement first is always apprehensive of the other side moving in to occupy the vacated heights.

"They have always changed the goalpost. At times, they would talk about the J&K status in an oblique manner, while sometimes they would point out how India is building infrastructure in the area – such as the DS-DBO (Darbuk-Shyok-Daulat Beg Oldie) road – that is threatening their interests," he said, talking about the meetings between the two sides. He added that there are a number of points the Chinese would put forth during the meetings, never say in a direct manner with only oblique references. Talking about the road ahead, Lt. Gen. Sanjay Kulkarni (Retd), who has served in the Tawang sector twice, agreed that there is complete lack of trust between the two countries after the Galwan clashes last year and the way forward for India is to be prepared. "But China has realised that Indian troops are deployed in equal numbers on the ground. We must build on that advantage, slowly and steadily modernise to ensure that we are fully prepared to take on China anytime," he said. He added that capacity building takes time, but intentions of the adversary can change overnight. "We must be prepared. If you are prepared, there will never be anything that would be fought on the wrong foot. That (preparations) must continue (for the LAC or the LoC)," he said."

With all that has happened and having come so far, the Indian leadership should ensure that the mountain strike corps is equipped with all necessities and then maintain its high level of political will to pay back the Chinese on all issues. This will require for Indian Army, Navy and Air Force to make it obvious to their Chinese counterparts that we have the means and the will to counter them and pro-actively like it was done on August 29-30, 2020, at Kailash Range.

NOTES

1 https://www.firstpost.com/india/history-tells-us-that-himalayas-hold-key-to-controlling-asia-india-must-continue-to-be-wary-of-china-9737541.html
2 https://www.chinadaily.com.cn/china/2016-02/01/content_23346907.htm
3 https://www.firstpost.com/india/history-tells-us-that-himalayas-hold-key-to-controlling-asia-india-must-continue-to-be-wary-of-china-9737541.html
4 https://www.google.co.in/books/edition/Communist_China_and_Tibet/F-yjBwAAQBAJ?hl=en&gbpv=1&dq=He+who +holds+Tibet+dominates+the+ Himalaya+ piedmont %3B+ he+ who +dominates+the+ Himalaya+ piedmont+ threatens+the+In dian+subcontinent%3B+and+he+who+threatens +the+ Indian+

subcontinent +may+well+have+all+of+South+Asia+within+his+reach+and,+with+it,+ all+of+Asia.&pg=PA210&printsec=frontcover

5. Source: https://www.firstpost.com/india/history-tells-us-that-himalayas-hold-key-to-controlling-asia-india-must-continue-to-be-wary-of-china-9737541.html?fbclid=IwAR3JOf_tSyXkkdbLNzfOcet9k9kPuJVhxrv3MjUnl75nNHPAC8wN5nNPUbM

Afterword

By Maroof Raza

The Chinese military's intrusions along the Line of Actual Control (in Ladakh) at three locations and one in Sikkim, in April 2020, had become the subject of much discussion in India. The central question was "why have the Chinese done this now (as India, like the world, was battling the Covid-19 pandemic) and what can India achieve or get back from the Chinese?" Much of that has been explained by Colonel Bhat in his detailed analysis of Sino-Indian relations in this book. However, from a geostrategic perspective, China's agenda appeared to be as follows:

First, the Chinese were keen not only to deflect the bad global press they have had after their shoddy handling—either by default of design—of the Covid-19 virus. This coupled with the situation in Hong Kong in early 2020, had made the Chinese leadership look bad in the eyes of their locals (i.e. those who have access to global news) and their vast diasporas across the world. Thus, the need for the Chinese leadership was to do muscle-flexing either in the South China Sea or the unsettled boundary with India, more so as India shifted steadily closer into the American camp and the 'Quad' of nations that also have the Japanese and Australians, other than US and India, all of whom are seen by China as adversaries.

Second, is the Chinese long-term strategic aim of limiting the rise of India and settling its boundary with India to its advantage, and the nibbling away of territory in the eastern parts of Ladakh, beyond the perceived boundary lines. The Chinese want to grab as much territory as they can in this area, to add more depth to their important road link (Highway 219) that connects Kashgar in Sinkiang to Lhasa in Tibet. The two border regions in Western China are really China's Achilles heel, and both have been at the receiving end of much state-sponsored brutality. That apart, the Aksai Chin area is part of a grand strategic design of the Chinese to extend their reach north of the Galwan river, where the confrontation took place after a visible intrusion, and link up with the Karakoram pass, where they have built a major road link to the Shaksgam valley, which they have occupied since 1963. The Shaksgam Valley was ceded to China by Pakistan to firm up the China-Pak nexus, which has been Pakistan's major diplomatic lifeline now.

Third, China is forever looking for more water resources in the Ladakh region, as the Indus river system originates from Tibet and goes via Ladakh to Pakistan's northern areas that we call PoK. The Chinese agenda is to have access to as much water in this region, as China needs an abundance of water to manufacture microchips. Silicon wafers require lots of water (10,000 litres for its 30 cm sq) to produce, and thus it is the waters of the Indus river system that China wants and Pakistan is expected to provide for its geostrategic and economic agenda. In 2018, China imported over $230 billion worth of Microchips from the US, Japan and Taiwan in 2018. It wants to make all this itself—through the fresh waters of the Indus and by melting of glaciers in the Shakgam valley. Thus, China had begun eyeing Kashmir's waters from the 1950s, and so it occupied Aksai Chin in 1954. Now the Chinese have agreed to finance five major Dams in POK.

These current incursions of grabbing territory open up that possibility further—since river valleys (like the Galwan valley where they'd pitched tents now) are normally defended by either side from the high ground around them. But India can defend them best by firing upon the intruder. However, Indian officials have in the past approached such Chinese intrusions on a diplomatic wing and a prayer! But that cannot be our standard procedure to have endless rounds of talks, only to announce that all is back to normal. But the threat of the Chinese to Indian troops endures, and more importantly so does the possibility of harm to our border road workers, who are unarmed and live and work in very trying conditions. The Galwan shock has now energised New Delhi into sanctioning over Rs. 12,000 crores worth of projects to improve roads and infrastructure. But that too is inadequate.

Sadly, India had not developed its border infrastructure for decades on the China front, on the stupid presumption that bad roads on the borders will slow the Chinese advance into Indian territory, in the event of another 1962 type invasion! A lot has changed since then, and this must be publicized if a national narrative is to be built. For a start, the Indian army is not the same as the one's that the Chinese rolled over in 1962, when the Pandit Nehru-Krishna Menon combine refused to allow it to fight even tactical battles. And though the Henderson Brooks report that looked at only the reasons for military debacle in 1962 (not the political failures) is India's best kept public secret. Our Generals have had access to it and learnt lessons from it. Hence, the tough stance at Nathu La in 1967 (that left short of 400 Chinese and 88 Indian soldiers dead) and then the swift airlift of troops by General Sundarji in 1987, when the Chinese intruded in Somdorung Chu. In both the cases, the Chinese withdrew.

Today, any hopes that Chinese will withdraw to the accepted Line of Actual Control (LAC) appear misplaced. India must be prepared for the long haul, like the Doklam standoff (of 72 days) or even more, since the Chinese found a way out of India's Doklam roadblock. China's leaders cannot lose face, every time. New Delhi's diplomatic approach of going through the talks and peace-making is a model that hasn't got us anywhere on the matter of settling for a boundary line, especially on the Ladakh front, as there are the differing perceptions of which line to follow. Will it be the LAC as agreed in 1993, or should it be the one proposed by the British in Simla in 1914—which the Chinese representative didn't accept—or the Johnson Line? It's about time we create a new mechanism to settle the boundary since 22 rounds of talks, have led us nowhere. If not, then is the 'tough' Modi government ready to talk tough with the Chinese? And could this lead to another Kargil like conflict? That is not quite off the table yet.

Communist China's presence in Aksai China has been known to New Delhi since the 1950s—notwithstanding India's historical claims—

and even after it became public knowledge, that China had built up its military presence in Aksai Chin, Pandit Nehru told the Indian Parliament on May 4, 1959, that India's "policy towards China remained unchanged and it would continue to support China's entry into the United Nations." Furthermore, on July 1, 1959, Panditji declared that New Delhi would not recognize the Dalai Lama as the head of a Tibetan government and that Tibet was a part of China. But all this wasn't enough for China. They wanted more territory, come what may.

In fact, from October 1958, the differing Sino-Indian claims on the boundary alignment on the Himalayas, had become a matter of public concern in India, with the news, that China had built a 180-kilometre long highway connecting Xinjiang (then Sinkiang) to Tibet via Aksai Chin that historically was a part of Ladakh, which India regarded as its own. India's claims were based on the boundaries suggested at the Simla Convention of 1913-14. This was signed only between the British government in India and the Tibetan government. The Chinese representative at the long-drawn-out conference had only initialized few maps, awaiting clearance from Peking, which never came. This final agreement defines the boundaries of Tibet with India, but only from east of Bhutan and onto Burma (now Myanmar). This came to be known as the McMahon Line. And though Nehru had asserted in Parliament to loud cheers,—"The McMahon Line is our boundary, map or no map... (and) we will not allow anybody to cross the boundary," the Chinese regime of Mao Tse Tung refused to accept any maps or India's claims. This is the case, even now, and hence the Chinese encroachments on the LAC and in Sikkim.

Under pressure at home, Pandit Nehru became increasingly assertive about India's claims. It eventually escalated into the 'Lonju incident' of August 25, 1959, that marked the first armed encounter between Indian and Chinese forces. Longju is located along the McMahon Line. And as reports of the 'Longju incident' became public knowledge in India, Nehru was further distressed to receive a letter from China's PM, Chou (Zhao) en Lai, in 1959 (September 8) that Indian troops had invaded and occupied a number of places, and that India was shielding armed Tibetan rebels with Indian aircraft violating

Chinese air space. And though Nehru gave reassurances to China that he regarded Tibet as a part of China, it didn't quite help resolve the tension. Soon their correspondence became acrimonious, and it led to battle lines soon being drawn over the conflicting boundary claims. *Shijie Zhishi*, a popular Chinese publication went on to assert (September 20, 1959), "The McMahon Line was 'illegal' and that the Chinese people will never accept it."

From then on, events moved rather too fast for anybody – even if they had the intent – to stall the slide into disaster. But whenever Nehru was asked about China's increasing presence in Tibet, their steady encroachment of territory and their claim lines as it were, which could lead to its stepping beyond the 'line' that India insisted was settled, Nehru would respond with "liberate Tibet from whom?" His "idealism" and belief in China's benign agenda had, among others, frustrated India's military commanders.

Even then differences between China and India continued to grow. In retrospect it is clear that **Mao's** China was looking for a fight. Yet another major cause of concern to the Chinese in the 1950s was the increasing footprint of the United States in the region—coincidentally it is again now—with the CIA having become a key player in India in supporting the Tibetan resistance that was to annoy the Chinese also. The CIA engaged the exiled Tibetans—from the Sino-Indian border town of Kalimpong—with the help and members of Nehru's administration. Historian Benjamin Zachariah, claims that BN Mullick, Nehru's IB Chief, worked closely with the CIA to train a number of anti-Communists as Indian intelligence agents, and to sponsor a Tibetan guerrilla force. Thus, as the US began to influence opinion of the 'Chinese danger' amongst India's politicians from the mid-1950s— even though Nehru was keen to abandon the British policy of the 'great game' the Himalayas—the CIA had begun to engage with Tibetan resistance leaders to challenge China's occupation of Tibet. And it was the CIA and its agents that closely monitored and assisted the flight of the Dalai Lama to India in March 1959.

Over six decades after the Dalai Lama's escape to India, on his 85th birthday, on July 5, 2020, the realisation finally sank into India's establishment that his escape from Tibet (in March 1959) and his exile in India, would never be taken kindly by Beijing. Even after China's occupation of Tibet, in the early 1950s, Pandit Nehru and his team of loyalists in New Delhi refused to accept China's growing territorial threat to India. In fact, on April 29, 1954, the Indian government had signed an (eight-year agreement on) Agreement on Trade and Intercourse with the Tibet Region of China and India. The very title of this agreement formally declared that Tibet was a part of China. This agreement also contained the 'five principles of peaceful co-existence' (*Panch Sheel*, as it later came to be known). But China eventually chose to ignore these efforts by Nehru, as India had also published a map in 1954 showing Aksai Chin as a part of India. Coincidentally, that led to claims and counter claims on the boundary and eventually the month-long Chinese invasion of 1962. Coincidentally, the recent publication of Indian maps showing all of Aksai Chin as part of the new union territory of Ladakh, is said to have upset Beijing.

Although we are nowhere near as ill prepared as in 1962, it would be prudent to take a leaf out of the experiences of our recent past. Having intruded past our border or boundary lines, neither China nor Pakistan have vacated the territories they have grabbed—in POK and Aksai Chin—since India's independence. It is now a given to assume that any territory that isn't physically held by troops—more so, if the claims of two countries are disputed—then, when an opportunity arises, it is grabbed by a country like China, that has no respect for the status quo. Maps and political claims will not get China to relent. More so, as China's territorial ambitions are known to those of us who study China seriously, the pattern of its intrusions were telling over the past decade. Unfortunately, India's establishment was both averse to intellectual pluralism (i.e. advice from outsiders) and has refused to learn from history.

Finally, the talk of China's withdrawal may sound good to people in India, anxious that things must get back to business as usual. But beware of a China's territorial creep northwards of the Galwan valley via the Depsang plains onto the Karakoram pass. This is to open the route to the flagship project of President Xi Jinping, the China Pakistan Economic Corridor. If China has control over Galwan Valley and the Depsang plains (north of Leh) it will greatly shorten the route by less than 1800 kilometres through very rough terrain taken by the Chinese to link up with the Shaksgam valley, that China first grabbed and then made Pakistan 'temporarily' gift it to Beijing! This valley, though inhospitable, has the largest collection of glaciers (252 to be precise), that China regards a source of water to further its agenda of world domination. China needs an abundance of water to manufacture microchips and silicon wafers, which requires lots of water. And it is the waters of Ladakh and Kashmir that China wants and has eyed since the 1950s.

At least India's military commanders—specially the CDS, General Bipin Rawat—have signalled that India would be willing to fight a 'two front war' with China and Pakistan, if push comes to shove. Unlike the 1950s, when it became public knowledge in the late 1950s that Chinese troops had occupied the Aksai region, and have stayed since then, the Indian government of Pandit Nehru, had made it known to the army that India's only threat came from Pakistan! China, they said, could be handled with diplomacy. This was even the belief in South Block until May this year. Only the recent clashes in the Galwan region in May 2020, had woken up India's establishment about the limits of Indian diplomacy.

With the build-up along the LAC and the Chinese reluctance to restore the status quo—which essentially requires that it should withdraw its troops to where they were deployed until April 2020—could the standoff lead to another border conflict? Would the Chinese use the unsettled global environment—with the Covid-19 distraction in 2020, like the Cuban missile crisis of 1962—to launch their forces, to try to 'teach India a lesson, once again? Among the several irritants for Beijing at present, ranging from India's growing military ties with the US to India being the only major country to openly oppose the Chinese Belt and Road Initiative (earlier the OBOR), the biggest challenge to China's territorial claims has been the Indian home minister's call to liberate 38,000 sq km of Aksai Chin following the creation of the Union Territory of Ladakh. This to them was the challenge to what they'd come to believe as the status quo. This too is similar to Pandit Nehru's assertive behaviour from 1960 onwards.

However, where the Chinese leadership has got it wrong—and that there are no parallels with the 1962—is that the Indian army has been allowed to respond to any further escalation in a responsible manner, on the front lines, and more importantly the Indian armed forces aren't a pushover anymore. And though the Chinese intrusions have once again given New Delhi a wakeup call to heed the military's demands for modern weapon systems, it has also revived the discussion on a number of issues of national security, just when many of us thought that India's only external threat was from Pakistan, and that the generals in Rawalpindi had been tamed by the IAF's air strikes on Balakot. However, dealing with China, would require India to respond on multiple fronts—military, diplomatic and economic—despite the brave fight by India's soldiers at Galwan valley or more recently the use of the aggressive tactics south of Pangong Tso and east of Chushul. But it may still not stall China's aggressive designs.

It has only made the situation possibly more explosive particularly in the Chushul sector. With the Chinese army (PLA) having deployed a large number of troops (of fighting, support and logistic arms) along the LAC, India too has had to substantially increase its military deployments along the LAC, and further north towards the Karakoram pass, where the Chinese would eventually like to link up their Aksai Chin controlled areas. Skeptics say that any Chinese talk of withdrawal should not be taken at its face value. India must verify and then believe it.

But given a thumb rule of mountain warfare, China has more disadvantages even if it moves in more forces, since every defending Indian division (of about 7500 men each) requires at least six Chinese divisions (45,000 troops) to push them out of their defensive lines. The defender in the mountains needs far lesser troops compared to the attacker, if deployed on heights as Indian troops are now, unlike in 1962. India thus, currently has an adequate number of soldiers deployed on the LAC. And of course there is the other part of the Sino-Indian boundary in India's east—on the McMahon Line that runs along Arunachal Pradesh—where China also has been asserting its claims.

And though China could deploy more artillery fire units than India, there is no mathematical equation available for how much an attacker would need. Moreover, to make substantial dent on Indian army's

Himalayan defences China would need at least 45 if not 50 army divisions (of 7500 men each). Though China can rapidly deploy up to 36 divisions across India's frontiers, in fair weather, not in the winters—with its well-developed road network across Tibet—it can only do so if it faces no other threat along its vast frontiers, as China shares borders with 14 countries, but territorial disputes with many more. And, there are at least three US aircraft carrier groups (made up of hundreds of frigates, ships and submarines armed to their teeth) operating along China's maritime front, near the end of 2020.

So, the PLA's best face saving bet is to try another Galwan-type encroachment along the LAC, without troops opening fire. But it could give a further blow to the Chinese army's reputation, as India's soldiers are now ready and waiting! Almost all Indian army infantry units (of about 700 men) have a 'Ghatak' platoon (of 36 men). These men are the most physically fit and trained as shock troopers, to even kill with their bare hands—as they did during the Galwan clashes—and are hardened after years of battling terrorism in the J&K. The Chinese army on the other hand, looks impressive in ceremonial parades and in doctored videos. But it has virtually no battlefield experience, unlike the Indian army, and is barely able to cope with the harsh winter of the Himalayas. Besides, with China's one-child policy, its soldiers are unwilling to die, while the Indian army's case is quite the opposite. The Indian army is ready to blow off the ghost of 1962, when it was humiliated, because Pandit Nehru and his civil-military cronies botched it all up.

The only edge China has is with rocket forces. These could cause considerable damage to the airfields—not aircraft—in Leh and Daulat Beg Oldie (DBO). India's air armada would be flying from airfields far away from Chinese arty and rocket reach—Srinagar, Pathankot, Agra, Bareilly, Siliguri and Tezpur—and all of these allow fighter aircraft to load their full bomb and fuel payloads (unlike Chinese airfields on the Tibetan plateau, which restrict air operational capabilities) and take off for their missions. Hopefully, if push comes to shove, India will not hesitate to use the IAF, because New Delhi hadn't done so in 1962, for fear of escalation! Sadly, it was only when the Chinese were across the McMahon line, and Tawang had fallen, did Pandit Nehru desperately seek American air support, but neither did the US respond (apparently based on the advice of the much trumpeted US envoy, John Galbraith), nor was the IAF used!

But recent history has shown us that in the event of escalation—like the Kargil conflict when the Indian air force became a game changer—the use of air power cannot be ruled out. Along with the limitations of high altitudes of the Tibetan plateau from where the Chinese airforce (PLAF) would have to fly towards India—with half their fuel and ammunition loads—the PLAF pilots have little experience of battlefield situations as they rarely exercise with other forces; unlike Indian IAF pilots who regularly train with the US, France and Russian air forces. And China's inventory of aircraft (the J-20 Chengdu included) doesn't give it an edge over the IAF that can currently be an effective match for the PLAF.

And as for China's maritime claims—with its stated aim to have the largest navy in the near future—the Chinese navy is at present fast expanding, but it has its limitations, if it were to operate near India's coastline. Its aircraft carriers are no match for those of the US and its nuclear submarines are known to be inconsistent with their underwater capabilities, as per a YouTube report on *Defence Updates,* in mid-2020. India's navy on the other hand, enjoys a considerable edge over the Chinese in these waters and could block Chinese ships from passing through the Straits of Malacca (a waterway near Singapore, between Malaysia and Sumatra). This can be a major pressure point against any long-term Chinese military campaign against India. Incidentally, Indian navy ships in the Asian waters now operate closely with the US navy (which has in the past said that the professionalism of the Indian navy was up to NATO standards). This is China's "Malacca dilemma," and as a counter, China has made considerable investments in a port in Pakistan (Gwadar) and the China Pakistan Economic Corridor (CPEC) that runs from Kashgar in Xinjiang via POK and through Pakistan.

But neither is the CPEC ready to help China move its oil and trade products, through Pakistan, from and to the Gulf region and even Africa, nor is Pakistan likely to get into a full-fledged war with India, in support of Chinese ambitions. The reasons are primarily two: for one, the Indian armed forces are adequately matched against Pakistan, despite the Chinese threat, and the other, is that during Indo-Pak wars (of 1965, 1971 and 1999) the absence of Chinese intervention, had foiled Pakistan's plans.

But short of that, Pakistan would be a major distraction for India, if Beijing moves to take greater control of Aksai China and even Ladakh, for the region's mineral wealth (including Uranium) and for the waters of the Indus and the Pangong Tso. But it also wants a link up with the Karakoram pass north of the Depsang plains—where it had encroached in the past too—so that the long and arduous journey towards the Shaksgam valley (now of over 1800 kms) is reduced considerably. Beijing had encroached onto the glacier rich Shaksgam valley well before the Pakistanis gave its control to the Chinese in 1963. However, any further ingress by the Chinese from Depsang plains from the LAC, will be met by not just India's infantrymen in their trenches, but a mechanized force of tanks and ICVs that have considerable room for military manoeuvres there. China has no doubt deployed a large mechanized force, but it needs at least three times India's mechanized force, to make any gains.

Some former Indian army commanders who have served in Leh ask as to how many of those Chinese tanks are actually operational and not dummies, and do they all have enough fuel and ammunition? Indian troops do certainly have an operational force, having been there since General Sundarji decided to move mechanized units (of ICVs) to Ladakh. His wisdom was questioned then, but certainly not now, with the Chinese looking for gaps in India's defence to exploit.

Even though the winter stocking of food and ammunition has been done, despite the additionally large numbers of troops deployed along the LAC, there is the crying need for round the year supply lines to Ladakh. That is a big challenge that India must address in whatever manner possible because that could be the decisive factor in the event of a Sino-Indian war. The two major mountain passes, Zoji La and Rohtang, are of little use from November to April. So, whatever is required by the troops, not just at the LAC, but in Siachen and Kargil, is pushed through by the end of October. The Rohtang pass now has the Atal tunnel, but Zoji La pass doesn't. This along with activating the Chushul airfield is essential. The move of the Indian SFF—a specialized force in mountain warfare made up of Tibetans and Ladakhis—that occupied the heights around Pangong Tso was perhaps for this purpose too and took China by surprise. Air lifts of essentials are the only lifeline for the troops in those freezing front lines. Thus, there is now the need to speed up work on the Chushul airfield, which was ignored all these years.

But India's big disadvantage versus Chinese capabilities is the lack of satellite capabilities and their inputs. Apparently, of the total number of satellites in the skies, the US and China have 45 per cent, and the rest belong to other countries. India's share is miniscule. So if we require satellite inputs, which we will in the event of a conflict, our sources, for now, would be the US and Israel and possibly Russia and France. Interestingly, some very useful data is available, for a price, from private companies in the West. But India may be reluctant to use their inputs, as this could give away India's intent. Satellite inputs apart, today's battlefield has a number of information providers from troops on the front, UAVs, helicopters and AWACs. But more so, than a 30 cm sq satellite photo isn't helpful in giving the correct status of the enemy's troops. Hence, we shouldn't dismiss the role of local spies, since they are often our eyes on the ground.

REWRITTEN

As the author has highlighted in the last chapter of this book, had it not been for the reaction and counter attack by Indian Army troops at Galwan on June 15, 2020, which had shocked the PLA and Beijing, the PLA would have kept pushing their envelope on the LAC, and it may have led to an outbreak of a limited war, at the least. And then Indian Army's unprecedentedly swift and surprise action of occupying the commanding heights of Kailash Range by a combat group with SFF troops of Tibetan origin, backed by the firepower of guns and missiles along with special equipment, had further shocked and frustrated the Chinese leadership, forcing them to deploy troops to spend the winter in those extremely cold conditions. However, the Chinese decision to partially disengage from the frontlines around the Pangong Tso region must be watched with caution. It has been argued that China chose to a partial and synchronised withdrawal, having achieved what it set out to do in the spring of 2020, i.e., to build its defensive potential between Fingers 4 and Finger 8, and to stall Indian patrols from occupying dominating heights there including a partial Indian withdrawal from the Kailash—so that Chinese positions south and eastwards of the Pangong Tso, aren't threatened. But this 'tactical' Chinese pull back, is the tip of the iceberg, literally. There are other areas of Chinese intrusions, north of the Pangong Tso, specially around the Depsang plains—that China sees of greater strategic value—that Beijing will be unwilling to vacate. These will require much greater give and take, with the likelihood of Indian gains there being limited. That apart, the possibility of another Chinese intrusion elsewhere, say along the McMahon Line, when complacency sets in and thus leading to another stand-off, cannot be ruled out.

PHOTOGRAPHS

PLA'S SPEEDY DISENGAGEMENT FROM PANGONG TSO IN FEB 2021

PLA'S SPEEDY DISENGAGEMENT FROM PANGONG TSO IN FEB 2021

PLA'S SPEEDY DISENGAGEMENT FROM PANGONG TSO IN FEB 2021

PLA'S SPEEDY DISENGAGEMENT FROM PANGONG TSO IN FEB 2021

1965_Sikkim map by CIA, accessed from Wikipedia

Brig MMS Bakshi, MVC (retd) in the conference hall at Nathu La

Brig MMS Bakshi, MVC (retd), exchanging greetings with Chinese soldiers across the LAC in Nathu La

Brig MMS Bakshi, MVC (retd), laying a wreath at the Nathu La Memorial

Brig MMS Bakshi, MVC (retd), saluting at Nathu La Memorial

Brig MMS Bakshi, MVC, during his command of the Nathula Brigade

Capt PS Dagar (arrow) seen with Lt Col Rai Singh and 2 Greadiers personnel during tense moments with Chinese PLA troops

Capt PS Dagar during a tense stand-off opposite a cHinese PLA soldier across the barbed wire at Nathula

Dagar Dwar, dedicated to Capt PS Dagar, VrC (Posth), 2 Grenadiers

Defence Minister Swaran Singh seen with Shri Kewal Singh, father of Capt PS Dagar, VrC, (Posth)

DO No A/23370/5-6/Org 3 (RR&C) (K)

OFFG. CHIEF OF THE ARMY STAFF
ARMY HEADQUARTERS
NEW DELHI

19 Sep 67

Dear Shri Kewal Singh,

I write to express the deep sympathy and condolence of myself and all ranks of the Army on the sad and untimely death of your son, Capt PRITHVI SINGH DAGAR. Your son gave his life for the sake of the Motherland - a noble death for any soldier.

I hope you will bear this loss with courage and fortitude with the knowledge that we share your sorrow.

Yours sincerely,

Shri KEWAL SINGH
Village MILAK PUR
P.O. NAJAFGARH
(DELHI)

Lt Gen SHFJ MANEKSHAW, MC

Gen Sam Manekshaw's letter to father of Capt. PS Dagar

Lt Col Rai Singh (with stick) and troops of 2 Grenadiers appear calm even as PLA soldiers confront them menacingly

Maj Harbhajan Singh, MVC
(Posth (1)

Photos show President Zakir Hussain speaking to father and brother os Capt PS Dagar, VrC (Posth)

Photos show Prime Minister Indira Gandhi with father and brother of Capt PS Dagar, VrC (Posth)

PLA officers and soldiers discussing at the LAC, Nathula, 1967

PLA troops with crude weapons approaching Kailash Range on 07 Sep 2020. They withdrew after being warned.

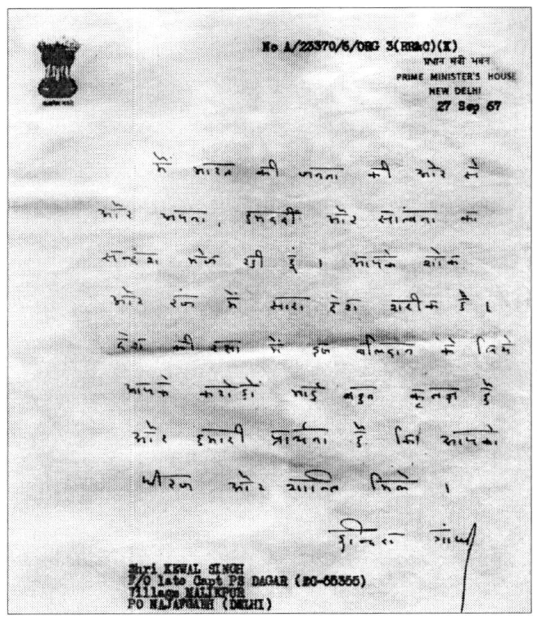

PM Indira Gandhi's letter to Shri Kewal Singh, father of Capt PS Dagar

President Zakir Hussain presenting to Shri Kewal Singh, father of Capt Prithvi Singh Dagar, his son's Vir Chakra (Posthumous) on 16 April 1969

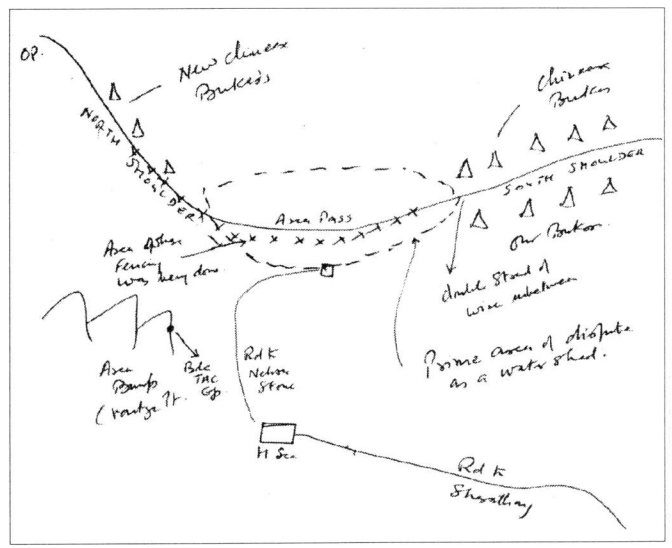

Sketch by Lt (later Col) NC Gupta

Tense confrontation & discussion between Lt Col Rai Singh with his troops and PLA personnel at Nthu La Sikkim, 1967

Tense confrontation between Lt Col Rai Singh and Capt PS Dagar (back to camera) with Chinese troops at Sikkim, 1967

The Dalai Lama being honoured by a Guard of 5 Assam Rifles which guarded and escorted him in India after he escaped from Tibet in 1959.

The Dalai Lama in India after his escape from Tibet in 1959

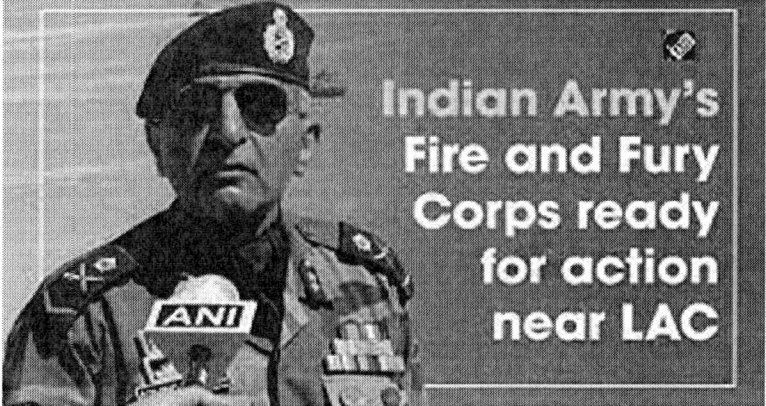

Video grab of Maj Gen Arvind Kapoor on ANI TV speaking about countering the Chinese Agression of 2020

INDEX

Acceleration Period, 160
ADB, 116
Admiral Arun Prakash, former Naval Chief, 181
Admiral Mountbatten, 21
Agni-V missile, 119
Air Chief Marshal RKS Bhadauria, Chief of the Air Staff, 189
Akash missile, 189
Aksai Chin, 8, 14-15, 18-19, 28, 30, 76, 208-10, 212
All under heaven, 181
Anti-Satellite Missile test, 161, 163
Antony, A K, the then India's Defence Minister, 96
Arpi, Claude, 22-24
Arunachal Pradesh, 1, 28, 69-72, 91, 96, 157-59, 179, 183-84, 203-4, 214
ASEAN, 118, 133
Assam Rifles (AR), 102
Australia, 96, 133

Bambawale, Gautam, 148
Bangladesh, 162
Beijing, 5-6, 79, 97, 119, 131, 135, 148, 156, 158, 162-63, 166, 169, 212-13, 217
Bhamre, Subhash, India's Minister of State for Defence, 152
Bhutan Issues DemarcheBhutan Issues Demarche, 130-31
Bhutan's Doklam plateau, 125
Border Defence Cooperation Agreement (BDCA), 99
Border Out Posts (BOPs), 40, 98
Border Roads Organisation (BRO), 204
Border Security Force (BSF), 102
Brig. Kundan Singh, 59, 60
Brig. M.M.S. Bakshi, 29-38, 42
Brig. L.P. (Bogey) Sen, 20

Caixin, 165
Capt. Manas Kumar Bhattacharya, 60
Capt. P.S. Dagar, 42, 47, 48
CCP-PLA combo, 179, 181-82, 184, 186, 190
CDS (Chief of Defence Staff), 21-22
Central Armed Police Forces (CAPFs), 184
Central Intelligence Agency (CIA), 23-24, 170
Central Military Commission (CMC), 156, 199
Chemical and Biological Weapons Control and Warfare Elimination Act, 1991, 167
Chemical Weapons Convention (CWC), 167
Chengdu, 72
Chhangu Lake Battalion Headquarters, 54
Chiang Kai-shek, 3
Chib Bhau Rajput, 57
Chicken's neck, 118
Chikungunya Virus, 173
China, 1-9, 13, 22, 24, 32, 69-90, 95-96, 98-99, 100-1, 104, 106-12, 115-21, 127, 139, 147, 154, 161, 164, 167-69, 171, 177, 215, 218

Setting up Wuhan kind Lab in Pakistan, 172-74
China Central Television, 131
China Development Bank, 115
China Military Online, 202
China Study Group, 193
China's
  Biological Warfare Program, 169
  Sweet and Sour Diplomacy, 158
  Maritime Claims, 216
China-India Treaty of Good-Neighbourliness and Friendly Cooperation, 160
China-Pakistan Economic Corridor (CPEC), 107, 112-13, 117-18, 120, 151, 216
Chinese Academy of Sciences (CAS), 164
Chinese Airforce (PLAF), 216
Chinese Belt and Road Initiative, 213
Chinese BW activities, 168
Chinese Communist Party (CCP), 171, 186
Chinese Government, 10
Chinese Journal of Virology, 164
Chinese Military Headquarters in Lhasa, 13
Chinese MMG, 48
Cho La, 27-29, 50-52, 64, 68
Chola Defence, 54
Chola Post, 55-56, 60
Chou Enlai, 14, 210
Chushul-Moldo, 197
Coastal Tourism, 114
Col. B Santosh Babu, 177-78, 180
Col. Bishan Singh (Retd), 45
Col. Danvir Singh (Retd), 187
Col. Krishnaswami, 55
Col. Long Shaohua, 202
Col. Vinayak Bhat (Retd), 142
Col. Wu Qian, 148
Confidence Building Measures (CBMs), 78, 80, 84, 87, 156-57, 170
  Protocols, LAC, 88
Convention between Great Britain and China relating to Sikkim and Tibet, 129
Covid-19, 207
CPC, 11, 165-66
CPC-PLA, 195

Crimean-Congo Hemorrhagic Fever Virus, 173
Cui Jie, 164

Dalai Lama, 12, 210-11
Darbuk-Shyok-DBO road, 178
Das, Durga,
  India from Curzon to Nehru & After, 15
Daulat Beg Oldi (DBO), 96, 102, 177, 183, 189, 193, 215
Dawn, 108
Deadly Agent Anthrax, 172
Defense Intelligence Agency (DIA), 170
Demchok, 177
Deng Xiaoping, 71, 76-77, 106
Dengue, 169
Depsang, 193
Desai, Morarji, the then India's Prime Minister, 69
Detection and characterisation, 173
Dhan Singh Thapa Post, 195
Digital Television Terrestrial Multimedia Broadcasting (DTMB), 114
Director General of Military Operations (DGMO), 156
Dogri, 56
Doka La, 125
Doklam, 29, 124-44, 150-52, 156, 158-59, 176, 182, 209
Doval, Ajit, National Security Advisor, 138-39, 155-56
Dr Li-Meng Yan, 171
Dr Ram Lal Markanda, 200
Dr. Li Wenliang, 163, 172
Dr. Subramanian Swamy, 69
Dragon-elephant tango, 159
DS-DBO (Darbuk-Shyok-Daulat Beg Oldie) road, 205

East China Sea, 120
East Turkestan (Xinjiang), 199
Eastern Ladakh, 97, 104, 107, 118, 179, 183, 189-90, 194, 202
Eastern Tibet, 12
Ebright, Richard, 169
Emerging Infectious Diseases, 173
Enlai's Statement, 16

Epoch Times, 163

Federation of American Scientists, Weapons of Mass Destruction, 167
Fernandes, George, the then India's Defence Minister, 84
Fibreoptic, 113
Finger 3, 196
Finger 4, 192
Finger 8, 196
Foreign Minister's Balancing ActForeign Minister's Balancing Act, 134-35
Fox News, 171
Frozen Period, 160

Galwan River, 199
Galwan Valley clash, 177, 180, 182, 192, 189-90, 193, 197-99, 203, 208, 212
Gandhi, Indira, the then India's Prime Minister, 30, 48, 194
Gandhi, Mahatma, 3
Gandhi, Rajiv, the then India's Prime Minister, 77
Gao Fu, 168
Gen. Bipin Rawat, Chief of Defence Staff, 140, 156, 187, 213
Gen. Cao Gangchuan, 90
Gen. Eric A Vas, 20
Gen. Krishnaswamy Sunderji, Army Chief, 72
Gen. KS Thimayya, Army Chief, 15, 18-19, 22
Gen. MM Naravane, Army Chief, 189, 197
Gen. V.K. Singh, former Indian Army Chief, 97
Gen. V.P. Malik (Retd), 132
Gen. Wei Fenghe, 150, 190
Gen. Wei Fenghe, China's State Councilor and Defence Minister, 159
Geng Shuang, 141
Geng Shuang, Chinese Foreign Ministry spokesperson, 157
Ghatak platoon, 215
Gilgit Baltistan, 138
Ginsburgs, George, 198, 201
Global Times, 119, 126, 135, 156, 191, 198
    Vitiated Response, 135-36

Gokhale, Vijay Keshav, India's Foreign Secretary, 149
Gokhale, Vijay, Foreign Secretary, 148
Gorkha JCO, 50
Gorkha troops, 59
GreatGameIndia, 169
Gupta, N.C., 44
Gurung Hill, 192
Gwadar, 112, 114

H5N1 Influenza Virus, 169
Han Cadre, 24
Hanuthang-Handanbroke-Zungpal-Turtuk road, 204
Hav Narinder Singh, 61, 62
Hav Surajbhan, 49
High Contracting Parties, 10
Hindi-Chini Bhai Bhai, 31, 38
Hindustan Times, 42, 199
Honeymoon period, 159
Hu Jintao, 94
    visited India, 91
Hua Chunying, 104, 140, 148
Hua Guofeng, 69
Huanan Seafood Market, 163, 164
Huang Hua, 69
Hubei Province, 164
Hussain, Zakir, the then India's President, 48
Hut Area Administrative Base, 57

IMF, 116
India, 5, 11, 119, 154, 157, 161, 163, 185, 193, 209
India's post-Independence history, 2
India-China Border Affairs
    Working Mechanism for Consultation and Coordination (WMCC), 104
India-China Boundary, 9, 186
India-China Peace Agreements, 189
Indian Army, 32, 42, 179, 193-94
    Statement, 202
Indian Defence Review, 187
Indian Express, 139, 159
Indian Foreign Secretary (Dutt), 8
Indian Navy,
    Coast Guard under, 102

India-US Exercise Malabar-7, 96
Indo-Japan-US trilateral relationship, 121
Indonesia, 162
Indo-Tibetan Border Police (ITBP), 102-4, 140, 184, 203
Indo-Tibetan Border Police, 137
Iran's chemical weapons program, 168
ISPR, 117

Jaish-e-Mohammad (JeM), 157-58
Jammu & Kashmir (Union Territory), 180
Japan, 162, 208
Japan Issues StatementJapan Issues Statement, 133-34
Japanese encephalitis, 169
Jiang Zemin, Chinese President, 80
Jiangsu Yongli Chemical Engineering and Technology Import/Export Corp, 168
Joint Study Group (JSG), 86
Joint Working Group (JWG), 72
Joshi, Manoj, 129
Joshua Philipp, 163
Journal of Defence Studies, 170
Journal of Fishery Sciences of China, 164
Journal of General Virology, 164

Kailash Manasarovar, 191
Kailash Range, 195
Kalha, R S, 24
Kashgar Prefecture, 110
Kenji Hiramatsu, 134
Khenzemane, 19
Khurshid, Salman, the then India's External Affairs Minister, 99
Klan, Anthony, Australian Journalist, 173
Kongka Incident, 13
Kongka Pass, 14
Kongka, 15
Kripalani, 16
Krishna, S.M., Foreign Minister, 98

L/Nk Krishna Bahadur, 63
L/Nk Moga Singh, 52, 53
Ladakh Scouts, 102
Ladakh StandoffLadakh Standoff, 137-38
Ladakh (Union Territory), 9, 28, 76, 177, 179, 184, 189, 213

Lanzhou, 72
Left Wing Extremists, 101
Lhasa Rebellion, 11
Li Keqiang, 100
Line of Actual Control (LAC), 2, 53, 64, 69, 75-78, 80-81, 87, 95, 101-5, 118, 120, 124, 126, 137, 149, 152, 158-61, 178-81, 185-86, 189, 191, 193, 196, 198-99, 209, 213, 214, 217
Line of Control (LoC), 102
Line of Existing Control, 193
Liu Bocheng, 17
Longju Incident, 13, 15, 19
Lord Ismay, 21
Lt Col. Rai Singh, 46
Lt. Col. Ajit Singh, 54
Lt. Col. Dany Shoham, 168
Lt. Col. Joshi, 57
Lt. Col. Mahatam Singh, 55, 58, 60-63
Lt. Col. Rai Singh, 48
Lt. Gen. B.M. 'Bijji' Kaul, 19
Lt Gen. Harinder Singh, 179
Lt Gen. J.S. Aurora, 40
Lt Gen. J.S. Bajwa (Retd), 102-3
  Modernisation of the PLA, 184
Lt Gen. Niranjan Prasad, 20
Lt Gen. P.G. Kamath, 144
  China Lies and India Believes: The Road Ahead, 183
Lt Gen. Prakash Katoch (Retd), 137, 196-97
Lt Gen. SL Narasimhan (Retd), 177
Lt Gen., later Field Marshal, SHFJ Manekshaw, 37
Lt. Gen. S.R.R. Aiyangar, 51
Lt. Gen. Sanjay Kulkarni (Retd), 205
Lu Kang, 142

Magar Hill, 192
Maj. Bishan Singh, 40
Maj. Chandershekar, 50
Maj. Cheema, 41
Maj. Gen. Arvind Kapoor, Chief of Staff of the Corps, 194
Maj. Gen. Dhruv Katoch, 102
Maj. Gen. Liu Lin, 179
Maj. Gen. Sagat Singh, 39, 41, 60

Maj. Gen. Sheru Thapliyal, 43
Maj. Harbhajan Singh, 42
Maj. K.B. Joshi, 51
Maj. R.K. Marwah, 43
Maj. Saroop Jamwal, 56
Maj. SC Dogra and
Maj. Subhash Dogra, 58
Malaysia, 162
Maldives, 162
Malhotra, Hansa, 24
Malhotra, Iqbal Chand
    Smoking Mirrors: The illusion of the LAC, 185
Mamallapuram, 161-62, 178, 180
Mao Zedong, 17
    Great Leap Forward policy, 11
Mao's China, 211
Mattis, Peter, 166
Maxwell, 27
McMahon Line, 70, 210, 214-15
Media Warfare, 166
Menon, Shiv Shankar, Foreign Secretary, 96
Menon, V.K. Krishna, 2
MERS-Coronavirus, 173
Michael Mathos, 198, 201
Middle Sector, 1
Militarizing CPEC, 116
Ministry of External Affairs (MEA), 128, 139-40, 142, 148
Ministry of Home Affairs (MHA), 102, 184
Mission Shakti, 161
Mithi, Mukut, Arunachal Pradesh Chief Minister, 98
Modi, Narendra, India's Prime Minister, 125, 147, 150, 158, 162, 183, 192
    visited US and Israel, 125
Monty Palit, 20
Morari Tso (lake), 97, 102
MoU, Defence Exchanges and Cooperation, 151
Mount Gya, 102
Mount Kailash, 191
Mukherjee, Pranab, the then India's Defence Minister, 90, 95
Mukherjee, Syama Prasad, 7

Naku La (Pass), 177, 183, 192
Nanjing Chemical Industries Group (NCI), 168
Nathu La Day, 50
Nathu La, 27-29, 39-40, 44, 46-47, 64, 68, 87, 176, 181
National Highway G219, 19
NATO, 11
Naxalbari, 28
Nayak, Amrita, 203
NEFA (North-East Frontier Agency), 17-18
Nehru, Jawaharlal, the then Indi's Prime Minister, 2-4, 8, 10, 12-14, 18-19, 21-22, 210
Nehru-Zhou Enlai Talks Failed, 15
Nepal, 162
New York Times, 166
News18.com, 196, 203-4
newsmax.com, 169
North Eastern Frontier Agency, 7
North Korea, 106
NSG (Nuclear Suppliers Group), 157

OBOR Economic Venture, 120, 125, 213
Observation Post (OP), 37, 70
Operation Falcon, 71-72, 75
Ormara, 115

Pakistan, 3, 31-32, 98, 100, 102, 106-18, 121, 138, 161-63, 172-73, 180, 184, 208, 213, 216-17
Pakistan Military's
    Defense Science and Technology Organization (DESTO), 173
Pakistan Occupied Kashmir (POK), 98, 151
Pakistan's
    Agriculture, 109-11
    Fibreoptics/Surveillance, 113-14
    Finance/Risk, 115-16
    Industry, 111-13
    Militarizing CPEC, 1161-8
    Tourism and Recreation, 114-15
Panchen Lama, 12
Panchsheel, 7-11
Pangong Lake, 101, 195-97

Pangong Tso, 137, 176, 180, 182-83, 186, 189, 195-96, 198-99, 203, 214, 217-19
Parthasarthy, G., 162
Patel, Sardar Vallabhbhai, 6
Patrol Point (PP), 197
peace and tranquility, 178
People's Daily, 18, 135
People's Liberation Army's (PLA), 6, 11-13, 27-28, 45, 68, 95, 98, 101-3, 105-6, 121, 124-28, 131, 136-38, 142, 149-50, 152-54, 156-57, 160, 165-66, 176-84, 186-90, 192-203, 214, 218
People's Republic of China, 6, 9, 73, 80, 87-88, 104, 166
Pran Nath Thapar, Army Chief, 20
Preparatory Committee for the Autonomous Region of Tibet, 12
President Clinton, 169
Pulwama Attack, 157-59

Qin Gang, 96
Quad, 207

Rao, Nirupama, 125
Rao, P.V. Narasimha, the then India's Prime Minister, 77
Recehen La, 192
Recovery Period, 160
Red Army, 4
Redeployment of troops, 186
Redux, 97
Regional Anti-Terrorism Structure (RATS), 154
Reuters, 140
Rezang La, 192
Rifleman Devi Prasad Limbu, 63
Rifleman Gagan Chand, 61, 62
Rijiju, Kiren, BJP MP, 95
Rohtang, 217
Royal Bhutan Army (RBA), 125
Royal Government of Bhutan, 128, 135

SARS-CoV-2, 164-65
SCO-Regional Anti-Terrorism Structure, 153
Second Lt. (later Colonel) NC Gupta, 29, 43, 45
Second Lt. Attar Singh, 50
Second Lt. Rana, 58
Senior Captain Zhang He, 138
Severe Acute Respiratory Syndrome, or SARS, 169
Shanghai Cooperation Organisation (SCO), 125, 153-54, 190
Sharad Pawar, the then India's Defence Minister, 77
Sharma, Ankur, 203
Shastri, Lal Bahadur, the then India's Prime Minister, 194
Shi Zhengli, 164
Shijie Zhishi,, 211
Shoham, Dany
  China's Biological Warfare Programme: An Integrative Study with Special Reference to Biological Weapons Capabilities, 170
Sikkim, 183, 207
Siliguri Corridor, 118, 128
Singh, Manmohan, the then India's Prime Minister, 96, 100, 162
  visited China, 95
Singh, Rai, 42
Singh, Rajnath, India's Defence Minister, 190, 195
Singh, Swaran, the then India's Defence Minister, 48
Sino-Indian border, 1
Sino-Indian War, 2, 3
Sino-Pak nexus, 160
Sino-Pak solidarity, 163
Sitharaman, Nirmala, India's Defence Minister, 153-54
Song Tao, 147
South Asia, 118
South China Morning Post, 165
South China Sea, 120, 207
South Korea, 162
Special Frontier Force (SFF), 187
Special Representatives of India-China 21st Meeting, 155
Special Security Division (SSD), 117
Spring Thunder, 28
Sri Lanka, 162
Straits of Malacca, 216

Subedar Nyima Tenzin, 188
Subedar Waryam Singh, 57, 61-62
Sumdorong Chu Incident, 70, 75, 103, 182
Sun Yat-sen, 3
Sutirtho Patranobis, 42
Swaraj, Sushma, the then India's External Affairs Minister, 134-35

Taiwan, 208
Thakur, Jai Ram, Chief Minister, Himachal Pradesh, 200
Tharoor, Shashi, 140
The Economic Times, 172
The Epoch Times, 163
The Hindu, 99
The Klaxon, 173
The Print, 171
The Tribune, 152
Thrombocytopenia Syndrome Virus, 173
Tibet Autonomous Region, 6, 72, 87, 199, 210, 212, 215
Tibetan Army, 12
Tibetan Crisis, 4
Tibetan Settlement, 5
timesnownews.com, 185
Tiwari, N D, 72
Tsewang Dorji, 198

Ultra-Light Howitzers (ULH), 203
UN General Assembly, 162
UN's Security Council, Human Rights Commission, 162
Unified Global System, 181
Unique Recreational Activities, 115
United Nations (UN), 169
UNSC, 126, 160
UPA government, 107
US, 133, 208, 218
    Intelligence Officials, 169
US-China Economic and Security Review Commission, 170

Vajpayee, Atal Behari, the then India's Prime Minister, 84
Verma, Shiv Kunal
    The War That Wasn't, 18
Vietnam, 162

Virologica Sinica, 164

Wagner, Ann, 151
Wall Street Journal, 166
Wang Yi, 156
Wang Yi, State Councilor and Minister of Foreign Affairs of China, 155
Wangchuk, Sonam, 185
Washington Post, 166
Wells, Alice G, 151
Wen Jiabao, 89-90, 95, 162
Wen Jiabao, Chinese Premier, 88
West Nile Virus, 173
West Pakistan, 2
Western Sector, 1
Western Theater Command (WTC), 126, 156
World Bank, 116
World Health Organization (WHO), 171
Wuhan, 143, 150, 158-59, 169, 171, 178
    Modi-Jinping meet, 148, 151, 159
    Summit, 147
Wuhan Central Hospital, 172
Wuhan Institute of Virology (WIV), 164, 181
Wuhan's National Virus Resource Centre, 174

Xi Jinping, 95, 104-6, 125, 141, 144, 147-51, 177, 185, 192, 199, 212
    visited India, 137
Xi's governing strategy for Tibet, 201
Xinhua AttacksXinhua's Attacks, 136-37
Xinjiang Production Corps, 110
Xinjiang Uygur Autonomous Region, 108
Xinjiang, 210
Xinjiang, Treatment of Foreigners, 23
Xinjiang-Tibet, 138

Yang Wenchang, 76-77

Zhou Enlai, 7, 17
Zhou-Nehru, 5
Zoji La, 103, 217
Zoonotic pathogens, 173
Zulung La (pass), 97, 102

*